T0113834

CHILDREN OF DIVORCE

DOUBLEDAY & COMPANY, INC., GARDEN CITY, N.Y., 1953

CHILDREN OF

DIVORCE

by J. Louise Despert, M.D.

LIBRARY OF CONGRESS CATALOG CARD NUMBER: 53-5288

Copyright, 1953, by J. Louise Despert
All Rights Reserved
Printed in the United States
At
The Country Life Press, Garden City, N.Y.

Designed by Diana Klemin
ISBN 9780385020015

146712470

This book is dedicated to the children of
Payne Whitney Nursery School,
who, during the years 1937–47, were my teachers.

I wish to thank Ruth Goode, whose professional
skill proved invaluable in the preparation of
this manuscript; Paul W. Alexander, Chairman
of the Committee on Divorce and Marriage Laws
and Family Courts; Lawrence H. Schmehl, Librarian
of the New York County Lawyers' Association;
Mary C. Bentley, formerly of the National Association for
Mental Health; and others who generously gave
of their time, knowledge, and interest.

FOREWORD

One of my purposes in writing this book is to help save marriages—the marriages of today's children whose parents have failed at marriage.

When a book on children of divorce was proposed, my impression, like the impression held by most people, was that children of divorce numbered largely in any group of disturbed children. I went directly to my files expecting to have this impression confirmed in the records of children who have been my patients and children about whom I have been consulted through the years, who together number well above a thousand. Most of these children were in such difficulties as to require therapy.

Astonishingly I found far fewer children of divorce among these than are found proportionately among the general population, which includes both well-adjusted children and children in difficulties. There was trouble between the parents of every one of the children in my files, but surprisingly few of them had been divorced.

Puzzled, I considered this discrepancy between impression and fact, and it became apparent that another element was involved. It is not divorce, but the emotional situation in the home, with or without divorce, that is the determining factor in a child's adjustment. A child is very disturbed when the relationship between his parents is very disturbed. This factor, which I came to think of as "emotional divorce," was always present.

As I pored over the records of disturbed children, another thought emerged: Emotional divorce always precedes legal divorce, but it is not always followed by legal divorce. Many a family is torn by dissension between the parents throughout the course of a marriage, and there is no divorce. On the other hand, whenever there is a divorce, we can be sure we shall find that emotional divorce was there before.

Thus out of the actual experience of unhappy children and their parents came both the reassurance and the warning which underlie this book. The reassurance, to parents faced with divorce or already on the far side of it, is that divorce is not automatically destructive to children; the marriage which divorce brings to an end may have been more so.

And the warning is that parents should look to their children not the day after the decree is granted, nor even the day before, but at the moment when they begin to be aware of trouble between themselves.

To parents who have come late to the realization that their children need their help, this is not to say that the damage which may have been done cannot be repaired. Indeed many of the children who move through these pages had to wait long before help came to them, and yet they can look forward to as bright a future as children who have not had to experience the collapse of their parents' marriage.

The drama of a divorce is of itself so compelling that parents tend to lose sight of what went before. Often it is only afterward, in the blank silence which follows the granting of the decree, that they feel rising within them an impulse to do something for their children. It is not that they have been unconcerned about their children until now, only that their concern has been pushed aside by their intense preoccupation with their own struggle.

But it is before the divorce, and often for a long time before, that the children have been hurt. If we could prevent some part of this grief and pain, these confusions and these costly misguided defenses, would we not bend every effort to do so?

In this book I have tried, not to pin-point merely the climax, the divorce itself, but to sketch the whole experience of marriage failure in its impact on the child. It is my hope that some parents, reading these pages, will have their eyes opened a little sooner, perhaps, to their children's unhappiness, and will move a little more swiftly and directly to their aid than they might otherwise have done.

Much effort is being invested these days in saving marriages, and this is all to the good, so long as we remember that what we are trying to save is not solely the form of marriage, but its spirit. A marriage can be saved at too great a cost, especially to the children. It is the children who pay the heaviest price, for they pay not only in present unhappiness, but also in future maladjustment and perhaps the failure of their own marriages to come.

So, while we strive to save the marriages of today, at the same time we must spare no pains to guide today's children toward more stable marriages in their tomorrow. Indeed we cannot afford to evade this task. Beyond the toll in personal unhappiness, there may be at stake the survival of the family as we know it, and of our way of life.

J.L.D.

IV
THOUGHTS ON THE FAMILY

I

SAFEGUARDING THE CHILD

1
DIVORCE IS NOT DISASTER

Divorce is not another word for disaster.

Divorce at best is an unhappy experience, and it may not even be a solution. Yet, in itself, divorce need not be either a bad thing or a good thing. It is only what the human beings involved may make of it.

All change is difficult, and divorce, whatever else it may be, is change. Convalescence, the change from illness to health, is also difficult.

If you who read these pages are facing a divorce or are already in the meshes of one, or if you are attacking the many-headed problems which come after divorce, there is one thing you may be sure of—you are not alone. Last year some 350,000 couples parted from each other in the divorce courts of the United States. About the same number will be taking the same step this year, and they will face many of the same problems.

Nearly half this number will be, like you, parents. They, like you, will be seeking ways to safeguard their children from the hurt of divorce or to heal the wounds already suffered. There are a million and a half children of divorce under the age of eighteen in the United States, and their number is being increased by about 300,000 every year. So you and your children are not alone in your trouble. You are part of a vast and growing special population.

Yet, comforting as the thought may appear in print, when you lift your eyes from this page you know that your difficulties are still your own no matter how many other men and women may have similar difficulties. Your problems are yours to face and yours to solve. Your children depend on you to protect them from the shocks and bruises of a stormy experience.

You can protect them.

Divorce is not automatically a destructive experience. It may also be a cleansing and healing one, for the child as well as you. Your support can help your child through its hardships. You can relieve him of guilt and fear; you can assure him that his parents' love for him is no less than it was before. With your guidance he can find security in the new setting of his life. He can come to accept his parents' failures as weaknesses. He can even come to accept the total or nearly total failure of a parent who, because of alcoholism, or mental illness, or other disabilities is considered "unfit."

We shall not pretend with each other that any of this is easy. Nor shall we pretend that children, any more than their parents, emerge from the divorce experience without some cost. All difficult experience exacts its price.

Yet divorce is not the costliest experience possible to a child. Unhappy marriage without divorce—what we shall call *emotional divorce*—can be, as we shall see, far more destructive to him than divorce.

You as a parent will not be dismayed to learn that safeguarding your child through divorce will demand of you your best wisdom, your most loving effort. If you have even given enough thought to these matters to look for help in this book, it surely means that you want to protect your child.

Perhaps you already know intuitively a curious fact—that if you invest effort for your child's sake during this period, it will bring you not less, but more, comfort, more peace of mind. You may also find, as many parents have, that in seeking insight into your child's emotional confusion you bring new illumination to your own; that in forestalling or easing his pain you can uncover and heal some unsuspected sources of suffering within yourself.

ACROSS AN EMOTIONAL NO MAN'S LAND   Many men and women in the divorce situation find themselves able to go far in helping their children once they begin to seek the way. Recently I was asked for a consultation about a little girl of six whose mother had re-married. The question was whether the child should be legally adopted by her stepfather.

On the hour of the appointment, instead of the mother or father of the child, or the mother and stepfather, to my surprise two gentle-men walked in. Before I could guess which was the father—and who the other man might be—they identified themselves as the father and stepfather.

This was a heartening example of how far parents and step-parents can join hands across the emotional no man's land of divorce and remarriage. The little girl had asked to have her name changed to that of her new father, since everybody in her present family—her mother, her new father, her baby brother—had that name and she alone did not. This request had led all the adults concerned to go further and consider how the child might be absorbed into her new family in other ways as well.

The stepfather offered to adopt the little girl legally and thus make the integration complete and final. The father, though under-standably very reluctant, nevertheless was ready to give the needs of his child first importance, and was willing to discuss the proposal. When they came together for consultation and advice, both men held the child's interest foremost. Eventually the situation was re-solved in that spirit.

The dilemmas of parenthood and step-parenthood in divorce and remarriage can be bewildering indeed. But they need not be in-soluble. They can be solved if the adults involved can find their way through their own emotional confusions and give rational con-sideration to the emotional needs of the children.

Nor must they find their way alone. If they want help, there is skilled and sympathetic help for them in clinics and social agencies and counseling services as well as in the private offices of psychiatrists. That the agencies available to parents and children are insufficient, we all know, and later on we will discuss the present resources, both public and private, and how they may be improved. But even with the existing facilities, parents can take the initiative, and seek help to smooth their own and their children's way through divorce.

WHY DO MARRIAGES FAIL?   Why has your marriage failed? No doubt you have asked yourself this question many times. Perhaps your questioning has led you farther, and you have asked why marriage in general seems so impermanent at this mid-point in the twentieth century.

When a man and woman fall in love, marry, and have children, they are following a well-worn path of human aspiration toward a permanent love, a permanent home, a permanent family. When they choose each other, they generally make the choice, so far as they know, for keeps.

Yet in the United States today nearly one out of three such efforts ends in the divorce courts. Throughout this century the divorce curve has been climbing sharply with only occasional pause, and elsewhere in the world it is following the same direction, though the trend is more recent and has not reached the same peaks.

Why is this so? We talk of the world-wide insecurity of our time, of the shift from farm to city, of the greater ease of travel and migration; of the dwindling of the family from the large kinship group to the small nucleus of father, mother, and children, often separated by wide distances from the place and family of their origin. We talk of the changing concept of marriage from a socially and religiously binding contract to a matter of individual choice and personal happiness. Men and women, and conspicuously women, now demand greater satisfactions out of marriage. They are less willing to put up with sexual dissatisfactions, less patient with them. And they have more freedom both socially and economically to break one marriage tie and seek success in another.

It is also said, and with considerable justification, that if marriage today is more demanding, men and women are in some ways less prepared for it than they were in an earlier day.

These changes are not sudden. They have emerged slowly from a centuries-long struggle for greater individual freedom, bringing with it greater personal responsibility. It is all part of our groping progress toward a democratic way of life.

To the individual man and woman, however, the impact of these historical forces is acutely personal. The family, though smaller and less sturdy than in the past, at the same time is subject to far greater strains. Each member asks more of every other member. Each relationship is intensified, each shortcoming more painful. The family today requires its adult members to have more enlightenment and insight toward each other as husband and wife, and toward the children as parents.

We are not surprised then to find that as marriage makes greater demands on them, more men and women fail at their first try. (The two-time and three-time losers are another story.) Little good can be done by forcing a man and woman to remain married when they have tried and are yet unable to make the necessary adjustment. Some divorces are, like some surgery, the only cure.

In the course of two days recently three families on the verge of divorce came to my office for consultation. One of these families can be restored, and I believe it will be, on a sounder and more durable foundation than it had before. One is doubtful. But the third divorce is necessary and long overdue.

"We should have done this eighteen years ago," the mother said, and she was right. There are three children, of whom the eldest is sixteen. All are unhappy. All have failed to make a wholesome adjustment to life.

This mother gave up a promising career at the outset of her marriage. Over the years she felt that marriage and motherhood did not adequately compensate for what was to her a great personal loss.

Many young women are confronted with what appears to be a choice between marriage and career, or more accurately motherhood and career. Yet it is not necessarily an *either-or* proposition, but a question of individual adjustment with a wide variety of possible solutions. This mother did not, however, succeed in finding her answer.

The husband, who had always tended to be domineering, in addition felt threatened by his wife's dissatisfaction and began to assert himself in ways which became overbearing. This too is not an unusual pattern in modern marriage. Many men feel threatened in their masculinity by what, consciously or not, they consider the rivalry of the wife in territory which for centuries has been fenced off as a male preserve.

Still, no matter how many men and women experience these conflicts, the resolution of them in each case narrows down to one man and one woman. The more insecure the man, the greater the threat which his wife's work or profession represents to him.

In this case neither of these two people was able to give ground to each other or to marriage, and both look back on the two decades of their existence together as unhappy, a waste of twenty years of their lives. They remained together, as they said, "for the good of the children," feeling that to break up the home would be too damaging while the children were young.

Children used to be considered a deterrent to divorce, in much the same way that marriage was the family doctor's prescription for the ill-at-ease, blushing young girl. Dissatisfied couples were inclined to resign themselves to situations which today would lead them to the divorce court. No matter how deep and permanent the breach might be, influences like the community and the church, the persuasions of friends and family, and their own concept of marriage as an inviolable contract pressed them to remain under the same roof. "For the sake of the children" was often the clinching argument in this drive to maintain the form of marriage though the spirit might be quite dead. The proof that the burial was only postponed is indicated by the peak in divorce among couples who have been married twenty years.

In some of these families the parents managed to achieve a way of living together which gave the children the emotional security they needed. In others, such as the last family mentioned, the attempt—always fraught with difficulties growing out of the personalities of both partners—was not successful.

Thus was added to these parents' unhappiness the unhappiness of their three children. And the important years, the years of infancy and childhood, had been marred for them by parental disharmony. These children can still be helped out of their emotional confusions toward a better adjustment, but much of their suffering could have been prevented by an early and wisely handled divorce.

In this case not divorce but unsuccessful marriage was the destructive experience. Divorce will come to these children, no less than to their parents, as a welcome release.

EMOTIONAL DIVORCE   Even so brief a sketch as the above calls to mind many similar marriages in which it is clear that other situations can be far more damaging than divorce. These are situations where there is emotional divorce, that divorce which exists in the hearts of one or both partners to a marriage even though legal divorce may never be considered.

Not all children of divorce are in trouble. Many have found a new balanced structure for their lives. Many have accepted the division of their time and love between parents who live apart, or have fixed on a step-parent or other satisfactory substitute for the missing parent.

Others are less fortunate. We know this, and we know that unless they are helped, some of them may join the throng of the delinquent or the mentally ill. Even at best, because of their inability to make the adjustments of maturity, some unhappy ones among the children of divorce will grow up to become tomorrow's parents of divorce, unless we can guide them toward healthier patterns.

But this is important to remember: the children of divorce who are unhappy and ill-adjusted are only a fraction of all unhappy children.

Later on we shall learn the story of one very unhappy child whose mother and father had both been divorced and remarried twice. These two young parents of Mary, about whom we are to hear quite a little, have so far been incapable of making a success of marriage, though each has tried three times. The cards were stacked against them even before they ever met and married; and we shall try to show why this was so.

Neither of Mary's parents was a child of divorce. Their own parents maintained, in both cases, the façade of an unbroken home. But though no breath of divorce ever entered either house, Mary's father and mother are suffering in adult life the consequences of their own parents' emotional divorce. Thus the source of Mary's unhappiness reaches back two generations.

What do we mean by emotional divorce? We must expect problems, both minor and major, to come between partners in all marriages, including those secure and stable marriages which form the majority of the population even in the most troubled times. Children everywhere pass through critical stages and periods of growth, and parents everywhere must meet unavoidable crises which may temporarily shake their serenity.

This is not what we mean by emotional divorce. Indeed, in most families these experiences are realistic learning experiences, valuable to the growth of the child. Ideally, the shared crises of living draw parents and children closer to each other in understanding and love.

Our concern here is not with the great majority of married people who manage somehow to face and surmount their crises together, but with those troubled parents and children who are emotionally severed from each other by deep and serious rifts.

Discord between husband and wife may be apparent on the surface. The children are often witness to bickering, sometimes even to physical violence. But even when there is neither quarreling nor fighting, they are aware of the chill silences and empty courtesies which cover disappointment and hatred. As one observer with wide experience in family counseling, Paul Tappan, has graphically pointed out, the child can more easily "learn to duck the family crockery than he can its intense resentments and contempts on a more subtle plane."

Even a very young child—and as a student of child behavior I will say, *especially* a very young child—responds to the true feelings of his parents for each other and for himself, however carefully they may be veiled.

This is not speculation. A clinical observer finds the same patterns of emotional disturbance in children of parents *who do not divorce*, although they have failed at marriage, as in children of divorced parents *who have not made their peace with divorce*.

We can be even more emphatic. The suffering of children where the divorce is emotional, but not openly expressed, is greater. Loyalties are as divided, security is as deeply shaken, and besides there is the anxiety about the uncertain, the unexpressed and inexpressible.

The child of emotional divorce cannot ask to have his confusions clarified and his fears explained away. He does not know what he fears and has no words for what he does not understand. The unidentified situation between his parents is far more threatening to a child than a realistic situation, however painful, which is squarely faced together with his parents.

Very little is concealed from children. More than once, observation of a child has led me to ask a parent, "Are you contemplating a divorce?" Often the question comes as a complete surprise to the parent, who feels that he has been found out by secret and mysterious means.

No, the child does not have a hidden microphone tuned in on his parents' innermost feelings, though often enough he behaves as if he had. We have countless demonstrations of how a young child unknowingly reveals—in his play, for example—that he is worried about his parents' relationship with each other, long before their discord has become an open issue.

Consider the question, "Are you going to get a divorce?" which, as many parents can testify, has been flung at them by a child after he has heard a quite ordinary marital argument. This does not necessarily mean that the child at that moment feels critically threatened. It may mean only that he has recently heard of a divorce in some other family.

A very young child, or a more anxious one, or a child in a temporarily disturbed period of growth may not be able to voice such a question. He *feels* disharmony, and whether or not the disharmony is serious, he tends to jump to the anxiety-filled conclusion that a brutal break is about to take place.

No wonder he is anxious in this matter which so closely touches his own future: "If Mommy and Daddy have a fight, maybe they'll get a divorce, and then what will happen to *me?*" At such moments his very survival seems threatened. A child knows himself to be small, needing care and protection. His fear of being abandoned is an ever-ready source of upsurging anxiety. He cannot help but leap ahead and even anticipate a break which the parents themselves may not have reached in their own minds.

THE SUCCESSFUL DIVORCE   When emotional divorce sets up nearly unbearable tensions, legal divorce often comes as a welcome crash of thunder. Momentarily shattering as the bolt may be, the storm at least has broken and the air cleared. The adult partners are freed of a failing enterprise. To the children divorce may bring a wholesome revision of their lives.

Nevertheless we must remember that even the most necessary divorce comes at the end of a bitter story; it is the closing of the books on a bankrupt marriage. We must examine the ingredients of the divorce, and of the marriage which went before, if we are to make this ending into the beginning of a new and happier story.

A man and woman may have been unable to make a success of their marriage. But they can yet make a success of divorce. With effort, with wisdom, with guidance where it is needed they can make of their divorce the maturing experience which their marriage has failed to be. They may free themselves not only of an unhappy relationship, but of some of the fears and hostilities, the confusions, the fantasies and misunderstandings which they unknowingly brought into their marriage and which doomed the marriage to failure from the start.

Above all they can make the divorce a success for their children. They can spare them the emotional damage which they themselves suffered in their childhood and which probably set them on the path to failure in marriage. They can break for their children the vicious chain of unhappiness which a previous generation handed on to them.

2

SOME EMOTIONAL PITFALLS
OF DIVORCE

To you, a parent involved in divorce, the plight of your children is probably the sharpest point of your present anguish. Guilt toward the children is an emotion you share with parents everywhere who must deal with the failure of their marriage, even those who have hardly guessed at the full depth of their children's agitation.

Many counselors report that this guilt is the first strong reaction expressed by parents. It shows itself in a variety of ways which nevertheless have a common denominator. "We must have failed somewhere—" "I guess I was not a good mother—" And from the father, "How am I going to face my son?" This self-accusation crops up in almost identical words in countless records.

Guilt is one of a number of emotional complexities of divorce, and one which it is well to be aware of. Divorce is not only a legal process. It is an emotional experience of explosive intensity. Grief and shock, fear for the future, feelings of failure, rejection, defeat; also resentment, frustration, self-pity, rage—all these may be expected to erupt in one form or another, singly or together, at any phase of the divorce process and especially at the beginning.

It is important to give these reactions full opportunity to be expressed and worked through. When they are buried they add enormously to the tensions between parents and children. And it should be your first concern, in guiding your children through the divorce, to let nothing come between you and them if you can possibly prevent it. The first aim of your campaign is to feel with your children, to keep their confidence and strengthen their reliance on your love.

Of course, children add to the legal complexities of divorce; their custody and maintenance are some of its spiniest problems. And the fact that there are children also intensifies the emotions of divorce. But thorny as the legal decisions may be, parents can cut their way through them toward a wiser agreement if they can first assess the emotions which may arise to confound their best efforts.

Guilt toward their children is the first of these emotions. Some parents may also come to resent their children for the very reason that the children add to their problems and make them feel guilty (and for other more obscure reasons which will be amplified later). How often have we heard: "If it were not for the children, it would be easy to start out fresh."

Some parents do not recognize this resentment. It may express itself as excessive concern, as overprotectiveness, as anxiety which beclouds issues and makes rational decisions for the child's welfare more difficult to achieve.

The resentment of one partner toward the other in the failing marriage also takes its toll of the relationship between parents and children. A man and woman who have hurt each other in marriage may unconsciously continue their war with each other through a divorce and afterward with the child as pawn. Many a harmful decision over custody, many a stubborn struggle over visitation privileges springs not from a concern for the child but from an unconscious wish of one or both parents to get the best of the other.

"The mother *wins* the custody—" This is the way it is put in both legal and popular parlance, as though divorce were a battle in which the reward of victory is the child. And all too often it *is* a battle, whether or not the true issues appear on the surface.

That a man and woman who have failed at marriage should harbor bitter feelings toward each other is, by all our experience of human behavior, to be expected, although the more mature the individual the less these feelings are able to dominate his judgment. If such feelings can be brought out instead of being buried, if their dynamic force can be released in a safer direction, then they will lose much of their potential power to do harm.

This is one of the values of having a person to confide in, especially one who can be objective as well as sympathetic and can support a parent in carrying out a wise course. This is the reason why marriage counseling services, clinics, and psychiatrists are often recommended—not necessarily for treatment, but rather for the release of emotional tensions and the opportunity for clarifying the issues. A parent may manage a situation without help of this kind, but he can usually manage it with less emotional cost to himself if he has some help.

A first step, then, in making a success of divorce is for the parents to take the time to find the help they need, then to understand and evaluate their own emotions in the divorce situation, both toward each other and toward their children. The extent to which parents are able to understand themselves is likely to be the measure of their success in making the divorce the beginning of a new and better future for themselves and their children.

A second step is to understand the child.

THE EMOTIONAL NEEDS OF CHILDREN   In bringing children through divorce and guiding them toward a happier future the first aim of parents should be to understand their emotional needs and to find healthy ways of meeting them.

The most serious danger to children lies in depriving them of the emotional support they must have to grow on. They can be deprived of all material luxuries, even of many physical comforts, and yet thrive and grow to wholesome maturity if their emotional needs are satisfied. This is a psychological truism which applies to all children, not only in the divorce situation. Clearly a divorce puts certain special strains on the child. But even through divorce, even through separation from a parent, even through drastic changes in the physical setting of his life a child's fundamental needs can be fulfilled.

This is true before divorce, during divorce, and after divorce. One reassurance which modern child psychiatry can offer to parents is that a child can absorb and survive almost any painful experience, if he is sure of his family's love. We saw this vividly demonstrated in the ordeals children were able to withstand during the London blitz so long as the love of the family continued to surround them.

During the stormy period of divorce, because of the stresses which have preceded and the adjustments which must follow, and because by its very nature divorce threatens those symbols of security most vital to the child, it is all the more necessary to be aware of his fundamental needs and give them first importance. There are returns for the parents in this giving of first consideration to the child. The more clarity they can bring to this joint problem the more light will be thrown on their problems with each other. In the effort toward objectivity for the child's sake there is likely to be a lessening of emotional tension all around and a general improvement in the climate in which the important decisions will be made.

The laws and the courts, which figure so largely in the disposition of the children, cannot be counted on as a sure guide to what is best for the child. Principles and practice differ widely from state to state, from town to town, even from court to court. While some states have made notable progress in providing aid to parents and to the judges who make decisions in divorce cases, others are still hampered by restrictions inherited from common law, from earlier social attitudes toward divorce, and outdated concepts about the property value of children. Later chapters will offer more specific information for parents on this tangled subject.

Before resorting to the courts, a father or mother or preferably both together can seek out agencies and make use of the available forms of guidance, social and psychiatric, in understanding their specific problems and deciding what is best for the child. Sometimes it is in the interest of the child to have a parent remove himself from the child's life to a large extent, leaving him to the custody of the other parent. Sometimes it may mean removing the child from both parents. Sometimes, and most often, the child needs something of both parents, and because of this they are asked to keep guard over their own emotions and their expression in word and deed, for the sake of the child.

In the previous chapter we saw how one little girl needed most of all to feel herself completely a member of her new family. She needed to belong. These situations are painful and solutions do not come easily. In this case the father, once he understood the child's need, was able to relinquish his claims in favor of the child's more urgent claim to a balanced family life.

In a reverse situation another little girl, also about six, was so much in need of maintaining a continuing relationship with her father that her custody was divided between her mother and her father and stepmother. In this case, through her understanding and love for the child, the mother was able to accept a situation quite painful to her, since she had lost her husband's love to another woman. She could have turned to the courts, which normally grant the custody of a young child, especially a girl, to the mother, with limited visitation privileges to the father. But her concern was primarily for the child's welfare, even at apparent cost to herself. (We say, "apparent" cost because in the long run the parent who follows a wise course is rewarded by a better relationship with the child and greater peace with himself.)

As a result of discussions with the counselor, it was decided in this case that the child spend week ends and all school vacations with her father and stepmother. The child's mother followed the recommendation in the spirit as well as the letter. She was able to work through her own resentment so that it did not trouble the little girl's relationship with her father and his new wife.

This mother was plagued by a further difficulty, one which is by no means unusual between parent and child. This was the child's outspoken hostility to her because she held her to blame for the separation from her father. The mother sought advice and through better insight into the reasons for her daughter's hostility was able to work toward an easier relationship with her.

We have mentioned some of the emotional pitfalls for parents in the divorce situation. For the child too there are many pitfalls, and hostility toward his parents is one of those most frequently encountered.

HOSTILE, GUILTY, AND FEARFUL   Practically the first reaction of the child, especially of a very young child who has no way of understanding the subtleties of an adult relationship, is that the parent who has left the home has abandoned him, and so he is likely to be hostile toward that parent. Hostility may also be directed against the parent who remains. As in the case of the mother and daughter just mentioned, if the divorce comes at that stage of a little girl's development when her father has a deep meaning for her, then it is her mother who usually becomes the main target for her hostile feelings.

Or hostility may be expressed toward both parents, singly or together, and in a variety of ways. For example, the child may deprive himself of food, refusing to eat, or of pleasure, refusing to play. He may behave in a general negative way, making an all-around nuisance of himself. Other actions may suggest an even more profoundly disturbed state.

If parents can feel guilty, so can children, and often they do. By steps mysterious to the adult but quite logical to him the child can arrive at the conclusion that *he* is responsible for the separation of his parents. He remembers, for example, that he has been naughty in the past; his misdeeds, trivial in the eyes of adults, to him assume serious proportions. He may say, "Daddy went away because I was noisy in the morning and he couldn't sleep." This is what rises to the surface, but the roots of his guilt spread deep into anxiety over unexpressed associations with "bad."

Or he may have heard his parents quarreling about him. He may have heard the implication, even the outspoken avowal, that "if it weren't for Bobby things would be so much easier."

To the child it follows from such evidence that the divorce is a rejection of him by his parents. This is driven home to him even more when he discovers that he can no longer live with both of them. Shuttling between them, he feels alternately rejected by each.

"Why doesn't Daddy live with us?"

"But Daddy has a new wife now."

"Why can't he live here with his new wife?"

To the young child, wanting to be close to both parents, the new wife is no obstacle to resuming the old relationship.

Exactly how a parent can relieve the child of guilt for the divorce, can reassure him of his parents' love for him, can re-establish his confidence and security despite the many changes in his life will depend on the age and sex of the child, on the individual situation, and the personalities of both the child and his parents. We will examine some of the ways of resolving these common emotional confusions of children which have been successful in actual experience.

Parents need first of all to be aware of these feelings in the child, to accept them, and give the child the opportunity to work them out. The ways in which a child may express these feelings are many, sometimes obscure, and not infrequently painful to the parents. It may help them to achieve understanding and patience if they remember that behind all these mixed feelings lies the paramount one of fear. The child, aware of his childish helplessness, is afraid—afraid of being left alone and uncared for.

SAFETY VALVE FOR PARENTS   It is not hard to see that in all these matters concerning children and divorce the demands on parents are considerable. Parents are asked to exert patience, objectivity, self-control to an unusual degree, and all this at a period when they are being subjected to emotional stresses of extraordinary intensity. How is this superior standard of parent behavior to be achieved?

It is not easy. There is not much in a divorce that is easy. But there *are* ways to help yourself.

Understanding, both of yourself and of the child will help substantially. If one is prepared for the difficulties, forewarned of the traps, and above all if one realizes that it is natural for oneself and one's child to experience such emotions as guilt, resentment, hostility —then the situation is relieved of a large part of its sting.

Yet these emotions must find their outlet. Children are expected to pour out their strong feelings toward a parent, and he is asked to accept these expressions, however painful, because of his greater maturity. But, because of his greater maturity and the children's immaturity, the parent cannot rely on them to render the same service in return. There are ways of rerouting the parent's feelings so that the children need not serve as their target.

Here is where the counselor, social worker, or psychiatrist, the minister or physician can do double service, both as guide and as recipient for the outpouring of troubled emotions. If no trained confidant is available, a friend or relative may have to serve. But it should be a wise and objective person, not one who, because of his personality or relation to the family, is likely to offer biased advice. The safety valve must be safe in the sense that it must serve to release the painful emotions, not to intensify them.

Once they have found such a safety valve, parents have a better chance to prevent these explosive emotions from coming between themselves and their children. And with the opportunity to open their own mixed and often contradictory feelings to the light, they can the better feel with their children in the stormy confusion which the children are also suffering.

We have tried in these preliminary pages to sketch a pathway for parents through those emotional barriers which rise from within themselves and their children and which may keep them apart at a time when they both need more than ever to be close. In the following chapters we will consider together some of the more specific questions to which parents in divorce situations seek answers.

3

WHEN DIVORCE IS COMING

Many practical decisions must be made in the management of the children's lives during divorce and afterward: whether to remain in the same house or apartment, the same community or school, if possible, or whether to break with the past altogether; how best to maintain the relationship with the absent parent or, in some cases, whether it should be maintained at all; how to establish the relationship with the new parent in case of remarriage. These and many others, including some you may not have foreseen, will be discussed in turn.

If you have not already taken the step, there is one question which dismays you now above all others: How should you tell the child?

This is one of the first questions and probably the most troubled one which parents ask a counselor. Consciously or not they give great importance to it; for them it is a question permeated with emotion. They anticipate that they will inflict pain on the child and are anxious, guilty, afraid of his reproaches. And most of them also feel to some degree that the way in which they present the situation to the child will help or hinder his acceptance of it. This is true.

Obviously the answer to this query involves quite a few preliminary considerations: How old is the child? How much does he already know or guess? What is his relationship with his mother, his father? Once parents arrive at the right answer *for them* to the question of presenting the situation to their children, they have already made a strong beginning toward bringing their children safely through the experience of divorce.

It would be unrealistic to minimize the element of anxiety here. So anxiously, in fact, do most parents anticipate the moment of telling their children that they feel strongly tempted to evade it altogether. Many do evade it, letting the moment slip by again and again, leaving the children to interpret for themselves what they see and hear.

Evasion is no solution. Children misinterpret, and parents grow more and more uneasy. Speaking practically, parents find in time that the failure to interpret the situation to the children has increased their own difficulties. For their own sake as well as the children's, parents must find a way to communicate with the young minds turning to them for interpretation and guidance.

Since you must tell the child, when is the best time? How much should you tell? Must you be unsparingly truthful? The total picture of a relationship between adults is complex, and much of it is not within a child's understanding. How shall you choose what to say and what to leave unsaid? How can you judge which are the important things to the child, the things which he most needs to know?

There is no single simple answer to this or to any of the questions which arise in the course of a divorce. Each divorce is different, each parent and each child an individual. The robot brain to resolve human problems has not yet been invented, and let us hope it never will be. The individuality of human beings may be inconvenient in a mechanized world, but it is the individual's most precious potential in his search for a better way to manage his life, singly and in his social group. It is on your own mature judgment, your wisdom achieved through understanding and clarity, on which you will come eventually to rely in your dealings with your children. Whatever the rules, you will be the one to apply them.

If there are no general recipes, still there are certain fundamentals to guide parents in their effort to establish the best emotional climate for the changes which divorce brings.

TO HAVE OR NOT TO HAVE A CHILD   It may seem odd, in a discussion of how to tell your child about your divorce, to begin by asking whether you are aware of why you wanted a child.

A divorce does not happen overnight. It begins long before parents consult their lawyers. It may have begun before the child was born. You may find some insight into your present relationship with your child if you ask yourself why you wanted to have this child in the first place.

All too often, when parents are consulting a counselor on what to do about a child in a divorce situation, it is revealed that they had the child in the hope of saving an already wavering marriage. Has such an attempt any chance of success?

It rarely has. When a man and woman have differences which they are unable to resolve, the arrival of a child on the scene is almost certain to increase rather than simplify them. A baby does not automatically call forth feelings of love and good will toward the partner in its creation. A baby is not even sure of finding a loving welcome for itself.

There are cases where a child has consolidated a marriage. We have seen instances in which the husband wanted children, while a young and pleasure-seeking wife had not yet arrived at the same level of maturity. The husband asked of marriage not only a wife but a family too, and the wife, caring for him, fearing to lose him, acceded to his wish.

This is one of the possible situations in which the coming of a child may strengthen rather than jeopardize a marriage. When such a marriage thrives we generally find that the young wife has been encouraged by the more mature personality of her husband into maturing a little faster. Thus she has come to enjoy the satisfactions of a wife and mother. This baby is wanted consciously by its father and also by its mother, who loves her husband enough to be willing to work at her marriage. A marriage in which the husband is the more mature partner is psychologically a healthy and promising one.

The only good reason for having a baby is that parents want the baby for its own sake. Wanting a child for itself makes a man and woman readier to accept the responsibilities as well as the satisfactions of parenthood, and being wanted assures the child in turn of the love it will need to grow on.

Parents who have a child for any other reason cannot be certain that they will respond to it with love. They are more likely to find their feelings of love complicated by such negative reactions as resentment and hostility (perhaps masked as overprotectiveness toward the child), plus the attendant anxiety which usually further beclouds a state of emotional confusion. And in the end they may be confronted with the breakup of their marriage anyway, plus the added complication of children.

Suppose you examined yourself searchingly now, and suppose you became aware that the hope of patching up your marriage was a motive in your wanting a child. If privately you hoped that his coming might cement your marriage, then today you can expect some disappointment.

You would not want to visit this disappointment on your child. To recognize this possible source of resentment in yourself is to take a wholesome step toward a better understanding with your child.

PRE-DIVORCE UNCERTAINTY   In any situation of discord between husband and wife there is likely to be a period in which the possibility of divorce hangs in the air, and nothing is certain except that there is trouble. This is a difficult time for all concerned, and particularly for the children. To the child of almost any age, the vague threat of change, unfocused and unexplained, is a trigger for anxiety. A clear and definite prospect, even one which they don't like at all, is easier for most children to bear than a pervasive and, to them, sinister uncertainty.

However, we do not ask parents to rush into divorce at the first sign of disharmony in order to save the child from uncertainty. Quite the contrary; relatives and friends, the minister, the social agency or psychiatric adviser, and many conscientious lawyers will often urge a disaffected pair not to be hasty, but to wait and consider whether it may be possible to save the marriage. Parents of the couple may point out that they too have weathered bad times. As for the husband and wife themselves, the more mature they are emotionally the more they will strive to avoid hasty action and win time for clarification and understanding.

This is not time lost. It may save a marriage and even strengthen it. Many instances could be related of husbands and wives who have found each other again after a stormy period, with a sounder understanding of themselves and each other and a better foundation for their marriage. If the private history of all marriages could be recorded, we would probably discover that among the most enduring partnerships a good many had been on the verge of foundering at one time or another.

Even if the decision is eventually for divorce, time out for consideration is well spent. A divorce entered upon in bitterness and misunderstanding is a destructive experience, but an enlightened divorce, one in which an effort has been made to straighten out differences and relieve emotional pressures, can be a positive step forward for all involved.

Meanwhile, what about the child? While his parents are struggling to resolve the crisis in their relationship, he cannot help but feel the tensions in the house even though the outward behavior of his parents toward each other is controlled. If they consult a counselor it is likely that their adviser will want to see the child. Though the child may not ask and may give no sign that he perceives anything out of the ordinary, it is safe to assume that he is aware and that he is troubled to some degree.

What should he be told?

First of all, while there remains any uncertainty about whether parents will separate, we should not trouble children by introducing the idea of separation. There is no need to inject the possibility of a breakup of the home until it is definitely decided upon.

Yet you must tell the child something, and it must be no fantasy or fairy tale, but the truth. Your first job is to bring out into the open the fact that there *is* discord.

The words you will choose to express this depend of course on the age of the child and his development. The words are less important than the atmosphere in which they are spoken. If you are anxious, distraught, confused, if you harbor resentment, these over-tones will strike the child more forcibly than words.

Especially in the pre-divorce period of indecision, when your anxieties are at their peak and your resentments have not yet been worked through, you will need to give careful thought not only to what you say to the child, but also to how you say it.

"Daddy and I [or Mommy and I] are having a little trouble. We disagree about some things. We are trying to work them out."

Perhaps there have been angry voices, quarrels. Perhaps there have been exchanges not necessarily in raised voices, but with the sharpness of hostility; wounding words, gestures of rejection. It is advisable to acknowledge these too.

Grownups sometimes get very angry with each other, as children do, you can say. Grownups also make mistakes. Daddy and Mommy feel they have made some mistakes. They are cross with each other because they are troubled. They may even be cross with their children because they are so troubled about these other things. Their crossness does not mean that the children have been especially naughty. It does not mean that they love their children less than before. It does not mean that the children are to blame for this disagreement between Mommy and Daddy.

These are the points you touch upon to reassure a child: It is true something is wrong, but that does not mean that everything is wrong. His parents are troubled and may be impatient with him, but that is not his fault. Grownups are not infallible; they make mistakes and want to correct them. His parents love him as much as ever, but because they are troubled they may not be as nice to be with just now. They must all be patient with each other for a little while.

The young child may seem content with this explanation. But we must remember that a young child does not absorb everything the first time. Even an older child who has understood what you have told him may later be overwhelmed by anxiety and need again to be reassured. Feeling your way, being careful not to plant anxiety, you can seek to keep the lines of communication open so that even if he does not ask, you will know when he needs another word of help.

He may ask. An older child may not be satisfied with your very generalized explanation. He may demand, "But what's the trouble? What are you disagreeing *about?*"

This is a dangerous corner. Such a question tends to open the floodgates of your own anxieties. It is a temptation to pour out, in the guise of explanation, feelings and grievances with which a child should not be burdened. Remembering that you are confused, probably hurt, certainly in the grip of many emotions, you will want to protect the child from any impulse you have to unload your troubles on his shoulders.

You will want to avoid mentioning any specific issues over which you are having differences, and you will especially want to avoid any involving the child. You will want to avoid any slighting reference to the absent parent, however much you may believe he is to blame, because this can only hurt the child. You will want to spare him the painful experience of having to take sides between his parents.

So your words will be brief in answering his questions. But your manner will be patient and leisurely because you do not want him to feel you are brushing him aside. You want to win and keep his confidence and make it possible for him to express his anxieties to you now and in the future. And you will not evade the truth, because an evasion now will return to plague you both some other day.

"We haven't been getting along well," you may say. "We are trying to find out how we can get along better."

"Is that why Daddy doesn't stay home very much? Is that why he shouts? Is that why you cry?"

You must be prepared for such questions and others like them because for the child too such a discussion may open the floodgates and let his anxieties pour through. Indeed this is one thing you hope to accomplish. For, although you will not seek to burden his immature shoulders with your problems, you do want him to turn to you with his. Your aim is to give him this very opportunity to bring his fears into the light so that you and he can examine them together.

Yes, you answer in effect, that is the reason for all the disturbing things he has seen and heard and felt lately. Daddy too is troubled, and when he shouts or scolds it is because he is upset. When he stays away it is because of these same unhappy feelings. Grownups are not so different from children. Grownups too have feelings which they do not always understand and cannot always control. But both Daddy and Mommy love him and are trying to work things out so that everybody can be happier.

Perhaps he can try, you tell the child, not to mind so much when his parents are impatient and cross. They don't want to be so, but sometimes they can't help it. He must try to remember that it is because of other things that his parents are upset, not because of anything *he* has done.

A child's anxiety turns on these points. What he needs to know especially is that he is not to blame, and that his parents still love him. Whatever eventuality he must later face, he can face better with your reassurance on these two counts, plus the acknowledgment that something is wrong (but not, as he fears, everything), plus the maturing realization that his parents are not gods but human beings who have made mistakes.

On these four cornerstones will be built your emotional support of your child through divorce, if divorce must come, and through the aftermath of readjustment.

A TIME TO DIVORCE? We come now to the point where parents have made honest, earnest efforts to save their marriage. They have sought and tried to follow advice on how to improve their relationship sexually, temperamentally, or in whatever areas they feel it has failed. In spite of all this, they have finally arrived at the decision that they cannot live together.

They now ask, is there a special time which is better than another to get divorced? Does the age of the children make a difference in their ability to adjust themselves to divorce? For the sake of the children, should they wait? And if so, how long?

Sometimes, of course, there is no question of waiting. A man or woman who has fallen in love usually is in no mood to wait. Or one who succumbs to the impulse to run away simply does so without thought of those left behind.

But when the situation is not urgent, there is something to be gained by waiting, especially when there is a very young child. The emotional focus of a child under five or six is his mother; his emotional stability is closely dependent on hers. The question parents of a young child should ask themselves is what the mother can be to the child when the father leaves.

Even though she has been unhappy with her husband, after he has gone it takes a while for a young woman to get used to standing alone, especially if she has the responsibility of a young child. At this moment she may have no prospect of remarriage. She may not have the home of her parents to go back to, or even if she has she may not think it wise to go there. Often it is better for her to manage without her parents. Going back to mother only postpones the day when she must stand alone with her child. Unless the relationship with her parents is an exceptionally sound one, the return to a dependent state may sap rather than strengthen her self-reliance.

Of the many possible causes of friction with her parents we need mention only one, the baby itself. Will the grandmother take over the rearing of the baby? Will Mother and Grandmother fight each other for the child? Add to this the discomfort in some communities of returning as a divorcée, the uneasiness with friends and relatives, the possible disapproval of family, and it is clear that there may be many reasons why a young wife may shrink from returning to her old home with her baby.

In an emergency, however, if she cannot manage alone, she must take help wherever she can get it.

If it is at all possible, it is usually better for a young couple to wait until the child is less in need of constant care, and the mother has more leisure to fill out her life with new interests and companionship. A nursery school might be considered, although this is only incidental, and there should be a lapse of time between the departure of the father from the home and the entrance of the child in school so that the child does not identify the two events and feel himself rejected by both his father and his mother. If it can be worked out, the child should be entered in school while the parents are still together.

In the same way, if the mother is going to take a job, this too should not be identified with the father's departure. Whenever possible it is better to establish these major changes in a young child's life gradually and one by one, giving him time to absorb each one before he is faced with the next.

The next step is the divorce itself.

TELLING THE CHILD   Before you decide how you will tell your child about the imminent separation, you must try to understand the child to whom you will be telling it. The child's age, sex, stage of development, especially in the middle and adolescent years, are some obvious considerations. The quality of the child's relationship with each parent is also a factor.

You should consider, besides, how much of the tension in the home may have been perceived by the child, over how long a period the discord has stretched, and with what intensity.

Be candid with yourself about this. It is understandable for you to feel additionally guilty if there have been angry scenes before the child, and when you feel guilty you may find yourself either minimizing the effect on him—or exaggerating it. On the other hand, coldness and hostility may have been expressed in subtler ways, and we know that children are keenly sensitive to the unvoiced signs of discord—the impatient gesture, the change of expression, the too-controlled manner.

It is often puzzling to perceptive parents that though a battle has been going on in plain view, the child has behaved like the three little Chinese monkeys, apparently seeing, hearing, and speaking no evil. As mentioned earlier, the more anxious child is often less able to ask questions. He may be too frightened. Or, like many an adult, he may be playing ostrich, hoping that if he hides his head and does not notice the thing he fears, it will cease to exist.

It is wise to assume that if there has been tension over any period of time, the child has been aware and is anxious about it even though he may be silent. Your very effort to mask a serious rift may have been his clue that something was wrong. A happily married pair can talk and joke about arguments they have had, and discuss their differences in the open.

Very important to remember is a point we made earlier in this chapter: unless divorce or separation is reasonably certain, it should not be mentioned. The suggestion of any breakup of the family is bound to be threatening to the child. If he has been told there will be a divorce, and then a happy unforeseen turn of events makes it possible to assure him that there is not going to be a divorce after all, that is one thing. But to subject him to alternate threat and reassurance is devastating to a child. In the end reassurance fails to reassure and he is left a prey to the sharpest anxieties.

So we may put down four guiding principles for your first discussion of the divorce (or separation) with a child of any age:

1. Acknowledge that there has been a decision to separate. He already knows there is trouble, and to talk with you calmly and simply about the impending separation will help relieve his anxiety.

2. Acknowledge that grownups can make mistakes, and that his parents have made them. He must one day accept the fact that his parents are human; it is part of his growing up. You may be hurrying him a little, but the truth is a more durable basis for his confidence in you than a fiction of your godlike perfection which in any case cannot be maintained.

3. Assure him that he is in no way to blame for what has happened between his parents. No matter what may have been said in anger or impatience, the trouble lies only between his parents and quite apart from him. In this way you help to relieve the guilt which most children take upon themselves when there is trouble between their parents.

But be careful, in freeing him from blame, that you *do not by implication lay the blame upon someone else,* that is, upon each other. "Bad" and "good" are words which have no place in this discussion. *His parents simply do not get along with each other.* This period of your own emotional confusion is no time to make judgments, and certainly not to a child.

4. Finally and most important, assure him in every possible way that despite your differences with each other, you both still love him as you always have.

THE CHILD'S REACTION Be prepared for a strong reaction from the child. The first open announcement is bound to be distressing, and he will probably show his grief. But the expression of grief, if it comes, is a release for him and you should not try to stop it.

He may flatly reject the reality which you are trying to lay before him. He may obstinately maintain, "I don't want it. You've got to stay together. I don't want anybody to go away." You have to persist gently in showing him the inevitability of your decision. His parents would also prefer it if the family could stay together, but this is no longer possible. It is hard for all of you now, but a way will be worked out to make everyone happier.

Also, the child will be disturbed by many questions, some of which he will not be able to utter. Whenever he does question, give him a frank answer.

Suppose he asks, "What's going to happen? Are you going to get a divorce?" If you are sure about this, you say yes.

He may ask now or later, "What will happen to me? Who will take care of me?"

Again, if his custody has been decided, you tell him. If it has not, you tell him you don't know yet. "We are talking about that. We want to take our time and work it out in a way that will be best for all of us."

If the decision is for a separation and you are not sure there will be a divorce, you have, of course, avoided mentioning divorce. But the child must be told of the separation. This need not carry the idea of finality. You can say, "We are going to try living separately for a while. We may be able to straighten things out. We hope we can. But whatever we do, we will try to do what is best in the long run for all of us."

Notice that you talk about "all of us." You do not talk about what is best only for him. You do not single out the child as separate from his parents. He needs to feel, now particularly, that he belongs to both of you, though from now on he may begin to think of you as separate people for the first time in his life.

At this moment he is afraid of being isolated, even in hearing about something that is for his own good. Let him know that he is not alone in any sense, but that you are all in this together.

We have talked of the child as *he* only because we have no single pronoun in English for both sexes. Naturally, in all of the foregoing, we have meant girls as well as boys. Later there will be differences along sex lines, and we will refer to these specifically as they occur.

Also, when we divide children into age groups in the following pages, it is only a general, convenient grouping, not to be taken as a rigid guide. A general pattern can never precisely describe any individual child. For many reasons, both of temperament and environment, children will be more or less dependent; some form a strong attachment to the father at an early age, some much later than the average.

We should not be surprised, furthermore, to discover a four-year-old trait in an eight-year-old. We have seen normal, competent men and women show a momentary resurgence of childish behavior, and a man among his friends may behave like a kid of ten with his neighborhood gang on Halloween. A parent reading any study of children must remember that the "normal" child is a fiction created for convenience, but his own child is real and individual.

Before we go on to talk specifically about children of various ages, one more caution is necessary regarding the child's guilt. The child takes on this guilt without your help. He interprets the trouble which has come upon him as a punishment for something he has done or perhaps something he has wished. You must reassure him, not once, but again and again, that he is not the cause of the divorce, that what has happened between his parents is quite apart from him.

This you cannot do bluntly, because a child is not likely to be conscious of his feelings of guilt as guilt, but only as part of his general fearfulness and anxiety. Be watchful, therefore, in talking with him or in his presence, of making references to the cost of supporting him, the difficulties of bringing up a child alone, of arranging for his future, or any other aspect of your problems which may reinforce his guilt and set up the very patterns which you are making your best effort to avoid.

4

DIVORCE AND THE YOUNG CHILD

To the young child the mother is the natural interpreter of the outside world, and so it is usual that the mother is the one to present the divorce situation. But we will begin our discussion of the young child with the father instead of the mother because in such situations the father is often left out. He is not sure what his role is to the child. He has fewer clues to the child's feeling for him. Ordinarily he has less experience than the mother in dealing with the everyday crises in a young child's life—and this is no everyday crisis.

Yet it is of great importance that the father's love be demonstrated to the child at this point. One of the ways of showing his love might be for the father to take a part in making the necessary explanations.

How shall he do this?

THE FATHER AND THE YOUNG CHILD   Sometimes circumstances make it difficult for the father to approach his child. If he has not been close to his son or daughter until now, he cannot now force his way into the child's confidence.

Sometimes, too, the differences between husband and wife tend to make the relationship of each to the child a competition for the child's affection. They must both guard against this. To the young child, his father and mother are *parents*, a single concept. Any effort to diminish his love for one in favor of the other is likely to shake his confidence in both.

The care of young children is generally considered the mother's job exclusively, by the father as well as by society, and sometimes it happens that a father, in turning away from his wife, turns away from his child as well. So closely does he relate the young child to the mother that he almost automatically rejects the one with the other. Often it is only later, when the storm of emotion is somewhat cleared and practical questions of custody and visitation privileges come up, that a father realizes he has temporarily cut himself off from his own child

It is possible to prevent this. Even though a young child may not have shown any particular interest in his father, his need for him is there. His father is part of the constellation which represents the child's security. It is just at this moment, when he is faced with the apparent loss of his father, that he most needs evidence of his father's love.

We suggest the possibilty of the father's closer approach to the child, at least as an attitude and an awareness, at the very beginning of the divorce situation. The concrete expression of this attitude depends, of course, on individual circumstances.

THE ASSURANCE OF LOVE   What can a father say to his young child whom he is leaving?

Put this way, the situation is almost too poignantly dramatic, and yet it need not become so. Fortunately a young child's concept of time and of the coming and going of adults is flexible, and fortunately, too, a young child absorbs his important knowledge less from words than from the subtler expression of feelings. Thus it is not necessary to say much. It is even better not to try to say too much.

You must tell him, since it is the truth, that you are leaving the home—but not with evasions about business or other fictitious reasons to explain your going. There must be no doubt left in the child's mind: his parents are going to live apart.

You can at once couple this with the assurance that you will come back to visit. You can pick up some thread of mutual interest to give the child a feeling of continuity in his relationship with you. Perhaps you have taken him to the zoo or some other favorite place in the past. This you can promise to do again together.

Above all you will make this a calm and comforting exchange. You will resolutely set aside the understandable turbulence of your emotions. You will avoid any reference to the differences with your wife, beyond the simple statement that Mommy and Daddy are not getting along and are going to live apart.

The young child is not likely to ask questions about this, but if he does, you do not brush them aside. You answer again, simply and in general terms: You and Mommy are working things out so that everybody will be happier. And you repeat, for emphasis, that you will come back to see him soon and will keep on doing the things that you and he have liked to do together in the past.

The word *promise* above calls for caution. Your best efforts to win the child's confidence will be in vain if you allow yourself, in your eagerness, to make promises you may not be able to keep. If you cannot be certain when you will come again, say only that you will come "soon." If you cannot be certain what form your visit will take, whether it will in fact be an outing, don't promise an outing.

Remember that to the child any promise you make is something to live on in your absence, as well as his guarantee that you mean what you say. If you don't come when you say you will, how can he believe that you love him though you say you do?

So be careful how you pin yourself down. He can accept *soon* as easily as *Saturday*, and, though he will miss you and the time may seem long, he will be spared the special hurt of a disappointment.

WHEN THE MOTHER HAS LEFT   We have been speaking of the role of the father when the mother remains on the job. What if it is the mother who has gone?

In such a situation the father has a considerable task. Distressed as he may well be, he can take it for granted that the young child feels far worse. The child has been rejected and abandoned by the one adult who meant most to him and in whom he must of necessity have placed his greatest investment of faith and love.

This child needs his father's immediate and convincing expression of his own love and reliability. Daddy is still here, and Daddy is staying. Daddy will not leave him.

As soon as possible the father usually seeks a substitute mother, a woman relative or friend or a housekeeper who can take the mother role not only in the care of the child but also in his affection. Few fathers can manage this care alone, since they must go out and earn a living, and certainly a father cannot be expected to become a mother overnight.

So much is clear enough. What is less plain, and often overlooked in the confusion of the home and the father's understandable resentment, is that the child also needs help in preserving as much of his mother as can be salvaged.

It is not good for the child to be told that his mother is a good-for-nothing who does not love her little boy or girl. There is time for the child to learn about his mother's weaknesses when he is more mature and can understand them not as a rejection of himself but as human frailty. Now he must cling to whatever comfort he can in his thought of his mother, and he must continue to believe in her love for him.

The father's job is thus not to break down the child's belief in his mother's love, but to support it. On the other hand there is nothing to be gained by embellishing the facts.

"But if Mommy loves me, why did she go away?" The child may ask this question, or he may not be able to voice it, but he wants an answer to it.

Mommy was "upset" or "feeling very badly" or "very unhappy," but she loves her little boy or girl.

"Will she come back?"

You hope so. Meanwhile, you and he can manage together. And this you proceed to do. Going on with the routine activities to which he is accustomed will comfort him more than long verbal explanations, and he will have the reassurance of his father's love, both expressed and demonstrated.

When a relative or housekeeper takes over the care of the child, impress upon her the importance of explaining the absent mother only in the same positive terms as you have done.

THE MOTHER AND THE YOUNG CHILD   Let us look at the more common situation, in which the mother remains and the father leaves. At the beginning her role is less difficult than the father's since she is closer to the child. But the child turns to her for repeated reassurance. He will show her his grief and anxiety in many different and perhaps troubling ways. She has almost constantly to be on her guard in his presence; she cannot give rein to her own distress without distressing him. And she must explain the absent father.

Suppose the father has left suddenly. Men often threaten to pack a bag and get out, a threat on which they rarely act. But when it does happen?

Generally the wife does not feel at first that her husband's departure is permanent. She says, and believes, "Daddy will be back."

But as time goes on and he does not come back she becomes less certain and her uncertainty is communicated to the child. The child may ask, "When is Daddy coming back?" and, "Why did he go away?"

Now that she is unsure of herself and beginning to be anxious, she will want to watch her answer. "Daddy was angry and upset. He was so upset he didn't do things the way he would if he were his usual self. Maybe he'll be back."

In cases of actual desertion and disappearance there may be an attempt to find the wandering father through the police. If it is necessary to explain this to the child, an answer might be, "Daddy was so upset; we hope he is all right. We're trying to find him and help him."

FACING THE NEW REALITY TOGETHER   Finally the mother gives up hoping for her husband's return, or he communicates with her and says that he plans to remain away.

Now her attitude can be definite and positive, facing toward the future. There is nothing to be gained by dramatizing the situation, and only harm can be done by attacking the absent father with bitterness and resentment.

She must say definitely that Daddy will not be back. But she can also turn her own thinking and the child's toward how they can manage best without him. Together she and the child or children must deal with the new reality. They will face and work out the situation together.

In the case of an experimental separation, when the father's absence is known to be temporary, there is no need to trouble a young child with the fear that it may be permanent. Very often such a separation is explained to the outside world as a business trip or a vacation alone. It is wise to keep the young child informed about the facts, but unwise to disturb him with uncertainties. If there is trouble in the family, admit it.

"We've been getting on each other's nerves a bit. It's good to take a rest from each other. Probably we'll find out that we're all not so bad together after all."

Often, of course, this turns out to be the case, and a man comes back to his family refreshed and with better perspective. If he does not, there is time enough to talk about the breakup of the family when it is certain.

DADDY IS GETTING A NEW WIFE   It is often less difficult for a mother to explain a father's absence, even his desertion, than his falling in love with another woman. A woman telling her children that their father has left her for someone he likes better is in a painful position. She knows herself to be rejected in favor of another woman. Her grief is deep, and she may also feel that she must somehow justify herself before her children.

She will be wise to seek an outlet for these painful feelings in a trustworthy friend or relative so that she can be calm and comforting with her children. The young child should not be involved in her struggle to regain her self-confidence; it can only confuse him. He needs to know that his mother loves him and that his father loves him no matter what has happened between themselves.

This mother can say, "Daddy has found a new wife. He loves her and wants to be with her, but he loves you too. He will come to visit you."

If there was tension before the separation, she can explain further: "Daddy was so unhappy he was making us all unhappy. It is better for us all to live separately."

The child may turn ostrich and refuse to face the new reality. He may insist that Daddy will change his mind and come back. The mother will do well to separate him gently and gradually from this fantasy. "Daddy made this decision after thinking about it for a long time," she can explain. "It is what Daddy wants."

A child can cling most tenaciously to his hope that all this business of separation, divorce, remarriage will one day pass and his parents will be together again. The little girl who insisted, "But Daddy can bring his new wife and live here with us!" is not unusual, except in the positiveness with which she could voice her wish.

Recently a very bright girl of eight, well anchored in reality on most other matters, reported confidently, "My maid saw in the paper that two people got divorced and married to other people, and then they divorced those other people and married each other again."

So great was this child's insistence on having her parents together, although both were already remarried, that if there had not been such a story in the papers she very likely would have invented it. She was living in the fantasy that all that had been done could be undone, and things would be as they used to be. She was ignoring the fact that her parents wished otherwise; she was refusing to make her peace with the reality of her new life.

Young children cling to the idea of the oneness of their parents. When there is separation and remarriage, it is the parents' task to help children give up this idea. They must take their parents as they are; after all, this little girl's father *is* married to a new wife, her mother to a new husband.

STEPFATHER AND YOUNG CHILD   Once he has accepted the reality of his parents as separate individuals, the young child may plunge into a new campaign, a campaign to find a replacement for his father, so that he may again have a unit of father and mother to-gether.

If his father has remarried, he may anticipate the obvious next step and ask his mother, "Will you marry another daddy?" It may cause amusement and sometimes embarrassment when he asks of every chance visitor, "Are you going to be my new daddy?"

Whether the question is openly asked or not, the mother may take it for granted that the child both wants a new father and fears that he may get one. She can reassure him on both counts by her own sensible attitude toward the possibility of remarriage.

They will not hurry, she tells the child. They will take their time and find a new daddy with whom they can both be happy. He will be a daddy the child can love too.

When she does find the new daddy, she may be dismayed to discover an apparent contradiction: the child has been looking for a father in every casual acquaintance, but now that she presents him with an actual father, he protests and makes difficulties.

Sometimes the child's protest is a reflection of the mother's own uncertainty. The mother might well ask herself how sure she really is about her choice. If she is feeling the glow and warmth of a sound attachment, the child is more likely to respond in the same vein.

There is also the possibility that even though the mother is con-fident of her choice, the child protests because he sees in the new father a rival to himself. Here the solution is largely up to the new father; he must establish his own good relationship with the child. When he becomes a positive factor in the child's life the element of threat which he represents will begin to fade. The new relationship of father-child displaces the relationship of rivals for the mother's attention.

The child's protest comes often because of a lack of preparation: a hidden relationship is suddenly revealed and the child is all at once presented with a brand-new father. This happens especially in a divorce which is followed quickly by the wife's remarriage, a divorce which may in fact have been brought about by the wife's interest in another man. For obvious reasons she could not display this interest to the child until after the divorce was agreed upon.

When the father has fallen in love with another woman, the young child is confronted first with the loss of his father and only later with the entrance on the scene of a new father, if the mother remarries. When the mother has fallen in love with another man, however, the child must give up his own father (in the home at least) and accept a new one almost in the same breath.

For the sake of her own comfort as well as the child's, and to give her new marriage a better chance of success, the mother will be wise to take her time and prepare the child for his new father. The situation demands a little more, too, of the prospective stepfather. He should begin to work at a friendly relationship with the child *before* he moves into the permanent position of husband and father.

ON BEING OVERZEALOUS   A frequent pitfall for stepfathers is that they are overzealous in their courting of their stepchildren-to-be. They press too hard. They bring too many and too costly presents. They make an aggressive effort at sharing the child's interests, or what they take to be the child's interests, before the child has gained confidence enough to reveal himself and his interests.

This is natural and understandable. A man in this situation has much at stake, and his very anxiety pushes him, sometimes to the point of overwhelming the child with attention. Naturally, too, he is hurt if the child draws back from him, and at the same time his anxiety about the outcome is sharpened. Thus his very eagerness to do well with the child raises further obstacles in his way.

Presents can be too grand. One stepfather discovered that the magnificent doll he brought to his future little daughter lay untouched in its box. But when he brought a bag of Mexican jumping beans and shared the novel toy with her on the floor, she gradually responded. Eventually she fetched her own favorite beat-up rag doll and climbed up to rest in his lap.

If the stepfather will give a moment's thought to the child's side of the relationship, it will help him plan his approach more realistically. To the child he is unknown and untried. The child wants and does not want him. An overpowering advance by a strange man brings mixed emotions. It is rather like the occupation of a small helpless country by a too-powerful ally. The child longs for the strong protector, but he is also afraid of being swallowed up.

The prospective stepfather will find that a waiting, welcoming friendliness will make quicker progress, though it may seem a slow and passive method. By his kindly awareness of the child he provides an open door, and sooner or later the child will come in. His own warm feeling for the child's mother, the comfort and happiness he brings to her, will be a magnetic force drawing the child toward him.

Here, too, a word of caution. Ardent embraces between adults are disturbing to a young child, especially if it is his own mother who is being embraced. Both the mother and the prospective stepfather will be wise to keep their overt expression of physical love to a minimum in the child's presence.

The new father must not be surprised, too, if the child's first approach to him is an aggressive one. It may take the form of that rough puppy play which releases hostility in the guise of fun, or it may be frank hostility.

The child has these feelings along with feelings of love which he would also like to express. His gestures of hostility are a necessary outlet for him, and they are also a way of trying out this new father. When the child discovers that his aggression, whether playful or direct, is met with patient good nature instead of punishment (even though the man in self-protection sets limits to roughness), the child gains confidence that he can also give his love to his new father.

Obviously this relationship takes time in the building. You must make haste slowly.

STEPMOTHER AND YOUNG CHILD   The stepmother is not usually too involved with the young child, since he remains with his own mother in most cases and is visited at home by his father. When the stepmother does meet him she may find him quite difficult to approach, because in these early years a young child is still so close to his own mother as to be almost a part of her.

How does the child feel? He sees the arrival of this stranger as a threat. Having already lost his father, he may fear that he is also to be parted from his mother by this unknown woman. If he has lost his mother, he may be more in need of this new mother, but he will probably also be more fearful and anxious.

The best chance of success for the stepmother is to offer the child warmth without possessiveness. A simple example: you bring the child a toy. He refuses to take it from you. He may even cry, "No, no!" and shrink away.

You do not force it on him. You say, "I'll leave this stuffed kitty here for you. Maybe you'll want to play with it later on."

Your pattern with the young child is one of giving, not demanding. You do not ask for his affection and friendliness. You only offer yours, as you offer the toy, for him to take when he is ready. When he seems to be coming closer, and you feel the time is right to explain yourself—or if his father has the opportunity to explain—it should be made clear to the child that you are trying to make his father happy, and you would like to be friends with him too; but you are not trying to take him away from his present home into his father's new family.

The stepmother's role becomes more important as the child grows older or when she comes into his life at a later age, and we will talk about this again in the following pages.

5

THE MIDDLE AND ADOLESCENT YEARS

During his middle years the child begins to expand his world beyond the four walls of the home, to include school, playground, and neighborhood. He makes independent acquaintances and perhaps friendships with other adults besides his parents; he knows his teachers, his friends' parents, some of the neighborhood tradesmen. He has schoolmates and playmates, and may run with a gang. A girl of middle years may begin to have "best friends." A boy may have one or several close pals.

Typically, though not necessarily in some individual cases, a child of middle years begins to be less dependent on his mother and to turn toward the father. A boy often has an active and growing companionship with his father. A girl may not express her interest in her father so openly, but she is increasingly aware of him and groping toward a relationship with him separate and apart from her mother.

Children now develop an increasing facility with words and depend more on verbal communication. At the same time they may at this age become less communicative in some ways. A boy, more often than a girl, is inclined to limit talking to his mother to the sheerly functional: "Mom, where's my baseball bat?" or, "Where's my clean shirt?" In his effort at manly independence he is likely to cut her off from his confidences. To bring his troubles to his mother seems to him babyish.

Because the child during these years often appears so self-reliant, coming and going by himself, arranging his work and play, choosing and visiting his friends on his own, we are inclined to assume that his emotional development has made equally rapid strides. However, he is not so independent of his parents as he seems. He is on his way to independence, but he has not arrived there, and he has the same fundamental need as the young child for the love of both his parents.

When there has been trouble in the home and the child has been feeling tension and discord between his parents, his need for his mother may be even greater. It is not rare to find in children who are troubled about their parents' relationship a greater outward show of independence to compensate for a greater inner need to be dependent.

How then do you go about helping children of middle years to accept the divorce? Remember, first of all, that even though they may ask no questions and may appear to want no explanations, it is important to take them into your confidence.

THE BOY WHO WON'T TALK With a boy, to communicate at all may take a little doing. In the stormy period of divorce you may notice that he is eating or sleeping poorly, dawdling about coming to the table, having trouble with his homework, and yet at the same time he may reject your offer of help. When you see that he is listless about going out to play, disinclined to join his gang in activities he formerly enjoyed, you ask him, "What's the matter?" "Nothing, Mom," is likely to be the answer.

It is safe to assume that you know what the matter is, and your first effort is to let him know that you know. Instead of repeating, "What's the matter—can't you answer?" you will get farther if you come right out and suggest that you know some of the things he is feeling. You understand that he is mixed up, upset. You are upset too. You and he can try to talk it out together.

You may not get an immediate response. Don't press him to talk;

your impulse to do so is an expression of your own anxiety, thinly disguised to yourself as an objective effort to draw him out.

But don't be discouraged. Be available to him when he is ready to turn to you. He wants and needs the comfort you can give him, but his feelings of anxiety, of resentment and guilt over what is happening between his parents act as a barrier between him and you. By showing him that you understand many of the things he cannot say you may help him to break through this barrier. The simple admission that you are troubled too, that you and he are in this together, will help him to come to you.

He can't quite say, "Why don't you grownups manage things better?" He can't ask, "What have I done to make you do this to me?" We know that our defenses keep us from uttering those thoughts and feelings which trouble us most. It goes even deeper, so that we may not even be aware that such feelings are there.

Your son may call you names. As you break the bonds of silence for him you may release the hostility he was unable to express or was trying very hard to control. Even in a secure home a boy of this age, struggling to free himself from his infantile need for his mother, may make her the target of his hostility. You must be prepared for a sharpening of this hostility under the emotional pressure of divorce.

He also has a drive to fix the blame on his father or mother in order to relieve himself of the guilt which is so hard for him to bear.

How can you help? First of all by allowing the child to voice these feelings, and second by making clear the realities of the situation. Again, as with the young child, you answer his unspoken questions: his parents are not getting along, but they both love him and he is not to blame for what is happening.

When he bursts out in accusation, for example, blaming his father, blaming his mother, you tell him that you understand how it can look that way to him. But relationships between people are more complicated than they seem. The two of you have tried to make a happy life together. It is not anyone's *fault* that there is trouble now.

You can draw on his own experience for an analogy. There are some boys he has never wanted to be friends with at all. Then there are others he thought he might like to have as friends. Per-

haps he has tried, and has been friends for a while with Tommy
Burns, for example, and perhaps the friendship has ended in a fight;
or he and Tommy have simply cooled toward each other. And how
much more serious and complicated than a friendship between
children is a marriage!

A girl's experience with her best friends will help her understand
how difficulties may arise in personal relationships, even though,
if she will think about it objectively, she will see that no one was
really to blame. It doesn't always have to be someone's fault when
people stop being friends, or stop loving each other as husband and
wife.

THE HOSTILE DAUGHTER   A girl's hostility at this period is often
very specifically directed at her mother. Her father has a great deal
of meaning for her; she has become more overt and aggressive in
competing with her mother for her father's love. She is likely to
feel that her mother has sent her father away, or, if she is a little
older, that her mother has not been a good enough wife to keep
him.

This hostility from a daughter can be most painful for a mother,
reinforcing as it does whatever guilt she herself may be feeling for
the collapse of her marriage. She sees herself a failure not only as
a wife but also as a mother. She feels she has not set a good example
for her daughter.

In such a situation she is naturally timid in approaching her
daughter. She is understandably reluctant to grasp this nettle. But
the girl, thorny as she may be, still needs her mother.

The mother should try to see the girl's position objectively. If
she feels she *was* inadequate in her marriage, there is no harm in
admitting it; the admission will help her as well as the child. For
the sake of both it is most important to give a voice to the girl's
hostility. The mother can relieve the pressure on the girl and on
herself to a great extent by making it clear that she understands her
daughter is angry with her and why. She has tried to explain why
Daddy went away, but she knows this is hard for a little girl to
accept. Instead of being cross with each other, why not talk it
out?

Parents should realize that a painful echo of the pre-divorce quarrels and arguments remains with the children, making them uneasy toward the absent parent and resentful toward the parent who stays—or the other way 'round. A wholesome air blows through this situation when parents can admit that there were quarrels, that they were angry and upset and occasionally did forget all consideration toward each other in the past. It is not hard for a child to understand this, having been angry and quarrelsome himself many times, and having known the headlong impulse to hurt someone, even someone he loves.

PROTECTING THE ABSENT PARENT   It is a sharp temptation for the parent who remains with the children to break down their love for the one who has gone. As we have said several times before, this may be a temporary relief to the parent who does so, but it can do only harm to the child. It only keeps alive the bitterness and misunderstanding which cause parents and children so much pain in divorce.

For boy or girl you must try to protect the image of the absent parent. It is not necessary or desirable to build an idealized version, or to gloss over weaknesses. But it can only hurt the child to hear, "Your father doesn't give a hang for you." No matter what the inadequacies of the absent parent, there are always some positive qualities which can be emphasized.

When the father and mother do emphasize each other's positive qualities to the children instead of breaking each other down, a practical benefit automatically comes to the adults. The very effort toward tolerance for each other, for the children's sake, makes for a more comfortable relationship between the parents. Since they must continue in some sort of relationship, if only because both will share in managing the children's future, a good one is surely to be desired.

It may help parents to resist the temptation to disparage each other if they will recognize this impulse for what it is—a sop to their own feelings of defeat and failure.

A girl especially may have a tendency to carry criticism of her mother to her father when they have their visit together. Thus put on the spot, a father should realize that while it is well to let the child air her feelings, it is not necessary to agree with her. He may sympathize with her, but he should not feed her resentments: "Yes, perhaps Mother is sharp with you, and perhaps she doesn't make home as pleasant for you as before, but you must realize that she is upset too. This is a change for all of us. We must help each other to get used to it."

Often a boy shows that he is apprehensive about the time he is to spend with his absent father. Here the mother can do much to help him. She need not "sell" the coming vacation. An insincere enthusiasm is quickly seen through by a child, and if he is made to believe the exaggerated picture of the delightful time to come, he will only be doubly let down when it fails to meet his anticipation.

What the mother can do, mildly and unobtrusively, is to counter the boy's fears with a reminder of those positive qualities which both know the father possesses, and of those pleasures which father and son have enjoyed together in the past.

Sometimes a mother is too eager to come between her son and his father. There is a relationship here from which she feels shut out, and about which she may be anxious. But if she does pry, if she is too insistent, it can only have the effect of driving the boy from her.

She can best protect her own good rapport with her son by maintaining it on its own terms and within its own wholesome limits. Her influence over the boy may be stronger, but it will be much less wholesome if she achieves it by chipping away at his attitudes toward his father. If there is anything about his father which troubles him, he will bring his worry to her—if she has established a good relationship with him. For this she must give him his emotional freedom.

"I'LL NEVER MARRY!"   The child of middle years may respond to the divorce with a wholesale rejection of marriage: "I'll never get married!" He is projecting into his own future with a child's judgment and a child's inability to grasp the complexities of adult relationships. He has been hurt. He has seen his parents unhappy in marriage and he has been made unhappy. Therefore, marriage is bad and he wants no part of it.

You can help him to form a more balanced judgment of what has happened. Tell him that you sympathize with the fact that he has been hurt, but also that you know that marriage does not need to work out this way. More marriages work out well. You have made mistakes; this acknowledgment, though difficult for parents to make to a child, is important to his full understanding of the situation.

When he is grown up, you tell him, he will have more experience in these matters than he now has, and there is no reason why he himself should make these mistakes. His parents have learned much from their mistakes. If they should marry again, they will do a better job of marriage the second time.

In apparent contradiction of his blanket assumption that marriage brings unhappiness the child may say exactly the opposite: "Frank's (or Joan's) parents are happy together—why can't you be like them?"

Here the child is expressing his feeling of painful uniqueness, of isolation and shame. In all the world only his parents can't get along together; only his family is having this trouble.

But, you explain, we cannot know how happy or unhappy other people really are. Perhaps Frank's parents are happy, and perhaps not, though they seem happy on the surface. People do not tell us everything about themselves.

Besides, you can reassure him with the facts: a great many people divorce. There are a million and a half children like him in the United States. Many of them, and their parents, manage to be happy. So will he.

THE PRE-ADOLESCENT AND ADOLESCENT CHILD   The child from the age of twelve onward has achieved physical independence, and he is also relatively independent emotionally. The effect of a separation from one of his parents is no longer so devastating to him. To the degree that he is able to separate himself from his parents, he is less likely to feel that their divorce is directed against himself.

What attains important and growing proportions in these years is the image the child forms of father and mother. This is what will influence him in his own adult role, in his attitudes toward the other sex and toward marriage.

You can do much to help or hinder your child in achieving success in adult life by the way in which you handle his experience of divorce during this period. The adolescent usually does not say, as the child of middle years says, "I'll never marry." Instead he may develop attitudes which will later cause him to fear any sexual experience or else to be promiscuous about it, to be afraid of giving love, to run from a permanent attachment, or to be cynical about marriage.

For boys or girls the best guarantee of a satisfactory future in marriage is a satisfactory parent image. Thus the main concern of parents with an adolescent son or daughter is to safeguard their image of father and mother.

It is not likely that the older child has been unaware of discord in his home although, preoccupied with his own busy life, he has probably been less affected by it. He may not have measured the true extent of the breach. He may have lulled his fears with the comforting illusion that "it can't happen to me." Or, on the other hand, he may have been engaged in positive efforts to keep his parents together, and may have succeeded to some extent. Certainly the child has felt some tension. He has observed peaks of disharmony occurring between levels of apparent peace.

In the pre-divorce and divorce period you may find yourself tempted to align the child's sympathies for yourself against the other partner. The child's discomfort in such a position is apparent. Yet, in spite of this discomfort, he may try unconsciously to push his parents into competition with each other for his sympathy. He may carry criticism of one parent to the other, tempting each one to fall in with him.

The snare is the more alluring for the parent who at this stage is understandably resentful of the other. But in their greater maturity parents should be able to look ahead and see the need to check the child's criticisms.

Why does he try thus to play one parent against the other? We have said that he wants his parents to stay together. At the same time he is striving to make certain of each parent separately. And he is also unconsciously trying to punish them. We must not forget that in the divorce situation the child, like his parents, suffers confused emotions and swings pendulum-like between opposing desires.

PLANNING FOR THE MIDDLE AND OLDER CHILD   Once the divorce is decided upon, plans for the older child should take into account the importance of neighborhood and school associations. The child may belong to a team, a club; he almost certainly belongs to a "crowd." These friendships become increasingly meaningful to him. Also we must anticipate the possibility that he may have a hard time keeping up with his school work under conditions of emotional stress, and we should spare him, as much as possible, the added strains of moving to a new neighborhood, a new school, and making new friends.

If the divorce occurs in the middle of the school year, any necessary change should wait at least until the end of the year; ideally it should wait until the child has completed one stage of his schooling, such as graduation from grade school, or junior high or high school. A change of schools is then not a dislocation caused by the divorce, but a natural step in his progress.

The child of this age may feel sensitive about being different from his friends because of his parents' divorce, and he may tend to withdraw from his normal activities. He exaggerates the reactions of his friends because of his own feeling that he is unique and isolated.

You can show him how far from unique his situation is: nearly one out of three marriages in the United States ends in divorce. Thus he can understand that the divorce is not always a disaster occurring to one family alone. It may also be a necessary adjustment of an unsatisfactory situation, and it happens to a great many.

If he points to the apparently stable marriages of his friends' parents, you can truthfully tell him that we do not know how happy any home or any individual may be beneath the surface. His own home may have seemed serene to outsiders. People very often conceal serious discontent until they are ready and able to do something about it, as his parents are doing now.

You may find your child fighting other youngsters over real or fancied slights to his parents' character. Neighborhood gossip may whisper that his father, for example, is not all he should be. The unpleasant details of a divorce may come to a child's ears from outsiders. Remember that under such circumstances a child feels that he must defend his parents. If there is a real basis for the gossip, however, it is better for the child to hear the truth from you.

You need not gloss over the facts. But you can honestly assure him that we cannot know everything about another person, his motives, his unhappiness. His father may have acted unwisely in some instance. No one is perfect. If we knew all about other people, we could understand and excuse many things which on the surface appear inexcusable.

As for his friends, they tease because they feel smug, and smugness is often a cover for doubt. They may need to feel and act this way toward him because they are perhaps not sure all is well with them in their own families.

It is worth your effort at this time to strengthen your child in an understanding and mature tolerance of the weaknesses of human beings, including his own parents and himself. In doing so you are helping him, now and for the future, to disentangle his judgment from the emotional confusion of motives arising at critical moments in any life.

Boys or girls in these years are old enough to observe many of the contradictions in human behavior. With a little guidance they can begin to interpret actions not as good or bad, black or white, but as the outward signs of complex and often conflicting inner drives.

What you will be teaching him is not to condone bad behavior, that is, behavior which is harmful to others, but better to understand the unreasoning and uncontrollable forces which drive people to behave badly to one another. You may be sparing him much pain and grief in his later life if you can thus make his parents' divorce not a destructive but a maturing experience.

6

AFTER DIVORCE

The aftermath of divorce brings a variety of sensitive situations about which it is wholesome for parents to do a little thinking in advance. Probably the most frequent and familiar duels between the former partners to a marriage arise over two issues: money is one, and the exercise of the father's visitation privileges is the other. Since the second more directly concerns the child we will take it up first.

The father's visits to his children in their mother's home is usually not altogether comfortable even under the best circumstances. He feels like an intruder. If the mother remains at home during the visit, even in another room, he may have the uneasy sensation that he is under unfriendly surveillance. And if she goes out, the children may convey their impression that his arrival has driven her away.

Time and events have come between the father and his children. He has lost the ease of daily contact. His feeling of guilt toward them may make him press too hard for a loving response from them, and any rebuff they offer is magnified out of its true proportion.

The children too are ill at ease. His presence may be a threat to the new security they have worked hard to build without him.

They are no surer of how to approach him than he is of his approach to them.

The general attitude toward these visits distorts them. As has been pointed out, the father's coming is not simply a visit. In legal language, it is a privilege of visitation which he has been granted, and it has the weight of the court behind it.

Both parents tend to exaggerate the significance of these visitations, the father hoping too much, and the mother fearing too much. It takes an effort for both to shake off the ponderous associations of their court experience, as well as their own mixed emotions, and to see the visit as simply a few pleasant hours spent by a father with his children.

A mother sometimes unwittingly builds up a child's apprehensions by her own resistance to the father's coming. The very tone in which she says, "Saturday your father will be here," may set the child's anxieties in motion.

By the same token, the father who anticipates the meeting too anxiously, either longing for it or wishing he could evade it, gives the visit a poor start.

There are ways to make these visits easier. For instance, the hours could be spent outside the mother's home, in some activity which both father and child enjoy. With a very young child this is not always easy to manage, but father and mother, realizing the value of these hours, should cooperate in planning them for the child's sake.

Even a young child can be taken out after his nap on an afternoon when the weather is good for a walk in the park or a trip to the zoo, or perhaps nothing more out of the ordinary than the playground in the neighborhood. The arrangements need not be very extraordinary. The father may simply take over the young child's afternoon airing as a matter of course, perhaps as naturally as he used to do on Saturdays or Sundays when he lived at home. An early supper together in a quiet, not too exciting restaurant might top off an enjoyable afternoon, and still get the child home for his regular bedtime.

It is for the father to plan his visit so that it fits comfortably into a young child's routine, just as it is the mother's part to adjust the child's routine within reason to the father's convenience. A father who capriciously upsets the child's day to suit himself is not think-ing of the child's welfare. And neither is the mother who rigidly sets hours which the father cannot meet without difficulty.

When both mother and father realize the child's need for a stable, continuing relationship with his father, they are less impelled to use calendar and clock as weapons against each other. The father's time with the child becomes no longer a visitation, either of angel or scourge, but simply a visit.

As the child grows older, time and place become more flexible. Where to go and what to do can now be planned by father and child together. Here the mother should not intrude. She can carry out her responsibility for the child's health and safety by unobtrusive supervision. She may genuinely feel that the child is being taken to unsuitable places or exposed to pernicious influences. It is difficult for her, however, to be objective; her feelings are bound to color her judgment of the information which comes to her. She can be reassured by the knowledge that the court stands behind her as the child's ultimate protector. But she must be sure that she has ob-jective evidence of harm being done to the child before she precipi-tates a new series of legal battles.

A smooth and sensible relationship with the child's father, how-ever, is her best guarantee that these excursions will work out in the interest of the child.

THE CHILD VISITS THE FATHER   The older child usually spends part or all of his school vacations with his father, and perhaps also some week ends. Here the father encounters a special dilemma. Unless he has remarried and has an organized household where the child can stay with him, he may—and some fathers do—unthinkingly expect the youngster to fit into his own bachelor life.

A boy may happily plod over the golf course with a father whose chief interest is his game and his men companions. He may be glad to go along on a fishing trip even though he may be a lone youngster in the group of men. But even such opportunities for a child to enjoy adult recreations are limited.

One father, a builder, thought nothing of taking his six-year-old daughter with him to his various building projects. The little girl would drag after her father as he inspected half-finished buildings until she was worn out, then spend the rest of the time wearily waiting for him in his car. Another father, eager to make his boy into a business executive, and perhaps also anxious not to waste any of his business day, took him to his office, where this four-year-old sat through meeting after meeting, until he finally slid down under the conference table, to be forgotten there until the end of the day.

Still another father thoughtlessly locked his two children up for the day in his one-room apartment while he went about his business. True, his business was very demanding, and he had to work hard to support two households. But we would not expect a father to treat his children in such an unimaginative and even callous way until we remember that he has probably not freed himself of his resentments toward his former wife. Know it or not, he is using his visitation privilege not to foster his relationship with his children, but as a weapon against their mother.

There are enough problems for a father to solve after divorce without the complication of unclarified attitudes toward his former marriage partner. It is hard enough for him to keep contact with his growing children over the widely spaced intervals between visits. It requires effort to share their changing interests and to keep their confidence. His visitation privilege is not an easy one to exercise. It carries with it an obligation to plan for the visits on the child's own level.

You can make these visits a positive and even joyous experience for both of you if you will stop to think what *your* child in particular enjoys, what his capabilities and interests are. As his father, you surely know your boy's inclinations, no matter how infrequently you are seeing him now. Does he like to build models or work with motors? You might start a bench project with him which could go on for months. Perhaps he has an aptitude which you might develop toward some branch of science or the arts. And there are his favorite sports, either as participant or spectator or both.

With a daughter, fathers sometimes feel more at a loss. How should a man know what a girl's interests are? But a girl, like a boy, is an individual. With a little encouragement your daughter will tell you or show you what she likes. Girls as well as boys are interested in sports, in science, in handicrafts; and boys as well as girls enjoy books, movies, theatergoing, music, and the arts.

For a girl or boy you can plan trips, picnics, swimming or ice skating, or whatever else the locality affords of outdoor pleasure. You may be able to offer the child companionship among the children of your friends and neighbors. Perhaps you may think of giving a simple party for your child so that he can meet these other children, or inviting your own friends with their children on a day's outing. Remember that your child is a stranger in this group, however, and that your thoughtful planning can help him to overcome his shyness with them.

A father may allow his potential pleasure in the child's visit to be spoiled by the emotional hangover of his divorce. Just as the child must learn to see his father and mother as separate individuals, the father too must see his child as an individual, apart from the mother and the marriage which has been dissolved. Freed from old and unhappy entanglements, father and child may still have an opportunity to build a rich and close companionship.

THE STEPMOTHER CONTRIBUTES   When we were discussing the stepmother's relatively small place in the young child's life (the more usual situation being that the child lives with his mother), we suggested that her role gains importance when the child is older. Here is such an opportunity in the child's visits to his father. Here the stepmother has a chance to show warmth and friendliness in practical ways which are meaningful and comforting to the child.

She can, for example, find out what he likes to eat. She would do the same to please any other guest. She would not serve lamb to him, especially at his first meal, if she knew he disliked it, and she would have chocolate pudding for dessert if it were a favorite with him.

You might try to arrange the child's room more or less the way it is at his home, but at the same time offer him a few choices. Too many choices will dismay him. He should not be asked to decide everything about his visit. But he may enjoy a feeling of independence in helping to make something about his room or his routine different here from the way it is at home.

Give him a chance to do so. Say to him, "I've fixed your room this way, but you can change it any way you like."

Don't be surprised if he brings something from home, a favorite toy or a special tool, something he is sure works better than the one you offer. This may seem finicky to you but he is only establishing a link with home to make him feel safer.

BOARDING SCHOOLS AND BOARDING HOMES   When the situation is very confused and difficult, parents may be advised to take the child out of it temporarily and place him in a boarding home or school. Sometimes the boarding or foster home is an economic necessity. A father may not be able to provide for both his family and his own separate maintenance, and the mother may be obliged to earn her living. The care of the children is then likely to be a problem which only a foster home can solve.

Boarding school is another matter. Parents often turn to it as a ready answer to the tangled question of what to do with the child. It is not without reason that boarding schools have cynically been called, "orphan homes of the rich." This is not to say that the boarding school may not in many instances be the right place for a child of divorced parents. It sometimes comes as a genuine relief to him to be physically removed from the scene of wrangling and discord.

Also the time after divorce when his mother is perhaps seeking increased social life may sharpen the loneliness of an only child, a loneliness already intensified by the loss of his father. A life at school among children of his own age may be a happy alternative.

But the comfort of being away is often destroyed for a child by the painful suspicion that his parents have sent him to boarding school to get rid of him. Teachers, housemasters, and parent substitutes at schools constantly have to deal with the reactions of children who feel they have been put out of the way by their parents. Some children cannot sleep or cannot eat; some remain withdrawn and friendless. Some fight, some whine, and some constantly get into mischief because they cannot study. Sometimes the child's guess is the correct one, too; boarding school may have been to his parents not the best but only the easiest solution, an escape from the fundamental issues.

How you explain to the child that he is going away, and the spirit in which he goes, may make all the difference between a good or bad experience at school. Let him understand that his parents are struggling with the changes brought by separation, and that they want him to be comfortable and happy while they get matters settled for themselves and for him. Let him have a voice in the choice of the school if possible, or at least let him visit the school before he is sent there to stay.

Parents should realize that even the best boarding school is not an ideal substitute for a home. When children are orphaned, that is one thing. But a child who has one or both parents living can only feel rejected if he is sent to boarding school without hope of ever returning to live with a parent.

On the other hand, a child who has been able, with his parents' help, to understand and accept their divorce may also be able to accept going away to school for a period. If his introduction to the school is wisely handled, a few years at a good country boarding school can be a rich experience despite painful readjustments in the family.

MONEY IS NOT THE ROOT OF THIS EVIL   The all-too-familiar wrangling about money after divorce often involves the children. Money seems to bring out the worst in people. Men and women who have behaved with great restraint toward each other during a divorce may be found a year or two later clawing at each other across a lawyer's table like cats on a back fence. A second wife who has been a model of perceptiveness and tact toward her husband's first wife may have all her careful self-discipline shattered by a surge of resentment over the alimony check.

We can better understand this almost universal reaction to money disputes if we realize that here, for once, money is not the root of the evil. Money has a symbolic value which gives it an exaggerated power in these tangled human situations. What it symbolizes is love.

When the alimony and maintenance checks go off to her husband's first family, the new wife feels love is being taken from her and her children. When the first wife fights a request (often an entirely reasonable one) for a reduction in her allowance because of the man's increased expenses with his new family, she is jealous less of the money than of the love which it represents, love which is being taken from her and given to her successor. The same pattern may be seen in reverse when the former husband demands a reduction in the maintenance he pays for his own children because their mother has remarried; he is resentful that the man who has taken his place in his wife's love may get the benefit of his maintenance checks.

However much she wanted the divorce, however antagonistic she may feel toward him now, a woman sometimes tends to regard her children's father as still part of the family. If she has unforeseen expenses, she feels he should promptly arrive on the doorstep with a check for the doctor's bill in hand. A man, for his part, may feel that his former wife's new family is better cared for than his own children, and at his children's expense.

Anger, frustration, resentment, jealousy—all the feelings we associate with rejection—are at the bottom of these squabbles over money, and it is these emotions, not the dollars involved, which make the scenes and instigate the court battles.

If only it were possible at the beginning to settle maintenance and alimony once and for all! These disputes seem to call forth emotions which might otherwise subside. But situations inevitably arise which make changes in the financial settlement necessary: illness in one family or the other, the growing expenses of children as they reach college age, a husband's diminished income, perhaps an opportunity for a good business venture which would mean added income eventually but at first requires some sacrifice on the part of his former wife—these are circumstances which might reasonably call for financial readjustment.

All parties involved know with their reasoning minds that two households cost more to maintain than one. All parties certainly know also that circumstances change and adjustments must occasionally be made. But emotion, not reason, takes command here. Each one has a strong drive to put obstacles in the way of the other household, to deny its needs because its very existence is painful to accept.

Where such strong feelings are aroused, the children can hardly escape being embroiled. Parents who have been most thoughtful in protecting their children through the divorce itself may unwittingly negate their own efforts in these later clashes over money.

Eventually the reality of the second household must be accepted. Not in the money itself but in the emotions reignited by it lie the sparks of contention. Once fact and feeling can be sorted out and recognized for what they are, the hardships which a decreased income may entail will be far less difficult to manage.

EASING THE DIFFICULT TIME   From time to time we have mentioned some of the reactions which parents may expect in children during and after divorce. Listlessness, poor eating, poor sleeping, difficulty with schoolwork, irritable and hostile behavior are as natural in a troubled child as their equivalent in a troubled adult. Many of the changes in a child's behavior are only what might be expected as a reaction to a specific unhappy situation. A mother complains that her boy refuses to go out and play with his friends, not realizing that she herself is following the same pattern of withdrawal, declining invitations, staying away from church or other usual activities, spending days and evenings alone at home.

A child who was in difficulties before the divorce may show considerable disturbance now. He does not have a well-adjusted child's resources to draw on when a crisis occurs, and he may need outside help. But the ordinary expected reactions of a child at such times need not be alarming unless you have done everything you know to make him comfortable and signs of excessive unhappiness still persist. At that point a consultation may be enough to reassure you, or to provide advice on how to help your child more effectively.

Are you surprised that your child is upset? Many parents are. They feel they have been watchful not to disturb the child's routine during the divorce. They feel they have devoted as much time and care to him as before. Yet he persists in unusual behavior. It is natural that he should. You yourself are feeling unusual emotions and perhaps, in the more restrained way of adults, showing this by unusual behavior. Everyone involved in a divorce is bound to suffer some pain.

It is not enough merely to maintain for the child the same routine as before, to pretend that life is going on as usual. This is the time to put in a little extra effort to relieve his preoccupation with his loss. You may not feel much like seeing people or entertaining friends and family. But make the effort for the child's sake, if not for your own; it will be better for both of you. There is a danger in too concentrated a relationship between you and your child. Expand your world instead of contracting it. Let him spread his affections over a wider area. A sudden burst of novel and overstimulating activity is not necessary or desirable, merely more of what the child has enjoyed in the past. Encourage him to have his friends visit more often, perhaps to stay overnight or for a week end. Have family parties. Invite more frequently his favorite relatives and those of your friends whom he likes.

You can spend more time with the child yourself on trips and outings which interest you both. Allow a little more time with him for the radio, television, movies. If you are fond of music, for example, or some other activity which can be shared, share it with him, but at the child's level and without forcing his interest. Turn about is fair play, too; if there is some skill or activity which he knows and you would like to learn, let him teach you. But give yourself the same consideration you give him. Don't force your interest any more than you force his.

Try to let your own common sense be your guide in small day-to-day decisions; it will give you a better chance to keep your anxieties under control. One mother, in the dazed condition immediately following her divorce, came to the husband of her best friend and pleaded, "Try to be a father to my boy." She was blindly following a counselor's advice that the child needed a father substitute, forgetting that the boy had had no previous relationship with her friend's husband, and that this man could not artificially establish a friendship with the child for this purpose. When she realized her mistake, she also realized that there were other men whom the child did know and like, some of them fathers of his own friends, and she sensibly began to invite these children with their parents to her home.

This is the time also to relax a little in the matter of routine and household chores. If your son forgets to take out the garbage or walk the dog, or perhaps refuses to comply when you remind him, let it go. If your daughter dawdles about doing the dishes or neglects to hang up her clothes and tidy her room, don't press her.

Will this indulgence set up bad habits? Many parents are afraid to let up on the rules even though their good sense tells them that the child is behaving this way because he is upset, and that nothing can be gained by making an issue of these small violations.

A child is not a little machine which won't work properly if you don't pull the right lever. There is no need to withhold sensible comfort from a child because of possible consequences in some far-distant future. When he settles down in the new life, you can work your way back to the routine again.

SHOULD YOU TAKE YOUR BOY INTO YOUR ROOM? The same is true for eating and sleeping habits as well. A child may eat poorly, or he may begin stuffing voraciously and putting on weight. Making an issue of his eating will intensify his resentments; it will not comfort him or help him to eat more, or less. He needs reassurance on the questions which trouble him, and he needs relief from his preoccupation with those questions. Give him what he needs, and see if his eating habits do not gradually return to normal.

A child may now resist bedtime, though he used to go to bed cheerfully in the past. A time of emotional disturbance often revives old fears or produces new ones. Your child may be afraid of things he has not feared since he was three. He may be unable to go to sleep, or be wakeful during the night because of his fears.

A young child may develop nightmares. When a child of middle years or older shows such an intense reaction after his father leaves, this indicates that he was anxious before, and the present situation has exaggerated his previous conflict. But your boy may only be finding it harder to go to bed, stalling, finding excuses for staying up until unreasonable hours. As sleeping time approaches the defenses are down. The child may only need his mother to sit with him a little while at bedtime and give him a little extra reassurance.

Suppose this is not enough. Should a mother take the boy into her own room?

There are special pitfalls for a mother left alone with her son. Even though she was not getting along with her husband, she had grown accustomed to the presence of another person, perhaps for years, and now she is lonely. Unconsciously she may turn to her son as a substitute.

The boy's problem is different. He misses his father, and he is anxious about his future life without his father. He wants comforting, but too much closeness to his mother is likely to stir up old conflicts belonging to his earlier sexual development which have already been pretty much absorbed.

A mother who is aware of this aspect of the mother-son relationship may withold comfort a child needs out of fear that she will be disturbing him. But if she is sensitive to the child's deeper need for independence as well as his immediate need for comforting, there is no cause to be afraid.

You can take a troubled little boy into your room for a while. Make it clear at the start that the arrangement is only temporary, for a few nights or until he is sleeping better and can go back to his own room. Try to avoid reproducing the father situation exactly. Move the boy's bed into your room. If that is not practical and he must use the other twin bed, rearrange the furniture. Or, if no change is possible, bring in his own spread, some of his toys, perhaps a chair of his, to make his bed look like a child's bed and his part of the room like a child's room.

A better solution is for you to sleep in his room; there may be a cot or space for a cot where a nurse or maid has slept. Again, make it clear that this is only for a while, until he can sleep by himself. Assuring him that it is temporary gives him the added comfort that you know this troubled time will pass. He is strengthened both by your readiness with help, and by your confidence that this is not likely to be permanent. Watch for him to relax, but don't press him to go back to sleeping alone before he is ready. The suggestion may even come from him, and not always in flattering terms.

"You snore too much," was one boy's way of re-establishing his independence. Another complained that his mother read too late in bed and the light disturbed him; still another that she kept the room too warm, or too cold. One protested against the scent of her cosmetics on the dressing table.

It hardly matters whether he is tactful. All you want to know is that he is ready to go back to sleeping by himself. He may not go back all at once to his old self-reliant habits. Let him leave his door open temporarily if he likes. Let him have a night light. He will not cling to these little safeguards against night fears once the night fears leave him.

THE CHILD WHO RUNS AWAY   A mother sometimes finds herself telephoning to all the neighbors in search of her child. Not infrequently, in divorce, this becomes a pattern. The child finds pretexts to linger at the homes of his friends and puts off going home although he knows his mother is expecting him.

This child is staying away from home because home is not what it used to be. This is one of the ways in which a child evades reality. Of course, evasion is no answer. The way to deal with this is first to acknowledge to the child the reason for his behavior. "I know you miss Daddy, and you like to go to Peter's house where there is a daddy. It's natural for you to feel this way."

Your very recognition of his feeling, without criticism, will help him to come home. At the same time you can try to provide more satisfying substitutes than these uninvited and often guilt-laden snatches at another child's feast. He need not stand like a child with his nose pressed against a shopwindow full of good things. Bring relatives and the friends he likes into the home, and take him to visit them.

You may have to resist your own inclination to seek your social life outside the home. Share your friends with him by having them visit you at home and by planning some activities which he can join until he is able to find his way in the new life.

A child may actually run away. When a child runs away from home, he does it for several reasons: he is running from a painful situation; he is rejecting his parents because he feels rejected by them; he is also, in fantasy, running to a new father and mother.

He will need your understanding more than ever when you get him back. This is not an occasion for punishment. There is no "bad" about what he has done. He was driven to do it by forces beyond his puny strength.

Give him sympathy. Make it clear to him that you know what made him run away. You are not angry with him, but you were very upset until you found him, because you love him and want to take care of him. You are sorry he has been so unhappy at home. Together you will try to make things happier for both of you.

THE DAYDREAMER   Daydreaming is also a running away, though not in body. The child who retreats into daydreams is also evading the reality he finds hard to face. Girls are more given to daydreaming, although boys are by no means excepted.

You must seek ways to bring her back to reality. Share her problems as she will let you; share your diversions and interests with her, in so far as you can. You might ask whether school work is also giving her some trouble—can you help her with it?

Principally, however, make sure she has the opportunity to talk out with you the things which trouble her, and help her to clarify her confusions. A blunt demand that she tell you what is bothering her is not likely to help her talk; but if you spend time with her, showing interest in the things which you know she cares about, she will gradually turn to you with her confidence.

You might enlist the school to help you brighten her life with new interests. Sometimes a frank talk with the principal or school guidance counselor will turn up suggestions for activities which will arouse the child's enthusiasm. Church or neighborhood organizations are other sources for new activities.

The mere giving of presents will not buy your way into her confidence. But a shopping excursion together can draw mother and daughter closer. A girl, like a woman, can feel her spirits lift when she has some new thing to wear, however small. Perhaps it is time to experiment with a new way of doing her hair; your friendly, not critical, interest in her appearance may be your open-sesame. She may like to cook or bake with you; you might teach her what you know, or try out new recipes with her.

The method you use scarcely matters. Knowing your child, you will find ways to reach her. What you are trying to do is re-establish communications so that you can comfort her and at the same time bring her back to reality and an understanding which will help her to accept reality.

WHAT SHOULD YOU KEEP OF THE OLD LIFE? People talk of making a "clean break" with the past, and beginning anew. Adults may get by with this, but children need roots in the past. Wherever it is possible, you will do well to maintain continuity with the child's way of living before the divorce.

Some changes are economically necessary. You may be obliged to move from your suburban house to a small apartment. You may be obliged to go to work. When drastic changes must be made, avoid making them simultaneously with the breakup of the marriage.

The mother of a young child may not be able to manage on her alimony. Should she go home to her parents? Should she take a job and put the child in a nursery school?

At first she would do better to take financial help from her parents or a social agency, to maintain the continuity of the child's life at least for a while. If she decides to take a job and put the child in a nursery school, she should approach that situation gradually.

Let the child visit the school a few times. Let him make friends with some of the children, with the teacher, with the school nurse. When he first begins to go to school, call for him yourself (or be at home when the school bus delivers him). Later, when you are working, a neighbor may keep him until you get home. Be sure to explain this to him in advance so that he will not be alarmed by your failure to be there yourself. In a rural community neighbors can often be counted on to help by keeping a child while the mother works, and this is valuable in maintaining the child's life with as little change as possible.

Should you stay in the same community? Your own impulse may be to run away. Perhaps you feel the community's disapproval, your friends' coldness. For your child, if you can manage it financially, it is better to remain; to continue with his Scout troop, his Sunday school class; to stay in the same school.

For yourself, although it may be hard at first, it is psychologically sounder to deal with reality by staying than by running away. If you must move for financial reasons, perhaps you can move to smaller quarters in or near the neighborhood so that the child is not sharply cut off from familiar friends and activities. As he makes new friends and develops new interests, he will gradually relinquish the old, but he needs time to do this.

In the new home keep as much as you can of his old furniture, his old toys. New things can come as a treat, but little by little, while he is establishing himself in his new emotional relationships. In time his old things will begin to lose their importance as a comforting tie to the past.

WHEN MOTHER GOES TO WORK   The possibility of going back to a job or profession, or of adventuring into a paid job, if she did not work before her marriage, may occur to a woman when her children reach school age, quite apart from divorce. In a united family a mother who wants or needs to go to work is likely to have a peaceful period in which to prepare her children for the change.

In the divorce situation time to prepare the children is more difficult to manage, but it is also more important. Any arrangement which a child may resent should be especially prepared for. If the groundwork for the new step cannot be laid before the divorce, then the child will need time after the divorce to accept the change.

Whenever parents can work together to carry out their divorce with the least friction—an ideal but not an impossible achievement—they can plan for the mother to begin her employment outside the home before the divorce proceedings are begun. Many a thoughtful mother takes her first step in this direction without advice. She will, for example, enroll in a refresher course in her field of work, or begin training for some new field. She may do this partly to assuage her unhappiness in her failing marriage, and partly as insurance against an uncertain future. Whatever her reasons, such a preliminary step is wise for both mother and child.

She should, however, keep the child informed. If divorce is not yet a certainty, she will not suggest to the child that a separation is imminent, but she can explain that his parents are not getting along very well, and that she wants the new interest outside the home now that the child is older and does not need so much of her time.

If the separation is decided on, an older child can be given to understand that the family is going to need more money when his parents live apart. It is good to prepare the child in this way before the divorce becomes final, better still before the father actually leaves the home.

When it happens that the father leaves abruptly, then the child needs time to absorb this change before he is faced with the next one. It may take some doing, but the mother should give him this time. She may need financial aid to tide her over. Some women can get help from their parents, some from friends, some from a welfare agency. Whatever emergency solution is found, the main thing is to time these changes so that they do not fall on the child simultaneously. The mother who tells her child, "See, your father has left us, and now I must go to work," or allows the child to draw this inference, casts an unhealthy air of martyrdom over herself and the child and of villainy over the father.

A reality situation has to be accepted, and parents can make the acceptance easier for the child by their planning. One mother, who had been a research worker before her marriage, took a refresher course before her divorce, so that by the time the separation was final her young son was accustomed to her absence from home and the new arrangements for his care; she, on the other hand, was well launched in work which interested her and also gave her a measure of financial independence.

A mother need not feel that her work must cause a painful separation from her child if she can share the experience with the child in positive ways. Nor does a child feel the need to resent his mother's job if he has been thoughtfully prepared for it.

LOOKING FOR A NEW HUSBAND   Let us not draw from this heading the picture of a divorcée clutching her decree with the ink barely dry, already on the prowl for a new mate. This may be a stock figure in fiction, but it is a long way from most women's reality. One needs time to absorb one's new status; there is a period of palpable loneliness, a pervading sense of loss. For a woman with children this is also a time of concern for them; she has a drive, perhaps as yet unfocused, to do something, plan something, in order to relieve their distress or make their new life more palatable to them.

But presently there does arise an urge to enjoy male companionship again, if not actively to look for it. Whether or not the wish for a new husband is recognized as such, with most women the desire to be married again revives even after a bitter experience. For the children's sake and her own a wise woman will act on this urge with discretion.

She will not, for example, rush out on dates every night to comfort her loneliness; she will remember that the child is lonely too. Nor will she present to her child every man she meets with the implication that he is a candidate for stepfatherhood. On his own the child may jump to this conclusion. As we pointed out earlier, the child is likely to be both looking for a father and fearing that he will find one.

It is important to guide him gently through this conflict of desires and relieve him of a feeling of imminence. You can explain to him that you have men friends, yes. You invite them to the house so that the child can also enjoy their company on occasion. But in the matter of choosing a new father you will not be hasty. You want to be sure first that the new family will be a happy one.

The pace of a woman's social life in this period is to some extent governed by the child's age and what his experience has been before the divorce. If father and mother were accustomed to going out a good deal and the baby-sitter was a familiar figure at night, the mother may feel nearly as free to come and go—and yet not altogether free, since she is aware that the child needs more reassurance of her love now than when the family was united. She will plan to go out somewhat less often, to have her friends visit her at home, casually including the man who seems the possible candidate for a husband.

If she was not previously in the habit of going out frequently, then it is a poor policy to expose a child suddenly to the experience of waking and finding his mother not there at a time when his security has been shaken by the divorce. It is not easy to explain to a two- or three-year-old that mother needs recreation and the companionship of grownups. A woman who feels with her child will try to continue the pattern to which he was accustomed, and have her social life at home as much as possible until the child is able to accept her more frequent absence in the evening.

To the older child one can, of course, explain. An older child can understand his mother's need for adult company, and he can also understand his mother's desire to marry again. But, though he may seem to accept the explanation in words, it may not be so easy for him to accept it emotionally. If he is an only child, moreover, although he may understand his mother's needs well enough, he may still be lonely and unhappy when she goes out in the evening, and she in turn may feel guilty at leaving him.

All these considerations will influence her to go slowly, to be patient with her child while he absorbs one new experience after another, to keep his confidence so that she knows when he is troubled and can reassure him. In this way she will be laying a sounder foundation for her new marriage when it comes, and for her own and her child's future happiness.

HOW IMPORTANT IS THE TRUTH? When we attempt to explain a complex adult situation to a child, we do so at considerable pains. Why do we do it? Why would not a simple fiction be enough, especially for a young child? For example, "Daddy had to go away on business," an uncomplicated explanation in which many a mother has taken grateful refuge when she had to tell a child that his father had left home.

To begin with, there is a practical objection. The fiction may satisfy the child at first, but it is not long before we are obliged to embellish it with more and more details until in the end it is a full-grown fantasy.

Recently a mother came for psychiatric advice about a little girl whose father had died suddenly. The mother, in her own shocked disbelief and also in an effort to spare the child, had explained merely, "Daddy has gone away."

The child was then two and one half years old. In the months since then, the mother has had to add to her first explanation in answer to the child's unsatisfied questioning: "We cannot visit Daddy in the place where he is; he cannot come home to see us from the place where he is." The little girl began to press the mother to move out to the country: "If Daddy can't come home to us here, perhaps he can come there."

From her persistent questions and also from the changes in her behavior, it was plain that the child had not accepted the explanation. To accept it would be too painful. Her father loved her. How could he go away from her? What could possibly keep him from coming back to see her? Can it be that he does not love her after all?

Similarly in a divorce situation, as we have already seen, the young child may offer what seems to be a naïve solution: "Why can't Daddy and his new wife live with us?" The motivation is the same, an inability to accept a too painful situation.

This brings us to the deeper reason, the psychological reason, why a loss, whether death or divorce, must be realistically faced. A child cannot accept the more agreeable fiction because it does not fit the emotional atmosphere which he perceives. If Daddy has merely gone away on business or for a vacation, why is Mommy so upset? And always the child's puzzled thinking turns back upon himself: "How can Daddy go away, and stay away, if he loves me?"

How much better if the mother had been able to give the little girl whose father died an explanation at least in the direction of the truth; for example: "Daddy got sick and had to go to the hospital." Then in time she could have given the complete explanation.

This mother believed she was shielding the child from a shattering encounter with a concept she was too young to grasp. In point of fact it was the mother's inability to accept her husband's death which kept her from telling the child. The knowledge that her father was dead would be less shattering to the child than an unexplained abandonment by a parent whom she loved and who, she wanted to believe, loved her.

The parent's own difficulty in accepting the divorce is often rationalized into an effort to spare the child. Recently I was asked about the curious behavior of a two-year-old, a toddler who had barely begun to talk.

This little girl had taken to looking behind doors and into corners. The act had become compulsive; in the middle of eating or listening to a story she would get up and go to open the door.

The father in this case had left for another state to get a divorce, and because the child was so young (but more because the mother was too upset to talk with the child about the situation at all), no explanation had been offered for her father's absence. So she was looking for her father. The need to find out what had happened to him was becoming so obsessive as to upset the whole orderly routine of her days.

Why, the reader may wonder, did this little girl not ask, "Where Daddy?" Words like these were already in her vocabulary. The answer is that her mother's anxiety effectively stopped her from asking. Even a two-year-old can recognize an emotional taboo.

So we must give the child an explanation, and it cannot be a fabricated one, but we must be careful to tell him only as much as he can absorb, and as far as possible in a setting of emotional calmness so that he will not be too disturbed to absorb it at all. We are trying to communicate something, not to his intellect, but to his emotions. We are trying to help him accept a situation which is difficult and painful to him, not because he cannot understand the simple words we use, but because emotionally he does not want to accept it.

The child must live in the real world. We help him to do so, little by little and in terms which he can absorb.

EXPLAINING AN INADEQUATE OR "UNFIT" PARENT   Some realities are more difficult than others to present to a child. Shall we tell him, for example, that his parents are being divorced because his father is a philanderer or an alcoholic? Or his mother is mentally ill? And if not, what shall we tell him?

We must give the child a valid explanation. We must assume that he has already seen something about his father that troubles him, although he may not know why, or that he has been upset by his mother's unstable behavior. There is a very good chance that, unless this is one of the extremely rare cases in which the deviation from the normal is perfectly masked, the child is already anxious about things he has not understood.

He needs an explanation which should do three things: it should set at rest his anxious puzzling about what is happening; it should help him to dissociate himself from his parent's weakness—in other words, to feel that what has happened is not his fault; and it should help him in his effort to salvage what good he can of his absent parent's image.

One boy, who had reached a state of speechless terror because of his father's tempers, has learned to deal with this violent trait in his father's personality. He has developed a protective psychological deafness to the scenes. He dodges the flung book and, more important, he dodges the emotional impact on himself. He has come to separate himself emotionally from what he now understands as an imperfection in his father, something for which no one, certainly not the boy himself, is to blame.

He no longer sees his father's wrath as that of an avenging Jehovah with thunderbolt about to destroy him for some unknown crime. Nor does he see his father as a bad man he must reject. He no longer questions his father's love for him; the man's furies are a thing apart. To this boy his father is a troubled man and his tempers are an expression of this trouble, like a symptom of an illness.

You cannot tell a child that a parent capable of violence or one who drinks to excess is ideal. But even a very young child can accept the explanation that his father or mother is unhappy, upset, or in some cases, sick.

The child may ask, or he may want to know although he cannot ask, why the parent does not try to get over his trouble or fix what is making him unhappy. Why doesn't he go to a doctor if he is sick?

Perhaps he is going to a doctor. If so, you can tell him so, and that you hope Daddy will get better. But if no effort is being made by the parent to deal with his difficulty, there is no need to mislead the child. You can say that some troubles are "hard to fix." You can explain that a person can be helped only if he wants to be helped, and sometimes he is too troubled to realize that he needs help.

We hope Daddy (or Mommy) will find a way to get better. But in the meantime we must make the best of it and not hurt the troubled person, and not let ourselves be hurt. A separation, if it has been decided on, can be explained as one way in which we can protect ourselves.

Whatever the difficulty, the child must learn to adjust himself realistically to what cannot be changed. Your explanation, sympathetic, gentle, and truthful, will set him on the path to that adjustment.

ARE THESE PROBLEMS NEVER SOLVED? Parents often express dismay at the discovery that however carefully they have dealt with one or another problem of a child's adjustment during divorce or afterward the same problem sooner or later arises to be dealt with again. But isn't this so with any phase of living?

We are familiar with advances and relapses in the process of learning, for instance. A child seems to learn speech, and then he seems to forget that he learned and must learn it again.

Emotional maturing moves along similar paths. Consider your own experience. You have dealt with your own particular specters of the divorce. You have examined your bitterness toward your former partner, let us say—have talked out and worked through your resentments, and have with considerable effort arrived at tolerance for the other's shortcomings along with recognition and acceptance of your own. You have been able to grasp, not only intellectually but also emotionally, the reasons why your marriage failed. Are there not still moments, perhaps even days and weeks, when the old unreasoning bitterness surges up again, for whatever cause, and you must retrace very much the same path toward clarity and peace of mind?

In the same way, your child has seemed to accept the situation as you patiently and repeatedly illuminated it for him. He has in fact made great strides. And yet, six months or a year later, perhaps when he is upset about something else (a friend has disappointed him or some achievement he worked for has eluded him), out of a clear sky he is speaking again of the divorce as if nothing had been explained or understood. He is criticizing arrangements made for him which previously he found acceptable, or he is flinging reproaches, or he is showing you, in ways you recognize, that he is feeling anew the grief and pain which you and he together worked so hard to absorb.

You need not feel that you failed with him the first time. You need not feel that you failed with yourself either when the feelings you thought you had worked through arise again to plague you. Each subsequent effort will be easier. This is how the human being progresses.

What pulls the switch and releases the old emotions again? Sometimes we know; sometimes we can only guess. The trigger may be trivial enough to pass notice altogether. A little girl who has been happy and contented suddenly begins to have nightmares. Her mother may remember that on that day the little girl was snubbed by a friend, or she lost a cherished toy, or suffered some disappointment unimportant in itself but just enough to revive her old grief for a more important loss.

What your child needs at such moments is more reassurance, more confirmation of your love and the love of the absent parent, more confidence in the stability of the present. You have said it all before. You must say it again if the child needs to have it said again.

Beyond this occasional resurgence of old feelings, like the twinges of an old wound, we also find that there are phases of adjustment to divorce just as there are phases of adjustment to other major changes in one's life.

Situations change, and our feelings change. We hope they will change for the better, but we cannot be sure that they will. How often have we seen a woman grow more, instead of less, bitter in proportion to the time which has passed since her divorce? How often does a man strive more and more to cut down his maintenance payments as the months part him farther and farther from his children and their mother?

On the other hand a man who has been distractedly seeking a new pattern for his life may find it hard to keep his weekly date with his young child. Once he establishes a new relationship his days fall into order again and he becomes more reliable. Or a woman who has been resentful toward her former husband becomes more tolerant of him when she herself has found a new love.

The parent who becomes more bitter and even vengeful is one who has not resolved these feelings in the first place. A mother whose resentment increases with time, perhaps because her husband has remarried and she has not, not only magnifies her own unhappiness, but also plunges her children into conflict. They find it hard to accept either their mother's unhappiness or their father's new happiness.

Often it is not a question of the principal actors in the scene, but of parents and parents-in-law, sisters, brothers, cousins who may stir up fires which, left alone, might have died away. And there are external circumstances which cause a setback in the progress toward adjustment. A mother may not find the job she counted on to fill out her days and her income. A father may suffer financial reverses or a misfortune in his new family. The diversity of possible combinations, inner and external, some troubling and some easeful, is virtually endless.

Finally the child grows and changes. A plan for a four-year-old's relationship with his father may no longer serve at six or eight. And the child matures and gets new insights. A boy whose parents were divorced when he was six said to me at thirteen, "I used to think my father was a skunk for leaving my mother. Now I know—my mother is a nag!" Strong language, but we must remember that he has had to take his mother undiluted by his father's presence since the divorce. At six this boy was wholly attached to his mother. Since then he has matured enough to grasp some of his father's point of view and to understand what drove him away.

Similarly, a girl who at first berates her mother for losing her father may come gradually to see her father's weaknesses and how they must have hurt her mother.

Change, both within and without, is inevitable in life, and we must be prepared for it. We can count on a child's comparative flexibility and resilience to bring about—with his parents' help—many changes for the better in his adjustment to divorce. Of more critical importance are the feelings and the attitude of the parents, for on their stability and their courage in facing new situations the child's adjustment depends.

WHEN YOU NEED HELP   Sometimes the situation proves too much for the parent who remains with the child. The parent is too profoundly troubled to be able to help the child, or the child's problems have advanced to the point where outside help is needed.

The parent in such case should not feel that he or she has failed. Nor is it too difficult to explain to the child that they are going together to seek help.

The parent can tell the child that, although they have both tried, their problems are too hard for the two of them to manage alone, and they will ask the advice of someone who has experience and special knowledge, a friendly person who will talk over their troubles with them and suggest how they can manage better.

In the following chapters we will look into the lives of some parents and children who have experienced divorce and have come through with more or less success, some with help and some without. Much pain can be saved both parent and child, as we shall see, in cases where the parent is sensitive to the moment when help is needed, and is willing to go out and seek it.

II
CHILDREN OF DIVORCE AND THEIR PARENTS

7

WHEN CHILDREN EXPERIENCE DIVORCE

Sometimes, when parents have come to me in grieved or angry baffle-ment at a child's difficult behavior, I have let my fancy wander, and conjured up some device by which the parent—for a day, even for an hour—could change places with the child. What a timesaver, labor-saver, painsaver—and child saver—such a magic wand would be!

If parents could stand in the child's place just once, could dwell in imagination within his body and mind, could know intimately his limitations—of comprehension, of capabilities, of physical size and strength—they would be able to *feel with him* the experience of divorce.

What makes it hard for us to project ourselves into the child's inner life is that we have been busy all our adult years blotting out much of our own childhood. This is how painful memories are ren-dered harmless.

How much anxiety, how many false starts would be spared parents if they could fully comprehend divorce in the child's terms! How differently, for example, would Donnie's father and mother have managed if they had known how Donnie first became aware of the idea of divorce.

Let us try to put ourselves in Donnie's place one night when he is awakened by loud voices in his parents' bedroom, next to his. He is lying very still in his bed. It is late, an hour when a boy of four should be sleeping. But Donnie has not been sleeping well lately, so it is not surprising that the angry argument in the next room has awakened him.

In the first moment of waking and hearing his father's voice Donnie squirmed out of his covers, ready to run and greet his father. It was a long time, as little children measure time, since his father had been home. Donnie knew that a newspaper man had to go away on "stories," but lately it seemed as though his father was never home. Presents came, big boxes which were fun to open. But it was not the same as when his father used to come home from a trip, bringing a present which they would open together. Donnie's mother kept saying that Daddy "would be home in just a few days," but her voice and face did not match the words, and Donnie, uneasy, had stopped asking.

So at first, hearing his father home again, Donnie was glad. But then the voice itself checked him. It was his father, no doubt about that, but he was speaking in the voice which Donnie did not like to hear.

Now he heard his mother. "If it weren't for Donnie I would have left you long ago!"

"Leave Donnie out of this!" his father shouted. And then he said that new word again: "divorce." Donnie did not know the meaning of the word, but from the way his father said it he knew it was something bad. And when, a few minutes later, the door of his room opened softly and his mother looked in, Donnie was in such panic that he shrank together under his covers and pretended to be asleep.

Thus, coupled with the word divorce, Donnie has already experienced fear, experienced guilt ("If it weren't for Donnie . . ." and "Leave Donnie out of this!"). With it he has already associated the unfocused but swelling uncertainties of the weeks when his father was away and his mother was anxious and worried. And in the morning, when Donnie wakes up, his father has already gone again, neglecting in his anger and distraction to think that Donnie might need just then to see him, to speak with him, to be reassured by him. And so there is included in Donnie's feelings about divorce one more feeling, that of being rejected, of having lost his father's love. Even if the strange word had not been mentioned, Donnie would already have been inwardly shaken by the events transpiring between his parents, though he might have given no sign of it. This will be the emotional setting of Donnie's experience of divorce —unless his parents can stop in their headlong flight from each other to give heed to Donnie. In Donnie's case, as it happened, this was not to be until after several unhappy years had passed.

300,000 DONNIES A YEAR   Your child, and Donnie, and between three and four hundred thousand American children each year must deal somehow with the experience of divorce. No two of them can have precisely the same experience, not even two children of the same family, as we shall see. Yet certain patterns, in broad outline, recur again and again.

There is the child who has been bruised by a rough experience, but has come through in good order, borne up on the love which one or the other of his parents has given him. Throughout a stormy time, this mother, for instance, has been able to maintain a strong and supporting relationship, spontaneously and without design, often without even an awareness of its importance to the child. Despite the turbulence of her own emotions, she has managed never to lose the thread of communication with her child, has somehow brought comfort and serenity into the hours spent together. And this solid, supporting love has been enough.

Another child may be spared many bruises because his parents, having decided on divorce, make conscious and efficient plans for his defense. They take pains to understand his needs and to meet them. Though the home is broken up and the changes may be drastic, they give thought to making the future setting of his life warm and secure, and they preserve their own relationship to him individually, though no longer together. If either or both parents should remarry, the child will be considered in this new relationship as well.

With such a child the changes in his life may appear more revolutionary than they really are. The important core, his emotional state, is not profoundly shaken, though it is revised. He must still accept the fact that his parents no longer live together, but the acceptance is less difficult because his parents have been foresighted. By their careful and timely explanations, by their continuously loving behavior, by their wise plans for him, they have forestalled anxiety and given him security in their love.

Still another child seems to have been completely forgotten by his parents during the time of their greatest personal disturbance. Obviously parents can "forget" a child only if their own emotional difficulties are such that they have little to spare for another's. Sometimes a child who has had to go through the experience of divorce without emotional support from his parents finds it in another adult, a grandmother or other relative, a teacher, a friend of the family; or he must build his own defenses. These may enable him to function somehow, but he may also carry into his adult life some permanent scars.

Or the child may show by his behavior that he is distressed, and his parents eventually come to realize that he needs help. An awareness has been steadily growing in the public mind that a child who has suffered a serious emotional experience may need help from outside his family to set him again on a healthy path. Perhaps of their own volition, perhaps at the urging of relatives, friends, or school authorities, parents who have been unable to help the child through the divorce itself not infrequently turn to a social agency, clinic, or psychiatrist to get help for him later.

In this chapter we shall examine the experiences of divorce in the lives of several children, illustrating these several patterns. Donnie, with whom we are already acquainted, is one of those children whose parents come later to an awareness that their child is in trouble and needs help.

THE ABSENT FATHER   The explosive quarrel which precipitated the divorce of Donnie's parents brought to a climax Donnie's long though unexpressed anxiety. He was born into a home in which anxiety was already insidiously working.

Donnie's father worked in a profession which required his frequent and sometimes extended absence from home. Journalism is only one of a number of professions which separate a man from his family for long or short periods: salesmen, buyers, some merchants, many kinds of technicians and industrial specialists; musicians, actors, and most members of the entertainment world; men in the armed services and in other branches of government service; all these must travel to some extent. Wartime of course exaggerates the problem of the absent father.

A father's absence can be accepted by his children if their mother, out of her own inner security, accepts it. But Donnie's mother did not have this inner security. A girl from a modest small-town background, she was at first dazzled by her husband's glamorous life, and only later realized that for her it had grave disadvantages. When he was at home, she found herself out of her depth among his friends. When he was away, she was lonely and without resources to fill the emptiness of her days.

Any marriage requires adjustment, but this kind of marriage demands a good deal more than the average, and Donnie's mother was unprepared. Carried away by romantic love, she had not anticipated the loneliness, the frustrations of such a life. She felt inadequate, and was unable to share the part of her husband's world which was open to her. Inevitably she felt rejected, hence resentful. She turned to her baby for solace, with the consequence that she gave him an overdose of motherly devotion, keeping him in her own room, watching anxiously over him.

Donnie was aware of the gradually widening breach between his parents although he was unable to ask about it. His father's returns were more and more often marred by quarrels, until the final explosion which confirmed this feeling that he was somehow to blame for his father's absence and his mother's unhappiness.

After the separation Donnie and his mother moved to a smaller apartment. Donnie went to nursery school; his mother took a business course, and through her former husband's affiliations found a secretarial job in a newspaper office.

For the first year after the divorce Donnie still groped for a reunion of his parents. He built a fantasy around the vacation he would spend with his father at his grandparents' home. He dreamed that his mother would come too, that they would all be together again.

His mother of course did not come, and the vacation was bound to be a disappointment for other reasons as well. Donnie had built his anticipation to impossible heights; at best his father could not satisfy his hopes. His father too had difficulties. It was hard to pick up the threads with the little boy who had grown and changed so much in the intervening months, and whom he had not known too well even before they were parted.

By the second year Donnie's mother began to bring friends home to cocktails and dinner, men from the newspaper where she worked, men not unlike his father. He regarded them with conflicting emotions, hoping he would get a new daddy, fearful that he might. A new daddy would close the door on his dream that his own father might someday come back. At the same time, though he liked these men who were rather like his father, he mistrusted them. They too might leave him as his father had done.

Toward his mother Donnie was increasingly hostile and difficult. Needing to be close to her, he also blamed her for the separation from his father. And he had the guilty fears of a boy who is too close to his mother, who has been kept in the mother-baby relationship past the time when he should have outgrown it.

Outside the home Donnie failed to make friends in his new neighborhood. To his schoolmates he boasted that his father was an important man—"he's on the radio"—and explained that his father was always away on a story; he could not admit that his parents were divorced. He did badly in school, and finally his disturbing, destructive behavior prompted the principal to call the mother in and insist that the boy could not stay unless he was given psychiatric treatment. His mother took him at last to a clinic.

Now for the first time Donnie had the opportunity to ventilate all those hostilities which he could not afford to express openly to his parents for fear he would lose their love entirely. Now for the first time, too, he could begin to understand that what had happened between his parents was not his fault, that though they had not been able to get along with each other, each still loved him as much as ever.

From a sympathetic neutral person with whom there were no emotional involvements, the realistic explanation came clearly and objectively. Little by little the differences between his parents, which until now had turned all against himself, took their proper place as a series of events in a relationship of which he was not the core. His guilt for his parents' discord gradually fell away.

His guilt for his excessive closeness to and dependence on his mother had tormented him in nightmares; he was now able to tell his dreams for the first time. He had dreamed of being with his mother, and suddenly she was not there. He had dreamed of being in a boat with her, and she drowned. Children normally have dreams like these, but a happier child awakens to familiar, comforting reality. Donnie's real world had not been reassuring because of the conflict which confronted him there.

Donnie became able in time to accept his mother's love without guilt, and to accept the reality that two people can marry with a hope of happiness and can fail to find happiness together. He became able to manage the division of his allegiance.

During Donnie's treatment, which lasted several months, his mother too was strengthened and relieved of her anxiety. His father learned something of what had been going on inside his boy, and learned what he could do to make the time which he spent with Donnie more satisfactory to both of them.

Donnie's father and mother have made new marriages, and Donnie gets along well with both his step-parents. What has happened to Donnie is that he no longer rebels at the real world, to retreat into fantasy. The reality which was unbearable to him before because of his emotional confusions, his anxieties and unrealistic fears, is now more acceptable.

In a sense it was fortunate for Donnie that his delinquency at school revealed his trouble and brought him help. Until then his mother had been too involved in her own confusion and unhappiness to see his need, much less to help him. A child's behavior does not always call attention to his needs so obviously. He may only become quieter, eat poorly, sleep badly, or do inadequate work at school. A child who retreats into himself and is docile and obedient at home and at school may not get the help he needs.

We have learned from experience that too much obedience can be a distress warning. The repressed child too is signaling to us by his behavior—"Somebody, please, do something!"

Such a child was Sidney, for example, whose parents' violent quarreling about money and about him drove him cowering into a corner both literally and emotionally. Sidney made no trouble to distract his parents from their intense conflict with each other. Sidney was a "good" boy, so good that his parents were not aware of the deep trouble he was in until, when he was eleven, he made an attempt at suicide. Only then, shocked by such an extreme gesture of despair in a child, did they realize that Sidney had been pushed beyond his strength and must have help. Sidney's story is extreme, but it reminds us that the too quiet child is also in need of help.

THE CHILD'S SELF-DEFENSE   Janie on the other hand has had no help at all. She has been left to build her own defenses, for better or worse. Janie's mother went to a guidance counselor, but not for guidance. What she sought was professional support in winning custody of the child. Bitterly resentful at the failure of her marriage, this headstrong young mother fought for Janie less for Janie's sake than to take vengeance on her husband for not measuring up to her unrealistic standards.

The story of Janie and her parents is so common and yet so frequently misinterpreted that it bears telling. Like so many divorces, the divorce of Janie's parents was the climax of a multitude of small but cumulative frustrations which, if they could have been dealt with separately and in time, might have been resolved.

These two young people married on the crest of an ardent love affair, and continued the carefree pleasure-seeking of an attractive young couple until Janie was born. Then at one stroke they were confronted with a different facet of marriage, its mature responsibilities.

Janie's father tried to fit himself into his new, oversize role. He tried to give up the round of parties, tried to be home for the baby's bath and supper, tried to get to bed early to make up for the sleep he lost giving Janie her night bottle and attending to her when she cried. He took a new interest in his job; the father of a family had to get ahead.

But Janie's mother was shocked to discover that a baby was not a doll to be put away when she was tired of playing with it, that she could no longer sleep till noon and be out for lunch, cocktails, dinner. She longed for her lost freedom. She was unready for the satisfactions of motherhood which compensate a more mature personality for the lighter pleasures she has surrendered. This maturity is not a matter of birthdays but of emotional growth, and Janie's mother had simply not yet achieved it.

Unconsciously seeking a way out, with the plea of higher family expenses, she soon began renewing her contacts as a fashion model. Gradually she slipped back into her old patterns, leaving Janie to the care of a succession of part-time maids.

By the time she was six, Janie hardly knew her mother, the lovely scented creature who dropped her a kiss in passing, but who unaccountably became a sharp-voiced enemy on the maid's day off. Janie was closer to her father, who had perforce taken over many of a mother's duties. But he too was becoming sharp and irritable as his lack of sleep affected both his work and his temper, and their scale of living kept him constantly pressed for money. He was anxious, tired, and inclined to blame his wife, and she for her part felt resentful and guilty. The infrequent dinners at home began to be accompanied by quarreling and tears. He rebuked his wife for the slovenly management of the household, for her neglect of Janie, for the thousand little irritations which daily built up the growing barrier between them.

"If you made enough money I wouldn't have to work!" she retorted, forgetting that her earnings barely paid for the indifferent maid, who took her place at home, for the extensive wardrobe she needed in her work, for the social activities which were part of her "contacts."

One final quarrel, and the young wife made good her threat. She took Janie and went home to Mother, to "bring him to terms." In fact she was retreating still farther from her responsibilities, as she had retreated from them into her modeling. Home to her was still the protective shell where she never had unpleasant chores to do, where her every wish was granted.

This pattern has become so familiar that we make a joke of "going home to Mother." In an older society, in which a girl was married much as a cow was sold, the troubled young wife also went to her mother or aunt, and found there an outlet for her dissatisfactions, but she did not also find fuel to feed the fires of her discontent. Unless her husband had failed in some serious obligation—and his obligations, like hers, were clearly delineated—she was rebuked as often as she was comforted, was reminded of her duty, and was sent back to fulfill it.

A girl in those days, moreover, had been taught her duty since childhood. "Love will come later," she had been told. Her husband was chosen, her future laid out for her, and she knew that she could make her own happiness only by fitting herself successfully into the role to which she had been reared.

Today the concept of marriage is very much changed. The words *duty* and *responsibility* are spoken softly, if at all, and *obey* is usually omitted from the marriage vow. The girl is no longer given passively in marriage. She makes her own choice of whom to marry and when. She is more responsible for her own future, and less prepared for it. As a child, she has had far more freedom than her sister of another day, and possibly more happiness as well, and this is good. But somewhere between the ages of six and eighteen the family pattern which should enable her to take her first taste of responsibility is not there.

Parents are apprised of sexual development in adolescence and what to do about it, but not of the development of personality which should enable a girl to manage her own life. In freeing the child from the real work of the family we are depriving her of the necessary emotional foundation for doing the work of her own family when she is a woman. How should she know that there are deep satisfactions in creating comfort and happiness for those she loves, when she has never experienced them, when up to the day of her marriage she has been always the recipient of care and never the giver of it?

So Janie's mother fled from the mature role she was not prepared to play, back to her own mother, back to the past and the longed-for state of a dependent child. In effect she was trying to be no longer a wife and mother, but once more a daughter. Yet the fantasy could not replace reality. She could not be a happy daughter, either, since she brought with her her conflict and its attendant guilt, resentment, and defeat. And there was Janie, a constant, troublesome reminder.

With the sure intuition of a child Janie slipped into her new place, becoming her own mother's little sister, competing for the love of Grandma, who was the only real mother in the house. So fierce was this competition, so desperate Janie's need for love, that the peace of Grandma's house was continually shattered by the child's screaming rages, the mother's furious discipline. Meanwhile Janie longed for her father, and tried her mother's already short temper still further with the monotonous question, "When is Daddy coming?"

Daddy came at last, not to set Janie's world right again by behaving like a father, but to plead with her mother to come back. He had not even unpacked his bag when Janie realized that he was saying good-by. She clung to his legs, aware even in her distress that her mother did not ask him to stay. (Janie's mother held firmly to "her terms," but what she really meant was that she could not go back and face again the realities of marriage and family.)

Janie's father, rejected and helpless, put Janie severely aside and departed. Janie thrashed about in frustrated rage, pounding with her fists against her mother, her grandmother, until her mother dragged her upstairs and locked her in her room to learn "to behave herself."

So there was a divorce. We know part of its aftermath and can project more. Janie's mother goes out with other young divorcées and unmarried friends, trying to enjoy herself, trying to expunge the seven or eight years of her marriage, but confronted always with the living symbol of them in Janie. She has defeated her husband and won custody of Janie, but it is a dubious victory. She will probably marry again; whether she will bring more wisdom to her second marriage we cannot know. The prospects at this time are not promising.

Janie meanwhile is building her defenses. She is learning to "behave herself" in sheer self-protection, but her somewhat better manners can only mask the stormy emotions underneath. In a child's terms she has had unmistakable proof that she is unloved, first by her mother, then by her grandmother, who has withdrawn from her out of pure inability to cope with such a difficult child. Finally she has lost the love of her father, whose leaving she could interpret only as a rejection of herself.

Janie is a fighter. Not knowing love, she can deal with life henceforth only by aggressiveness and hostility. Her native intelligence, her determination to reach a goal, especially in opposition to parents and parent figures, her toughness in the face of challenge—all this suggests a familiar pattern. She may one day become a successful career woman, an aggressive business executive. But she is not likely to make a life yielding emotional satisfactions to herself or to others around her.

THE PLANNED DEFENSE OF THE CHILD   Stories like Donnie's, to whom help came, though late, fill the clinical records, and Janie's is a story which may come out years afterward on the psychoanalyst's couch.

But there are happier stories, which do not appear in the clinical records, of those children whose parents planned in advance for their defense from the possible ill effects of divorce.

Peggy's parents, for example, carefully and thoughtfully arranged for her future before they considered the arrangements for their own legal separation. Peggy needs and will need no help outside her parents. The stories of children like Peggy come to the attention of psychiatrists and social workers only when their parents ask for advice in planning for the children.

Peggy's parents knew before she was born that their marriage was not an unqualified success. A bluff, hearty, outgoing man, fond of merry company; a gentle young woman with rather serious tastes and a need for peace and order in her home—it is not too unusual for such opposites to marry. It was not so farfetched an attraction. Both were warmhearted and affectionate. During their courtship he enjoyed the dependence of this demurely loving girl, while she appreciated, though she could not actively participate in, his exuberance and high spirits.

Once they were married the differences in their tastes became troubling to both. The get-togethers she had enjoyed in his company were now in her own house, and she took her management of them too conscientiously. The frequent and unexpected arrival of friends now became a strain. Try as she would, she could not help being upset when in the midst of preparing a simple dinner for two she was all at once called upon to serve cocktails and snacks to the half-dozen friends her husband had impulsively brought home.

Seeing her distress, he began to stay out with his companions instead of bringing them home. He realized that this was equally destructive to their marriage, but he was too much of an adolescent to see the charms of a quiet home life. Meanwhile the example of other young, carefree couples—the couple next door, for instance—impressed her with the realization that other women could manage a gay social life, and she felt inadequate and unworthy.

When she became pregnant, both hoped that the coming of a child would solidify their marriage. Each tried to change so that the other would be more comfortable. As a result he felt constrained; his zest for living was paralyzed. She was fatigued, depressed after each effort to join him and his gay cronies. Once the baby came, he enjoyed and welcomed the satisfactions of fatherhood, but the sound of the baby crying at night was not his dish. He admired his wife's willingness to take over the whole task of child care and homemaking, but could not participate in it.

Fortunately these two people cared genuinely for each other. As individuals, they were emotionally mature enough so that feelings of rejection and inadequacy did not poison their affection for each other. As he confided a developing interest in an attractive divorcée, she, on her part, told him of the renewal of her friendships in the church group to which she had belonged before her marriage, and in particular with a man of quiet tastes whom she met there.

As each began to develop a life apart from the other, together they considered a legal separation. Intuitively he grasped her need of continuing emotional support from him until the baby was out of the diaper-and-formula stage and there would be more leisure for the mother to pursue other interests. He saw too that it would be better not to interrupt the continuity of life for her and the baby, that it would be better if he were the one who went to another state to get the divorce.

All was done as planned, without haste. When little Peggy was past her second birthday she was entered in the church nursery school where her mother had already made a place for herself as an assistant. Thus the child had the opportunity to spread her affections among several mother persons—the teachers, the nurse—while having the reassurance that her mother was there with her. Going to school did not take on the aspect of being thrust out of the home, rejected by her mother, as in similar circumstances it often does for a young child. Peggy was thus able to develop a good measure of independence.

Peggy's father took an extended vacation to get the divorce. His absence was comfortably explained to Peggy by her mother, who had no difficulty explaining, since she had long before accepted the plan and had no anxiety about it. When her father did not come back to live with them, but only to visit, Peggy was ready for a further explanation, and was given one:

Daddy and Mommy liked different things, and found it hard to be happy together. Daddy liked to laugh and play and be noisy; this Peggy understood very well, since this was the way Daddy played with her. Mommy liked to be quieter, to read and talk and play music, to keep house and sew for Peggy. This Peggy also understood, since it was apparent in their serene life at home. But Mommy and Daddy cared for each other, as Peggy plainly observed in their affectionate, considerate behavior when they were together.

Above all, Mommy and Daddy loved their little girl—and this Peggy had never had occasion to doubt. In her mother it was steadily demonstrated. And her father, in his exuberant warmth, made his visits an uncomplicated delight to the child.

Peggy cried at first when her father left. But she accepted his reassurance that, although he must go now, he would come again next Saturday. She accepted it because he did unfailingly come when he said he would; he was careful not to make a promise he was not sure of keeping.

As the weeks went by, Peggy asked more questions. What would happen to her? She and Mommy would stay here together as they had before, and Daddy would continue to come to see them. When she was older, Daddy would take her out sometimes to interesting places.

Then, as her father's remarriage approached, that too was explained. Daddy was getting a new wife. She would go to visit him in his new home and be friends with his new wife. Someday she might have a new sister or brother in Daddy's home.

Would Mommy get a new husband? Mommy's friend was a frequent visitor. He brought books for Peggy and read them to her. Peggy went walking with him and her mother on Sunday afternoons. He was very different from her father—this was reassuring; if he were too much like her father he might also go away. But he was familiar and kind, and incidentally he was careful to temper his courtship so as not to disturb the child by displaying ardor toward her mother in her presence.

When Peggy asked, "Is Mr. Rogers going to be my new daddy?" her mother's answer was mild.

"We want to be sure. We want to know each other very well so that we can all be happy together."

Now Peggy began pressing her mother to marry Mr. Rogers. She liked him, enjoyed his stories and the quiet games he played with her, and she wanted a man in the house. With this evidence that all promised well, when Peggy was four and a half her mother and Mr. Rogers were married.

Peggy's mother and new father love their quiet orderly life. Peggy has thrived in the serene family setting, in which she feels she belongs. She bears no resentment toward her father, who has shown in his bluff way that he loves her, and who, with the satisfactory new life he has made for himself, brings no resentments of his own into his relationship with Peggy.

Peggy may expect new brothers and sisters, and we are safe in assuming that she will continue to feel that she belongs in her new family even as it expands.

No two divorces are alike. But in all divorces in which children are involved the children need to be defended. Whatever the dynamics, whatever the relationships, the defense of the child is important to the child's future, and to the parents' peace of mind.

DEFENDING THE OLDER CHILD   What Peggy's parents did for her almost before she was born, Bernard's parents arranged for him at fourteen. Peggy's parents did not, however, need to repair any damage already done. The period of uncertainty preceding a decision to divorce was brief in their case, and as nearly without rancor as such an experience can be.

For Bernard the more usual pre-divorce tensions were present. An older sister, away at college and enjoying it, was out of reach of the acute situation at home, but Bernard was caught in the middle of it. Add to this the fact that he was going through his own adolescent tensions, and that his father, a traveling salesman, had been away from home for long periods during his entire childhood.

Bernard's parents had been married nineteen years. Usually a father's professional absence is a contributing factor in the insecurity of a marriage, as it was in Donnie's story, told earlier in this chapter. In Bernard's family the father's travels had had a reverse effect, maintaining a relationship which would very likely have crumbled long before.

During most of the marriage Bernard's father had found his well-kept home comfortable, his wife's companionship adequate for the comparatively brief periods of his stay, and he had opportunity to satisfy his need for heartier company during his travels. Now, at fifty, he had retired to an office position, and his wife's sexual coldness and other incompatibilities distressed him. He was already interested in a woman who could give him the warmer affection he needed.

Bernard's mother for her part found her husband's new permanence at home confining. Through the years she had enjoyed her freedom to go out with her women friends. She also felt a strong urge to launch out seriously on a career of welfare work, in which she had dabbled for some time.

Both these mature people had the feeling of urgency about satisfying their needs—the "last-chance" feeling—which often comes over men and women in their middle years. Both felt acutely the tensions growing between them, and the man in particular feared for his health. Heart attacks had already claimed some among his friends.

Bernard could not escape awareness of the situation. He saw his father going out alone in the evening, or if his father stayed at home his mother went to her room. She had moved into the absent daughter's room, to an adolescent a disturbing sign that his parents avoided intimacy with each other.

Bernard worried in silence. He could not talk to his parents, partly out of the fear that a thing once talked about becomes real, partly because he had never had a close enough relationship with either parent to voice his really important problems.

When a child's disturbance is a reaction to the specific acute situation, and the resolution by divorce or separation can give him relief and the promise of a good future, then psychiatric treatment may not be indicated. The child must learn to deal with new situations, and he can deal with divorce with his parents' support.

So it was with Bernard. While his relationship with his parents was not close to the point of frankness, it was basically healthy. He was troubled by anxieties specific to the situation. What would become of him if his parents separated, as they semed on the verge of doing? If he lived with his father, toward whom he inclined, how would his father keep house for him? Would he have to hear bitter words from his father about his mother? He shrank from that; he loved his mother too. And how could he hurt his mother by openly preferring his father? Suppose his father remarried, what would the stepmother be like? He worried about the details of life without his mother, who knew the food he liked, bought his clothes, managed the entertainment of his friends.

On the other hand, if he lived with his mother, it pained him to think of his father living in some furnished room, lonely and comfortless. He did not think his mother would remarry, so no stepfather problem was likely. But he was uneasy at the prospect of such closeness to his mother without the leavening of his father's presence. And finally he felt a rising hostility toward both his parents. Why couldn't they get along? Why couldn't they at least wait until he got away to college like his luckier sister?

Thus he pondered, and his work at school, which had been good until now, began to suffer so that the school principal called his mother for a conference. Was there anything wrong at home? This brought matters to a head for both parents. They agreed that they must resolve their situation, promptly and in the best way, so that Bernard might not suffer unnecessarily.

The mother consulted a guidance counselor, and Bernard was invited to conferences, first alone and then together with his parents. Alone with the counselor, he was able to air his anxieties, and later to discuss them with his parents in a joint conference, frankly and without fear of blame, since he had the counselor's sympathetic and objective presence to support him. Out of these conferences came the plan which settled Bernard's future, and in fact rearranged the lives of all the individuals of this family toward greater satisfaction.

Bernard went, as he really preferred, to live with his father. The counselor relieved him of his guilt toward his mother, assuring him that this preference was natural and wholesome at his age. His father at first had a housekeeper to look after their needs; later came the expected stepmother, to whom Bernard had little difficulty adjusting, as his relationship with his own mother became increasingly comfortable. His mother found the outlet she needed by plunging fully into the career of her choice, and Bernard was further relieved at seeing how occupied and contented she had become.

Bernard and his sister spend their vacations with their mother. Freed of tension, all three can now really enjoy the time they have together, the children taking a lively interest and pride in their mother's work because they no longer feel threatened or shut out by it. And in his new home situation Bernard reaps the full benefit of his father's relaxed and happy second marriage.

LOVE, THE INTUITIVE DEFENDER   Side by side with planned protection of their children by parents contemplating divorce are the experiences of children whose parents sustain them without conscious plan but with quite as much success by the steady support of their love. Such an experience was Patty's.

We have already learned the end of Patty's experience of divorce in the early pages of this book, when her father and stepfather came together to discuss Patty's adoption. This little girl was able to demand the final cachet on her feeling of security in her new family, the change of her name, largely because she had been so well protected through the divorce situation by her mother's love and, as far as he was able to give it, her father's love as well. A glimpse into the events leading up to Patty's adoption by her stepfather reveals some further facets of a child's experience of divorce.

Patty's parents married young. They loved each other and worked at their marriage, but in spite of their efforts it was not a good marriage for either of them. Patty's mother needed a strong mature husband to support her in her own groping toward maturity. This need Patty's father was unable to meet. When crises arose and decisions had to be made, he escaped, taking a vacation or arranging a busines trip in order, as he believed, "to gain perspective." In reality he was evading the need for action, leaving his young wife to cope with the situation alone.

The experience of growing up together, which is the crucial factor in the success of youthful marriages, was not possible for these two. Often such maturing comes in the wake of an early first marriage but not until after it is ended. Patty's mother turned to a childhood friend, a stronger and more mature man who had been a friend of her family and who reappeared during the intervals of separation from her husband, offering innocent companionship.

Patty welcomed her mother's friend even at the beginning. She saw the comfort and reassurance he brought her mother, and she too felt comforted. Meanwhile Patty's father, whose inclination had been toward lighthearted and less responsible friendships with women, was fortunate in becoming attached to a more mature woman whose influence on him was wholesome and steadying.

As her parents' periodic separations lengthened and progressed toward a final parting, Patty could not escape entirely the unsettling effects of uncertainty and imminent change. But her mother, though young, was calm and sure of herself in her relationship with her little girl. She found solace in her child through the painful period of breaking up, but not possessively. She and Patty drew comfort from each other.

Evidence that Patty was not deeply shaken by the divorce was clear in her behavior. She was neither hostile nor too obedient. She resisted her mother only in those small rebellions which are the normal expression of a young child's self-assertion.

Yet, following the divorce and remarriage, there were the inevitable tensions. Patty's father loved her, but when he came to see her he felt like an intruder in the home where Patty herself so obviously felt she belonged. All his gestures of love somehow took on a perverse twist. Patty refused to go out with him, refused to get into his car.

He was also aware of his irresponsibility in the past, and his own guilt increased his feeling that Patty's mother was turning the child against him. This was not true, except that she did find it difficult to speak favorably of him, and therefore did not speak of him at all. The silence itself had a destructive effect.

Still he tried earnestly to maintain his relationship with the little girl. He planned in advance each coming visit, mulling over what he had done the previous time, determining not to make the same mistake, resolving not to press Patty to go out with him. Yet when the moment arose, pushed by his own guilt and tension, he found himself saying and doing the same things again.

Patty's mother meanwhile longed to be rid of the ghost of her first marriage. Yet she sturdily resisted the pressure of her parents, who had not forgiven the young man's irresponsibility in the marriage and urged her to exclude him from her own and Patty's new life entirely. Patty's mother knew intuitively that to banish the child's father would not be good for the child.

Trying to erase a friendship or a relationship which has failed is no solution. We cannot slam the door and thus end all feelings. They continue within ourselves, churning up guilt and resentment and recriminations whether we will or no. Patty's mother and her new father understood this not only for Patty but also for themselves.

Patty, meanwhile, was thrown into conflict; her feeling for her father became increasingly troubling to her. She felt snug in her new family, and her father was a threat to this safety. She feared he might take her away, "kidnap" her from her secure home. She remembered his previous absences. At the same time she felt guilty toward him for these fears, and for accepting her new father so completely.

She had begun by designating her two fathers as "my daddy that I was born of" and "my daddy now." Presently "my daddy now" became simply "my daddy," an apt expression of her feelings.

When the new baby was born she was really in distress. She felt secure in both her mother's and her stepfather's love, but the new baby was a symbol of a closely knit family and she was not sure of her place in it. Her mother, her baby brother, her stepfather were all called Barton. But she was still Patty James.

Her imagination fixed on the name as a kind of magic, and one day in school she gave her name as Patty Barton. The children giggled, and she was startled and upset. "It was an accident," she explained. But it was the kind of accident which must be interpreted as a significant revelation, and it was so interpreted by her mother and stepfather.

All this came out in the discussions with Patty's two fathers and later with her mother. It was necessary to examine the whole situation and each individual's part in it before a solution could be found which would provide the best answers for everyone involved. The discussions themselves had the wholesome effect of airing each person's confusion between his own desires and his guilt toward the others.

The father in such a situation is almost bound to be hurt by his child's rejection of him. But this can be soothed by relief that in agreeing to her adoption he contributes to her happiness.

For Patty's father the relief was great. His position had been a most painful one. To give up his child for legal adoption freed the relationship of its greatest source of tension—the child's concept of him as a threat—and made it possible to keep the best part of his daughter's feeling toward him.

On the counselor's advice he gave Patty time to absorb her new status as Patty Barton. After a lapse of a month or so Patty would want to see her father. Now that he was no longer a danger to her security, she could regard him as a very special friend, someone with whom she would go on happy excursions, someone with whom a visit was a festive occasion rather than a tug of war. Whatever her legal status, Patty could from then on allow herself to give him a daughter's love. A relationship of importance to both had not only been saved, but was given an impetus to blossom through the coming years, because a wise move had been made, and made with understanding on all sides.

The element of understanding and clarity for all parties is a crucial one. The wisest action, if taken in haste and emotional confusion, may have effects quite different from those intended.

Good intentions are not enough. Good emotions must provide the climate for success. We have only to imagine how Patty's adoption by her stepfather might have turned out if it had been forced on her father without a clarification of his own and the others' feelings.

Guilt, resentment, hostility would have been intensified. These painful emotions cannot be annihilated by a legal gesture. Unless they are resolved, they remain to fester and throw off their poisons, corrupting every relationship. In Patty's case it is apparent that the aftermath of a wise decision unwisely executed would have damaged not only Patty's future happiness but the happiness of both the families which claimed her.

If this is true in the resolution of a child's future after divorce, it is true through all the stages in the breaking up of a marriage. The effort to clarify emotional confusion, to find one's way through the tangle of human reactions to a deeply felt crisis, is never wasted. So much pain, so much error, so much waste and even tragedy can be avoided for parents and children if men and women can restrain the hasty action, if they can take time to consider not only what is to be done, but in what manner it can be done for the good of everyone.

This is not to say, in the words of the fairy tales, that they will all live happily ever after. These stories of some children's experience of divorce show how the crisis of divorce itself has been surmounted with more or less success. We cannot promise that all these children and their parents will dwell henceforth in a paradise of mutual love and happiness.

We can be reasonably sure, however, that for Patty, Bernard, and Peggy, and to some extent for Donnie, divorce has done a minimum of damage. It may even have been a maturing and clarifying experience. And we can feel confident that a child who has been thus successfully defended through divorce will be no less able than other children to meet the situations and ride out the storms which are part of every human life.

8

ARE THEY BOUND TO FAIL?

What future can we expect for the child of divorce as an adult?

We have been told repeatedly that divorce is a major cause of juvenile delinquency. Yet a study of approximately 18,000 delinquent children by M. C. Elmer revealed that only one tenth of delinquent boys and about one fifth of delinquent girls came from families broken by actual separation and divorce. From what kind of homes, then, did nine tenths of these unhappy boys and four fifths of these unhappy girls come?

Not, we may be sure, from well-adjusted families in which both parents were on the job. Some came from homes broken by the death of a parent, but not a large proportion, as we know from other studies. Some are the product of homes broken by desertion; these figures do not appear in the statistics as legal separations. But the largest proportion of these children who fall foul of the law come from families which are emotionally broken, *without* having their disharmony overtly recognized by a recourse to law.

From among our juvenile delinquents, both those who are detected and those who escape detection, from among children who may be under institutional or private care, and finally, and in greatest number, from among children whose maladjustment is not recognized until they have to face adult responsibilities—from among all these come the adults who make society suffer and who suffer themselves the varying penalities of maladjustment.

Divorce is not responsible for most of these unhappy men and women. Many of them would have been the better for it if their parents had brought their disharmony into the open with divorce. While the physical separation of parents brings many urgent problems in its wake, it is not the severest blow to children. The emotional separation of parents from each other, and of parents from children, works its destruction on children in homes where the word divorce may never have been breathed.

Even theoretically, then, considering the poor prospects of many children who have not experienced divorce, the chances of children of divorce for a successful future are comparatively not so bleak. With actual divorce we are likely to find the situation opened to the light of day. Parents who have arrived at a decision to divorce must also decide what is to be done about their children. For many parents this is the first time that they become aware of their children's difficulties. It is the time in many cases when they turn to the minister, the doctor, or a clinic or psychiatrist for help.

Divorce also often brings the child's buried anxieties to the surface. The divorce has not created these anxieties. They have been there throughout the period of dissension. They may have been born long before. The remoteness between parents is usually accompanied by a parallel emotional remoteness between the parents and their children. The divorce is not the cause but the catalyst. The separation between his parents in actual fact often brings the child's hidden troubles out to the level of open behavior which his parents cannot ignore.

A child who has been able, with his parents' or outside help, to weather a divorce has a better chance for healthy maturity than a child of unhappy marriage who has not come through this stormy experience. This is rather like Hobson's choice; we would much prefer that parents loved each other and their children simply and wholesomely, and that homes remained intact emotionally as well as legally. But since unsuccessful marriage cannot be wished out of existence, in those situations which nothing short of divorce can resolve it is reassuring to know that under certain circumstances the divorce can bear good fruit in the child's future. It can do so, however, only if the parents are able to work toward such results.

We need not speculate on how children of divorce can grow up to healthy adulthood. We can look at some grown-up children of divorce and see.

TWO SISTERS   Betty and Alice are sisters. When their parents were divorced, Betty was in high school. She was a self-contained girl with an air of being always calmly and purposefully bent on her own affairs, popular with boys and apparently a successful student.

Only Alice knew that Betty cheated on examinations, and that she was not ashamed of this. Only Alice saw Betty's selfishness, her coldhearted cynicism. Their father was a man of spectacular achievement, and a perfectionist. He thought Betty beautiful, brilliant, quite faultless. He would not have believed that the fine character he ascribed to her was a garment she put on only for him. So high were his standards for himself and his family that either one had to comply, at great cost, in order to be accepted by him, or else rebel, at equally great cost.

Betty's mother's opinion of Betty is unknown, nor would it have mattered to Betty. Unable to meet her husband's high standards, this mother was a fugitive from her unsuccessful marriage long before divorce freed her to marry again and live in another city. "Sick headaches" and a variety of minor ailments were her overt reasons for her remoteness in the marriage. She left Betty's upbringing almost entirely to her husband. With her father's unwitting help, Betty at an early age formed an image of her mother which was not one to win a little girl's faith.

Now Betty is twenty-two. Her hair is a little too garishly blond, her make-up a shade too theatrical. From high school she went away to a first-rank women's college, but came home in the middle of her sophomore year. She had been working too hard, her father said indulgently, and gave her a long vacation at a ski resort. The next fall she decided with her father that she would enroll for special courses at the university near by.

For two years Betty deceived her father into believing that she was faithfully attending her special courses. The truth is that she very early succeeded in seducing a young instructor who let her copy other students' records to present to her father. She lived for more than a year with a wealthy married man whose home was in the suburbs and who maintained an apartment for her in the city. But she deceived him too. Students, instructors, almost any likely male were welcome to her favors. She has had two abortions.

One of the young men in her retinue, a student, took her too seriously. When he threatened suicide Betty married him. But no permanent relationship can content Betty. She is a queen bee, devouring males. It was easy to persuade her father that this marriage was a mistake, and he was glad to pay for the divorce to extricate her from her youthful error.

So Betty was off to Reno for the first but probably not the last time. She has found her career, not in scholarship or professional work, not in marriage and motherhood, but in divorce. Her brilliant mind and great capabilities are, by all present signs, destined to be wasted. Her mother failed her, and her need for her father's unqualified approval drove her to cheating and deception, the only means by which she could meet his unrealistic standards.

There is little hope that Betty will ever be other than an immature, exhibitionistic, social and sexual delinquent, as well as one of the perennial repeaters enjoying the benefits of Nevada's easy divorce laws.

Not so with Alice.

ALICE-SIT-BY-THE-FIRE   By contrast with Betty's dash and vivacity, Alice was a plain child, even a little dull, and it did not need the brilliance of Betty's school achievement, real or fictitious, to reveal Alice's slowness in learning. Indeed it was this inability to cope with her schoolwork which led her father to seek help for her after his divorce.

As we write of her, Alice is nineteen, entering her second year at college with a good record in her studies. She is friendly, with a wholesome kind of good looks. She is not engaged, but is planning to marry a young man who is now away in the service, a stable, well-organized youth, a sound choice for Alice among the several boys who have courted her. Knowing Alice's steadfast character, we can believe that she will wait for him and that together they will make a good marriage. She is not tempted, as Betty was, by sexual experiment to appease powerful but unidentified hungers. Her emotional needs are channeled, her judgment mature. Alice is a successful girl on the brink of a successful womanhood.

Is it hard to believe that two children, of the same sex and not far apart in years, born of the same parents and subjected to the same divorce experience, should turn out so differently?

The truth is that they did not have the same divorce experience. They did not have the same family experience while their home was still unbroken. They did not have the same parents—or, to put it more exactly, the relationship of each of these girls with her father and mother was so unlike the other's that they might have been born of different parents.

We know that Betty was her father's girl, and her relationship to her mother was almost entirely negative. For Alice the parents had quite other values. Alice was her mother's girl. She was loved by her mother with a possessive, jealous love, while her father all but ignored her.

Alice's mother conceived her, partly in competition with her husband's possession of Betty, and partly in the hope that another child might help her to keep her husband. Thus even before she was born Alice was robbed of her birthright, the right to be the child of both her parents.

Superficially Betty had the better deal; the stronger parent was on her side. By contrast with Betty's busy, stimulating life Alice's childhood was dreary. She was occupied in soothing her mother's unhappiness, and later covering up her mother's inadequacies, at the same time as she strove vainly to win her father's approval, which to her was synonymous with his love.

By the time she was twelve and her parents had parted, she was a solemn child who seemed unable to play, a child for whom her teachers were sorry because she tried so hard and seemed unable to learn. "You're too dumb even to cheat," Betty used to tell her.

But Alice was not really interested in school or play. Her whole small being was internally focused on one purpose only: she was trying to keep her parents together.

When her mother broke into petulant complaint, Alice whispered, "Shh, Mommy, Daddy's tired." When her father raged over a suit unpressed or some other trivial omission Alice soothed him: "Mommy's been so busy, she just forgot to send it."

She was alert to forestall irritation, to nurture kindness and consideration. It was she who remembered birthdays, including her father's, she who arranged with the cook for a special dinner menu, a birthday cake. Betty might be off to a dance, their mother lying down with one of her headaches, but Alice would wait patiently for her father to come home to his birthday dinner, knowing that she might be disappointed and her tender planning all for nothing, because more and more frequently he might not come home to dinner at all.

When her mother departed at last, first to Florida for the divorce and then to marry and live far away, twelve-year-old Alice was the only mourner. The effort of keeping her parents together, to which she had devoted all her childish strength, had failed. She had never had her father; now she had lost her mother as well. She became even more silent and withdrawn. Her few friends drifted away. Her schoolwork went from bad to worse.

The father of these two girls was not an unkind man, and far from an irresponsible one. With Betty apparently launched at college, he turned his attention to his younger daughter's troubles at school. He had only to scratch the surface, in his first discussion with her teachers, to realize that the roots of Alice's trouble lay not in school but at home. He could not yet imagine the dark well of anxiety and defeat, of rejection and lovelessness, which lay beneath her reserve.

Her father preferred Betty. To her mother it was imperative that she do as well as Betty, for to her mother Alice was a competitive pawn in the battle for her husband's regard. From all this Alice could only conclude that achievement was the price of her parents' love, and she was unable to achieve. Undermining her yet further was her knowledge that her sister, the model held up for her to follow, was a sham.

Alice could not take Betty's relatively easy, though eventually destructive, escape from reality into deception. Alice was anchored in reality, grim as her reality may have been. She could not dismiss her mother as Betty did, since her mother was all she had. She could not aspire to meet her father's standards; from the beginning he showed no interest in her and gave her no encouragement. She could have no illusions about the stability of her family, which was cracking even as she was born into it.

Betty never wanted help, could not afford to take help. She made her path through trickery and evasion; she must keep her father's esteem at all costs. But Alice craved help. She could not cope with these realities alone.

Alice's father got help for her. In the psychiatrist's office she was able to air her conflict and give a voice to her anxieties, thus freeing herself of intolerable tensions. She needed to see that her desperate effort to achieve, her fear of failing, made her even less capable. She needed to understand and accept her mother's inadequacy, and her father's drive to set such high standards for his own achievement no less than for his children's. She came to see Betty's cheating not as a superior skill but as an index of weakness. Betty was not luckier or happier than herself. She was no longer tortured by the impulse to tell on Betty and the horror that she might tell.

None of this was easy for Alice. What we sum up in a paragraph could not be absorbed in one installment. Alice was perhaps more receptive to these truths because she had stared unblinking at reality all her young life without knowing the values which lay behind its façade. Armed with insight into herself and her family, she now had gained the power to cope with it.

When the time came for Alice to go to college, she did not elect a distant college—that would be running away—but chose to live at home with her father and go to the near-by university. She has achieved a good relationship with him at last. A lonely man, he takes pleasure in her company and has come to depend on her. With her new emotional balance and her growing self-confidence, she is not overwhelmed by this long-awaited response from her father. She has a life of her own to live and she is sensibly preparing to live it.

Could Betty also have been saved? It is a question no one can answer. We must first ask whether the father of these two girls, whose own inner anguish was the most dynamic factor in their lives, could have come to realize the destructive role he was playing while desperately trying to "do the right thing."

This outwardly successful man was tortured by anxiety, obsessed with an undue sense of his own worthlessness; he was driving himself to meet those same perfectionist standards which he set for his family. Since his eyes did not focus so sharply on Alice, she was a more distant target for his drive. He was a product of a passive father and a strong mother who had been merciless in driving her children, all of whom have earned recognition in their fields, but at great cost to themselves in personal unhappiness. There is more to his story than this, of course, but enough here to recognize the outlines of a familiar pattern.

What Betty and Alice make clear to us is that divorce is not the destroyer. Betty was tobogganing on the thin ice of deception long before, and to Alice the divorce brought recognition of her misery, and eventual release. Only when divorce freed her father's energies from the struggle with his marriage, and gave him custody of Alice with the attendant responsibility for her welfare (which a man of his caliber would not shirk), only then did plain little Alice, the family's Cinderella, have a chance to find her happy ending.

THREE YOUNG MEN   We know that boys in emotional difficulties outnumber girls by a ratio variously given as two to one and sometimes three to one. We do not have all the explanations for this disparity. Here are three young men whose lives may give us a glimpse into those conflicts more special to boys.

Jack, Hal, and Walter have never met. Nor, if such an unlikely meeting were ever to take place, would they find that they had anything in common. Jack is a reform school product, a juvenile delinquent gone straight. Hal, an intellectual and an aesthete, was graduated with honors from an Ivy League college. Walter, a high school football hero, is a successful sales manager in a large Midwestern city, a genial, handshaking, hard-drinking man with a host of friends.

These three could scarcely be more unlike each other. Yet they share one deep personal problem. Each of these three young men was abandoned by his father. Each in his own way shows the effects of that abandonment. Each, according to his own pattern, reveals a permanent inability to live a satisfactory adult life. Each is deprived, emotionally maimed, and unable to meet the requirements of society.

Jack's father was the kind of man a boy can love. Cheerful, easygoing, handy with tools, he could always fix a bike or a skate. When Jack was ten his father disappeared.

There are statistics of families broken by legal separation and divorce, but there are only estimates for desertion. In the United States there are more married people living apart from their spouses than there are divorced people (one and one quarter times as many wives are absent, and 1.3 times as many husbands, according to the 1950 census), and most of these separations are presumed to be permanent. But we have no way of discovering how many of these absent men and women are deserters, those who one day become fed up with the burden of a family and simply vanish. Sometimes these immature, irresponsible adults go on to assume a new personality, begin a new life, and perhaps establish a new family. Sometimes they abandon the second family too, and a third. Now and then a migrant husband is discovered to have wives and children dotted all across the country.

AFTERMATH OF DESERTION   Jack's father left behind him four children; Jack, the eldest, was ten, and the youngest was five. Jack's mother was faced with a monstrous uncertainty. Any day her husband might turn up again, repentant. Meanwhile she had to find some way of supporting herself and her children.

She took a job as a domestic worker, but then her children were truly abandoned to the streets. Next she tried staying at home, accepting crumbs from the city welfare department and various social agencies until this became intolerable to her self-respect. More and more she leaned on her eldest boy. She tried not to burden him, but she was in fact overwhelmed.

When his mother was working, Jack became nursemaid to his

sisters and little brother, and the boys on the street shouted, "Sissy!" When his mother was not working, Jack got himself a newspaper route. He saw homes more comfortable than his own, women less burdened than his mother. He began to steal a little here and there. He was caught once, twice, and at sixteen he was sent away to a reform school.

Jack had not aimed for a criminal career. He wanted to be a good man, the kind of man he used to think his father was. Yet if his father was a good man, why did he leave his family without a word, without a thought for the struggle they must face after his desertion? This is the question buried deep in Jack's unstable personality, the doubt at the bottom of his insecurity. He cannot find a satisfactory answer, any more than he could find a satisfactory male figure to pattern himself upon.

At twenty-five Jack no longer steals. He is a fair mechanic and a friendly, likeable fellow, and in times of ordinarily good employment he has no trouble getting a job. But he is the kind of worker whom industry abhors, a floater. He begins each new job in high hopes; it is just the job he has been looking for. But soon he is having trouble with the foreman or a fellow worker, generally a senior. Sometimes he is fired, but more often he quits.

Jack's mother shrugs; it's in the blood. He'll marry, if any girl is foolish enough to take a chance on him. He'll have children. And he'll desert his wife and children. He is his father's son.

The course of this boy's life is so revealing that we need not call on heredity to explain it. The pattern of steady, responsible manhood was destroyed for him by his father's desertion. The destruction had in fact begun long before. The desertion brought him a sudden awareness of fleeting impressions which had already made him uneasy.

When Jack was stealing during his early adolescence, he convinced himself that he did it to help his mother. But he also stole to get even with his father, to flout that authority which a father represents to a child. To the child parental authority and support are two sides of the same concept; together they form the framework of his security. In Jack's case both authority and support were suddenly, unaccountably withdrawn. He lost at one blow his security, his dependent role as a child, and the image on which to pattern his manhood.

Not all boys with Jack's history turn out as Jack has done. Some become chronic lawbreakers. Some, like Sammy, whom we shall meet later in this chapter, grow up to be responsible citizens. When the whole story of these more fortunate ones is told, one often finds in it a third character—a teacher, a settlement-house worker, a relative, perhaps a neighbor or a playmate's father—on whom the boy could fix his love. Not a father necessarily, but a father image, is the essence of a boy's need.

ON SOCIETY'S TAINTED FRINGE   Hal is twenty-seven, a soft-spoken young man with perfect manners and a scholar's stoop, who wears English tweeds and smokes a pipe. He is half owner of a successful antique shop on a fashionable avenue and is something of an expert on English silver. He shares a tastefully furnished apartment with his partner, who was his classmate at college.

Hal has done his best to arrange his life well, but it has a sinister flaw. He has had one brush with the police, possibly not his last, although the disorderly behavior with which he was charged was not his own but his friend's. He is listed on the police blotter as a homosexual.

Hal's parents were divorced when he was nine. Long before that, he had begun his progress toward the abnormality which dooms him to live on the tainted fringe of society.

Ironically, when divorce was not yet even a cloud on the family horizon, Hal's mother interested herself in children, especially troubled children. She was active in organizations for better motherhood, better childhood, better family life. Like many women of strongly masculine tendencies, she made her gesture toward motherhood on the large scale, in terms of Children, an abstraction, rather than her own two children with their challenging individual differences and their demands for the individual mother-child love which she could not give them. To her, as to many modern women, motherhood was not so much an emotional experience as an executive job.

Hal's father, a gentle man, accepted the passive feminine role she carved out for him, taking refuge in literature and the arts, retreating to his bookshop. Incapable of making the trivial day-to-day assertions of himself, he allowed his discontent to mount through years of baby-sitting while his wife attended club meetings, until it erupted into a wholesale destruction of his relationship with his wife and his sons as well. He abandoned everything and fled, characteristically, to his own mother.

His wife managed the divorce, the custody of the boys, and took a position as housemother in a boarding school for children of broken homes, thus assuring their support and education too. Everyone admired her courage and resourcefulness.

Hal's brother, three years his senior, achieved some independence of his mother by being assigned with his age group to another dormitory. Hal was part of the group his mother supervised, and thus he was subjected to the continuous frustration of physical nearness and increased emotional separation. Sharing her with an abstraction had been hard enough. Now he must share her with twenty other real boys.

Rejection breeds hostility, and Hal turned from his mother, gravitating toward his brother's group of older boys. The school was coeducational, but he avoided girls. He went on to college and distinguished himself in literary and dramatic activities. His social life narrowed to youths like himself, a small, arrogant, literary-artistic coterie who scorned football games and proms.

By graduation he had been introduced to homosexual practices by a more sophisticated friend who became the feminine member of the relationship. This friend, now his partner in business as well as private life, dominates him entirely, holding him in thrall like a capricious and heartless woman. As is often true with the feminine member of these relationships, his friend is fickle. Hal has already tasted the first bitter consequence of his friend's addiction to chance acquaintances and antisocial behavior. This path can only lead downward. When his present friend leaves him, he will look for another, and one day he may find himself a seducer of young boys.

A GLANCE AT THIS HOMOSEXUALITY   Hal's tragic situation brings up a concern which may haunt more than a few parents of boys, although many are too fearful to speak of it. They are frightened by lurid newspaper reports which give a distorted prominence to homosexuality. Its linkage in these stories with gangs, narcotics, and delinquents is factual enough, but not representative. Homosexuality is both closer and more widespread than we like to think; on the other hand, it does not generally reveal itself in this exaggerated, sensational form.

We cannot do more than touch on this complex problem here, and only tangentially as it meets our subject. Parents are quite generally aware nowadays that in the course of normal development the boy is at first exclusively dependent on his mother. Then gradually he shifts away from his mother to identify with his father and, still later, other males. Hero worship for a teacher or older boy is part of this attraction toward members of the same sex and as a passing phase of adolescence is recognized as normal.

It is also well known that personality characteristics of the sexes are not in absolute contrast. Men and women are more like each other than we used to think; there is a little of the female in the male and vice versa. We now accept it as a fact that a father can give tender care to his baby and remain virile. We are quite accustomed to women with qualities once called masculine, such as executive or scientific ability. We now take it for granted that a man need not be all aggression, a woman all meekness.

In the normal individual masculinity and femininity strike a balance. The admixture is not always so healthy. A boy, for instance, may continue too long to identify with his mother, and his masculinity fail to emerge, a deficit which will remain to trouble his adult life. Sometimes circumstances may help set the stage for such a development, as when a mother is left to bring up a boy alone.

Similar problems arise to trouble girls, although the lines of development for girls, while parallel to those of boys, are not identical. The paternal and maternal images play as forceful a role, but with different connotations. It would take us too far out of our way to go into the subject as a whole; we can attempt here only to give the reader a better orientation for the story of Hal.

In these pages we meet mothers who have held their boys too closely. We can observe how some mothers have thwarted masculine development in their sons by their tendency to dominate and manage them and live their lives for them. We see clinging mothers who lean too heavily on their sons, also thwarting their growth, though in different ways.

Overt homosexuality such as we found in Hal's story is infrequent. But there are all degrees of "sissifying" or, to be more technical, of emasculating.

A mother reading these pages is already aware of the losses her boy has suffered if his father has left the home. Her awareness of this lack in his life is one protection against her making these mistakes. She is alert to his need for adult male companionship. A variety of solutions will occur to her; some are suggested in these stories of other mothers and their sons.

She will guard against her own anxious tendency to manage the boy's life too much. She will refrain from disparaging his father; on the contrary, she will make efforts to sustain for the boy the positive side of his father's character. She will refrain from intruding on his relationship with his father, because this too is a protection for the boy against too much feminine influence.

More of the subtle variations in the mother-son relationship will appear in stories which follow, and also some of the ways in which the dangers have been successfully overcome.

MOTHER'S BOY   While Hal is the victim of too little mothering, Walter has had too much of a special kind. Walter's mother lavished everything on her only child. She still keeps his room as a shrine, with a little museum of his athletic trophies, clippings, snapshots, a lock of his baby hair, a baby shoe. She boasts that she never said *no* to him or laid down a rule for him. He was perfect and could do no wrong.

From the beginning she excluded Walter's father from the communion between herself and her son, and Walter's father, a tinkerer and a putterer, was content to say, "Okay, Mom," and retire to his workbench in the garage, relieved of the necessity for taking a stand on anything whatever.

Walter was a beautiful baby and a handsome boy. His studies suffered on account of his need to make a constant display of his charm and prowess. He was not happy unless he was bathed in admiration, unless everybody liked him and most of the girls

were in love with him. Walter himself was never in love. He flitted
from girl to girl, reasserting as each attachment fizzled out that
mother was right and no girl was good enough. After high school he
progressed from job to job and then to the near-by big city, where,
separated from his mother, he fell tempestuously in love with the
first attractive girl who resisted him and, in order to win her,
married her.

His marriage had an odd effect on his parents. Having lost
Walter, his mother turned on her forebearing husband, nagging,
criticizing, trying to change his easygoing ways until the man
rebelled and left home. Outraged at his defection, she divorced
him.

Meanwhile trouble was beginning in Walter's own marriage. With
the excitement of conquest settling into sober routine, Walter's eye
began again to wander. One woman's love was not enough, and
the pressure of adjusting himself to another human being imposed
a discipline he never had to learn. His wife, however, was unwilling
to sacrifice her marriage because of his flirtations. She managed a
reconciliation, and she became pregnant. It was a risk; having a
baby to cement a marriage is rarely successful. Still she thought
there was a possibility that if a child came while Walter was close to
her, he might be able to accept the mature role of husband and
father.

The young wife lost the gamble. Walter had only to visit his
mother and bask in her uncritical adulation, and the painful effort
toward maturity seemed not worth the candle. No sooner was his
son born and he was presented with a living symbol of paternal
responsibility—and worse, a rival for the center of the stage—
than he fled.

And so we have another divorce, and still another little boy,
Walter's son, abandoned by his father. Walter himself may marry
again, and divorce again. Or he may remain the gay bachelor,
the extra man so useful to hostesses, the charmer somewhat dangerous to young girls and discontented wives. Walter is the classic Don
Juan.

And what of Walter in his fifties, when his charm can no longer
cover the fact that his hair is thin, his waistline thick, and himself

an empty, aging man? Then in sheer weakness, seeking the mother protection of his childhood, he will probably let himself be captured by an amazon. Thus he will be tamed at last, and become a hollow replica of that passive weakling whom he has scorned all his life, his own father.

BUT MANY WIN THROUGH Boys like Jack, Hal, and Walter offer an unpromising forecast for the sons of broken homes. But we can counter their stories with those of boys who have found their way through the emotional morass created by a father who has failed his son. Some were guided by a mother whose love was not only strong but wise; some had professional help; some found father substitutes. It is not inevitably fatal to a boy to be deprived of a father's love.

Andrew's case seemed hopeless. Andrew lived his childhood in a petticoat kingdom, surrounded by women. His parents' marriage was emotionally sterile, and when Andrew was about four there was a divorce. His father quickly remarried and moved to a distant city, there to establish a new family as though the first had never existed. He vanished completely from Andrew's life.

Andrew's mother, who also seemed to brush off her marriage, had no interest in remarrying nor even in having men friends. A woman of much charm, very feminine, she was inhibited by sexual frigidity; her response to this was to settle into a false comfort of exclusion.

She went into business with an unmarried woman friend who eventually came to share the household. With the housekeeper and his young sister, this made four females for Andrew, and never a male around the house with whom a boy could even have a game of catch.

His mother tried to fill the lack. A good athlete, she played ball with him, taught him to swim and play tennis. But the more she tried to take a father's place, the more antagonistic the boy became toward her. He resented attention from any of the "skirts" in his home; this was one of his many names for them and almost the only printable one. He took to running with a tough gang which engaged in petty thievery and in roughing up girls. At twelve he was hanging around the corner drugstore, smoking, drinking when he could get liquor.

Thus Andrew tried to assert his manhood against an overwhelmingly feminine world, running as far as he could from his dainty mother and her frilly home, aping the most harshly masculine behavior. At the same time he would wake up screaming from nightmares in which he dreamed he was a girl, wearing his sister's or his mother's clothes.

Unconsciously Andrew was fighting a strong pull toward homosexuality, and in his battle he also was well on the way to becoming a thorough delinquent. Fortunately he found an ally, the young minister of his mother's church who had organized a baseball team in the community to win over difficult boys like Andrew, and who also ran a camp in the summer. For the first time Andrew found a man to admire and love.

Andrew begged to go to the minister's camp, and his mother consented. At camp Andrew made friends with the minister's children, a boy and two girls, and accepted with them the mild discipline of their cheerful, sensible mother. When the minister was removed to a distant parish, Andrew was momentarily in despair. At this point the clergyman offered to take the boy to live with his family for a year, and Andrew's mother, greatly relieved, agreed to the experiment. She had seen Andrew come home from camp healthier, friendlier, and full of enthusiasm for the minister and his family. Realizing that her boy was showing her the solution to his difficulties, she accepted the long separation from him because it was what he needed.

The respite from his mother's petticoat realm, the experience of living in a complete family, and above everything else the presence and affection of a man whom he could admire and with whom he could identify in his striving for masculinity proved to be the turning point for Andrew. At eighteen he is in his first year in a large university, enjoying his studies and his friends. He plans to become a doctor and has begun his premedical training.

SAMMY FINDS HIS BOYHOOD   While Andrew's solution was to find a substitute father, indeed a substitute family, Sammy's was to meet several father persons and to see himself for the first time as a boy among other boys.

Sammy's father was an alcoholic. Like Jack's father, earlier in this chapter, he walked out on his family one day and some time later notified his wife that he was divorcing her and marrying again in another state. She had neither the resources nor the wish to prevent him. His going released her from an intolerable life.

Like Jack's mother, Sammy's mother took domestic work to provide for her three young children, and Sammy became her devoted helper. At eleven he was both father and mother to his younger sisters; his mother praised her "little man of the family." But as he grew more and more solemn and withdrawn, with the face of a little old man, she became worried. Groping for the help which her love told her the child needed, she went to a social agency for advice.

When the social worker recommended a stay at a summer camp for the boy, she was appalled: how could she manage without Sammy? The social worker showed her how by arranging for the mother and the two little girls to stay at a boarding farm for the three weeks which Sammy would spend at camp.

Refreshed, with a new perspective on her problems, Sammy's mother was amazed and joyful at the change in Sammy. His cloak of resignation had slipped off. The horizon which had been bounded by crowded tenement rooms and paved city streets was suddenly expanded. He could not contain his happiness over his simple physical discoveries: "When you walk on the grass, it's so soft!" Best of all, he had met kindly, friendly men, the camp counselors, and had been a boy among boys.

With the social worker's help Sammy's mother found a way to continue Sammy's outside contacts through the winter. She took cleaning work in office buildings, working evenings when Sammy had to stay at home anyway to do his homework. In the afternoons and on Saturdays Sammy was free to join a near-by settlement-house group, where he struck up a friendship with a shop teacher. He began to talk about his own plans for the future and thought he would like to become an electrician. He was beginning to see himself as an individual, no longer imprisoned by his duties to his mother, but free to prepare for a life of his own.

Sammy is now a graduate of vocational school and has his first job as an electrician's helper. His boss likes him; he is steady, reliable, a good worker. He still comes to the settlement house on Saturdays to help out with the younger boys. He contributes to his mother's budget, and has something left over to take a girl to the movies once a week. While Andrew groped toward his own solution and showed his mother what he needed, Sammy was helped by a mother sensitive to his needs who sought and found help for him.

THE RUNAWAY   Joel is the third of this random selection among many boys who have won their way back to safe shores. Andrew was a delinquent, Sammy a prisoner, but Joel was on the way to serious mental illness.

Joel's father did not abandon him physically. He was a man who had an obsessive sense of responsibility, along with other, less constructive elements of his personality, such as a violent temper and a need to turn martyr and withdraw when the family arrangements did not center around himself.

"I work myself to death for this family and I don't even get a decent dinner," he would complain, forgetting that he habitually came home late, with no excuse except his own compulsions. Night after night his children saw him leave the table with his reheated dinner untouched while a cloud of guilt settled over their un-comprehending heads.

The older child, a daughter, escaped the concentrated destructiveness of this father's unhappy personality by virtue of her sex and a more compliant temperament. But in Joel the father saw himself, his own fears, his own confusions, and it was upon Joel that he projected his unvoiced dread of insanity.

In a favorable emotional setting Joel might have been a lively, spirited, inquisitive child, but under the pressures generated by his father normal childish rebellions exploded into temper tantrums, an inquiring mind became an erratic one, and liveliness was transformed into violence.

"That boy is going to kill someone someday," his father would say when Joel's protest took a destructive turn and he flung his toys and broke household objects. The child's solution was to run away.

He would disappear for hours while his parents took opposite roads in search of him. He would return disheveled, inarticulate. Sometimes he had merely hidden in the bushes near by, lying curled up, mindless, in a dark safety like that of the womb. Sometimes he would walk without direction or purpose, returning only when he was exhausted. At bedtime in his room he could be heard talking to imaginary companions; sometimes he called his mother in terror, crying that weird creatures were disturbing him with their noise, threatening him.

By the time Joel was eight his father was seriously campaigning to send the boy to an institution, and, finally, following several family discussions, Joel's mother brought him for psychiatric treatment.

Now and then in the following months hints were dropped which the father quickly interpreted as accusations against himself. He left the home and proposed that his wife get a divorce, not without the characteristic drawing of the robe of martyrdom about him: "If I'm such a burden to this family, if I'm so bad for the boy . . ."

Meanwhile Joel in his visits to his psychiatrist was working through his severe conflict. He boasted about his father's achievements, struggling to build up the image in which he needed to have faith, and at the same time revealed his fear of his father, portraying his father in various ways as an awe-inspiring figure of whom he was in great dread. Just as the father recognized himself in the boy, so Joel saw himself in his father, and was frightened at what he saw. On a child's level, with his tempers, his destructiveness, his running away, he was unconsciously patterning his behavior on his father's.

Joel's imaginary characters took form in verbal descriptions and in drawings on the blackboard: part animal, part human, they were equipped with dangerous teeth and hidden pockets full of poison, a further expression of his need to destroy a world so inimical to him. In similar situations children may attack a teacher with a chair, or suddenly aim a weapon at some adult. One boy was known to have had a six-inch knife concealed in his suitcase when he went to visit his father shortly after his parents' divorce. Children who do violence are responding to an impulse not intellectually controlled; theirs is a direct eruption into action of emotional pressures which have reached explosive force. Occasionally they can tell afterward what preceded the explosion; not infrequently this turns out to be an incident related to the child's very source of conflict, such as a scene between his parents.

Joel showed with classic clarity that he hated his father, feared his father, and yet loved his father and longed for his father's love. This confusion of emotions was unbearable, and so he ran away, partly to escape by becoming a lump of unthinking flesh shut away from his anxieties, and partly to punish his parents by worrying them.

What part did Joel's mother play in his life? Obviously she had her own personality difficulties, though outwardly they were not so apparent as her husband's. She was torn between her need to respond to her husband's emotional demands on her as a mother and the needs of the children. Her husband was in effect a sibling rival to his children, and no matter how this wife-mother exerted herself to meet his demands, it was never enough to satisfy his craving for a mother, a craving which he had never outgrown. A neurotic need can be tyrannical for the very reason that it is out of time and place, without relation to the realistic situation—in a word, neurotic.

Still, Joel's mother was able to rise to the boy's need once she understood it. In addition, the separation of Joel's parents was a liberation both for them and the boy; a hopeless family situation had been dealt with surgically. By her husband's departure the mother was relieved of the conflict between his demands and those of the children. Furthermore, she was brought into therapy herself as part of Joel's treatment.

It was recognized early that the father was inaccessible to treatment, for reasons too lengthy to expand here. As in many such cases, he flung himself more completely into his work as an escape from the emotional tensions in himself which family life aggravated rather than satisfied. Both parents were thus better able to give Joel the help he needed, the mother with her encouraging and understanding support, the father first by staying away on the psychiatrist's advice, and then by a gradual re-establishment of a relationship with Joel by way of visits and shared interests which both could enjoy.

Joel was graduated from college last year, and is now working in his chosen field. He made a good record in his studies, enjoyed his college experience and formed several enduring friendships. He is in love with a wholesome girl and looks forward to his own home and family.

Joel has owned to some diffidence during college in relationships with his professors, and toward his seniors in the office when he first began his job—an understandable remnant of his fear of his father. He recognizes this for what it is and has so far been able to work his way through it. He is aware also that it is hard for him to take criticism and occasional failure; this too he understands as part of his need to win his father's approval.

During the college years he found his vacation visits with his father progressively easier. The man who used to say of his son, "He's hopeless—there's nothing to be done for him," was taking pleasure in the boy's progress and—more important—was even able occasionally to express pride in him.

Joel knows that his father is far from ideal. He has had to accept his father's limitations and make the most of a difficult man's positive qualities, such as a devotion to his work and a sense of responsibility which saw Joel through college. Perhaps most precious to Joel is the fact that his father was able to reverse his former judgment. Where previously the man had vented his own self-doubts in predictions of doom for his son, he can now instead encourage the boy in his progress toward health.

CAN A MOTHER COMPENSATE FOR A FATHER'S FAILURE?   In all three of these stories it is apparent that, whatever other factors came to the boy's aid, the mother's understanding and support were always present.

When a father fails his son, it is possible for a mother to support and strengthen the boy in his struggle to achieve a well-adjusted manhood. Some mothers, who have been left to bring up a boy unaided, have discovered this for themselves, a fact which may serve as encouragement to mothers reading this book. But we must also post a warning that, in compensating for a father's failure (or his absence from the boy's life for various reasons), a mother must be aware that she is embarking on a delicate piece of navigation.

She cannot step into a man's shoes and become father as well as mother to the boy. Andrew's mother tried this, and it was Andrew's good fortune that he could pull away and fasten his affection on his minister. Hal's mother assumed the dominant role in her marriage and afterward, as did Walter's mother, with damaging results to both boys.

A child needs his mother to remain a mother. When she attempts to be both mother and father she is likely to end by being neither. The converse, we might point out in passing, is also true, as Betty's father discovered too late; he had excluded the mother from Betty's childhood and assumed both roles himself.

More important than anything else is the mother's effort to understand what is going on inside the boy and to let him know that she understands. She can see how he is caught between his resentment against his father and his longing for his father's love. He is guilty, frightened, needing comfort and yet fearing to take it from his mother because this is a threat to his masculinity—and this fear, breeding its own guilt, may lead him to reject her proffered help. She cannot press him to take the comfort she offers or overwhelm him with love to compensate for the father love he misses. She can, however, open the door for him to air his struggle. By her recognition of what he is suffering she relieves him of some of its pressure.

We must remember that the mother is also troubled and confused. At best she is suffering from the dissolution of her marriage, and she cannot help harboring some resentment against her husband. Further than this, she usually has her own inner difficulties, or she would not have made this marriage in the first place. A woman who is well integrated and emotionally mature is not often drawn into a neurotic marriage, and the same is true of a man. Such a mother may herself have had a weak father and a mother who overreached her maternal role.

While with her sympathy she encourages her son to express his bitter feelings, she must be watchful not to take sides with the child against his father. To do so may relieve her own feelings, but it only hurts the child. This is his father, after all, and it is within her power to help the boy see and accept his father, weaknesses and strengths together.

She must remember that as a young child the boy has regarded his father not as a fallible human being but as a god, a god who for some reason punished him by refusing to love him and care for him. Her part is to guide the boy into a more realistic and mature view of his father, foibles and all, as an individual not godlike but human.

A child can learn to duck the blows of a drunken father. In the same way he can learn to duck the emotional blows of a father whose inner conflicts reveal themselves in more subtle forms.

The mother trying to help her boy may defeat herself by unwittingly coloring the father-child relationship with her own feelings. Is the father really behaving so badly to the boy? Perhaps because she feels he is cruel to her, she may unconsciously distort his treatment of the child. The effort to be objective is hard, but it is necessary.

There are further ways in which a mother can support her boy through a father's failure without going outside her own role as a mother. Rather than keep him at home for protection, she seeks practical opportunities to provide him with a father substitute in male relatives and friends. She encourages him to join a boys' group where he will find an adult leader and also leaders among the older boys.

In all three of the more cheerful stories we have told, the mother achieved a measure of understanding of the boy's need. In Joel's case the effort was noteworthy. His mother had profound emotional dislocations of her own to cope with, and it was a hard pull for her to achieve insight into herself and her own attitudes toward her husband. After the divorce this became easier for her. No longer did the walls of the house shake with violent scenes; she had quiet and solitude in which to think.

Still, though it was easier, it was never easy. It cannot be easy for a mother in this situation, any more than for the boy. (Nor, we must add, is it always easy for the father who has failed, for, though some fathers seem to take an easy way out of their obligations, many suffer the tortures of the damned and cannot help themselves.) But Joel's mother and father too—for he helped as much as he was able—are repaid for their effort by the satisfaction of knowing that their boy, once badly hurt and possibly in danger of irreparable damage, is now a young man with as good prospects as any young man for a full and happy life.

THE BOARDING SCHOOL ORPHAN   We have seen children who have had too little or too much mothering, too little or too much fathering. In the cases of several who have come through, we have seen how one parent has helped the child to accept the failure of the other. We come now to one who has had neither fathering nor mothering, who has been nobody's child, an "orphan of the living," to borrow a description coined by Professor Raphael Lemkin of Harvard.

Joyce is eighteen. For eleven years of her life she has had neither home nor parents. Since she was seven she has lived in a succession of boarding schools. Joyce's troubles really began when her father, a successful man already middle-aged, married a vivid, spirited young girl. Joyce was born, and four years later a little brother, but the young wife was unable to mature into the responsibilities of motherhood. She wanted out.

After the divorce, Joyce, already a difficult child, became downright unmanageable. She began to use foul language, to lie, to steal from the housekeeper, who, as the available substitute for her mother, became the target of her hostility toward the one who had failed her. She was rude to her father's sister, in fact to all women, but to the housekeeper she was outrageous.

The peace of his household was more important to Joyce's father at that moment than the needs of his little girl. Confronted with a choice between his daughter and his housekeeper, he kept the housekeeper and sent Joyce away to school.

Yet Joyce's father would be deeply hurt if you were to tell him that he had neglected his daughter. He would feel, and with some justification according to his lights, that he had done everything possible for her. For one thing, he did not stint financially where Joyce was concerned. No sacrifice was too much. And who is to sit in judgment and say that he should have done otherwise? We might wish that he had been able to rely less on the power of his checkbook and give more of himself to Joyce. But we can see how difficult it must have been for him. By the time her parents parted and she became solely her father's responsibility she was already bristling with defenses. The situation was too much for a busy man who had never been close to his daughter anyway. He sent her to the best schools. He put her, he believed, into the care of people who knew how to handle a child better than he did.

Joyce went from one school to another. When she found a teacher or principal who showed particular interest in her she did better, but for the most part she added failure after failure to her already heavy burden. When she was home for vacations, she tried awkwardly to win her father's affection. But he found all his satisfactions of fatherhood in her younger brother, and seemed to have nothing to spare for Joyce, who felt further isolated by this father-brother communion.

Now that Joyce is eighteen, the ordeal of boarding schools is over, but she has nowhere to go. She can go to college, her father tells her. Stubbornly she will accept no college but the best, and her scholastic record is far from good enough. She begins to knock around.

Her father is alarmed. He sees Joyce following her mother's wild pattern. But it is too late now to win Joyce's confidence. She has tried desperately not to be like her mother. She resents bitterly the suggestion that she is going the same way, and throws up to her father, with some justification, his lack of understanding.

After a long week end away from home Joyce brings in a young man, her husband. The partner to her impulsive dawn elopement after a party is an entertainer who has already been married and divorced several times.

Her father pleads with her: such a marriage has no chance for survival; better to have it annulled at once. Joyce blazes. "Who are you to talk? Look what happened to your marriage!" And she goes, to make the best of the only escape she could find from an unloving father and a home which has never been home to her.

Joyce will keep doggedly trying, but she is not likely to succeed in her search for love and security. Her way is misguided and immature. She cannot know how to create a home and family and an adult way of life, for, though she dreams of these things and longs for them, she has never experienced them.

Joyce is not exceptional. Boarding schools are often the readiest solution for parents who, for good and not-so-good reasons, cannot give their children the help they need through a divorce. Many boarding school heads find themselves struggling to keep their schools from turning into orphan homes for children of divorce.

One principal writes:

"Our own youngsters are the only children from a unified happy home. Our pupils come from broken homes, or homes in the process of splitting, or homes that should have been taken apart by a kindly judge for the good of the children."

Here are some of the children in this school described in the principal's rather pungent words:

"Beth's dad had fled to foreign parts when he learned that she was on her way into the world. Doug's dad had thrown over his family for art's sake and Mom was husband-hunting. Freckles' mom and pa had refused to face divorce for five years and had just come to the starting line for Reno; Jack's and Jill's parents ditto. Nell's parents had been held together by financial considerations. Nell had to go to court to testify against her father.

"Red's home was such that he ran away. Ginger's mother was a hysteric, her father an alcoholic. Ginger has been at boarding schools from the age of four.

"Slim's dad and mom brought him to school, girl friend sitting with dad, Slim with mama. After that, dad visited one day, mama another. Mama has settled down with boy friend, and all show a kindly if not a loving interest in the boy.

"But what goes on inside the boy?"

This school presents a somewhat concentrated picture, because it accepts rather more children with problems (though not problem children) than the average boarding school, and provides a family setting in which the children may be able to get their bearings away from the disturbed home situation.

Answering his question, "What goes on inside the boy?" this principal recorded a dinner-table conversation among the children. We give it below, but with a key; such a conversation is almost too pure a culture, and cannot be taken at its literal value. Children can seldom be so open and specific and particularly so detached about matters which trouble them. Sometimes one child is stimulated to make a challenging opening, and the others take the dare; each one tries to counter or top the one before. Something of the sort seems to have happened on this occasion, when Whitey blurted his rather shocking opening remark:

WHITEY [who is frightened, disguising his fear with flippancy]: Gee, I'm glad my dad killed himself. It was so much better than if he had lived and mom had to get a divorce.

PETE [apparently a successful divorce]: Oh, I don't know. Mom and Dad are divorced and they seem to get along a lot better now than they did before.

FRECKLES [covering his anxieties by sticking to the practical]: Well, Dad and Mom started not living together and they may get divorced but the worst thing is that I have to keep traveling to two different parts of town to see them.

SLUGGER [anxious and doesn't care who knows it]: It looks as though I was in for it. I wonder what Dad's new girl friend is to me, a going-to-be stepmother? Or isn't she any relation?

Joyce was not heard making such unsparing comments on her parents, but her feelings were in no way different. For Joyce, the boarding school was no solution nor even a refuge, but only another evidence of her rejection. We cannot turn the clock back and revise human experience. But there are enough similarities between Joyce's experience and that of other children so that we can see in retrospect how Joyce might have been helped.

Going to boarding school of itself need not have been a bad experience for Joyce if she could have understood it in any other terms than a rejection. If it had been possible to get a helping hand into her situation at an early stage—if, for example, her father had been able to perceive that there might be something behind Joyce's stealing and bad language, something less like wickedness and more like anguish—Joyce might still have gone away to school, but with quite other feelings.

She needed to know that, though her mother had left her, her father cared for his little girl. She needed to be given some insight into her parents' problems, to be reassured that these were between themselves and not directed at her. She needed to be set free as a separate individual, affected, of course, by her parents' troubles with each other, but not implicated in them.

As it was, she saw herself only as the focus of her parents' troubles, the object of their wrath for some guilt she did not understand; her mother's going and her father's sending her away were her punishment. While Joyce's towering difficulties might not have been completely surmounted, nor all her conflicts resolved, yet she might have been liberated enough to find good friends in some of her teachers at school, to develop her potentialities in positive directions, and to make the most of a childhood spent away from home and parents.

THE CHILD OF IMMATURE MARRIAGE   A large proportion of today's divorces come after only a few years of marriage, and we know that many of the marriages which suffer early dissolution are immature ones.

Probably the majority of high school marriages, like the majority of all marriages, turn out well. Human beings of any age can usually learn by doing. Many young people, however, pay a considerable price for their experience, and divorce is all too often part of the price. Not infrequently there is also a young child involved.

In this chapter we have been looking into the lives of some children of divorce grown up. Let us see how such a young child might fare in the custody of a mother who is herself hardly more than a child.

I was called in one such case to a Midwestern city to give what is legally called "expert testimony" in court. The question at issue was the custody of a little girl between three and four years old. The child's mother had eloped at seventeen with a dashing flier who, although he was older and far more wordly than his child bride, presently revealed himself as unready to give up his gay bachelor's life.

The girl's parents had tried to prevent the marriage. But once it was accomplished, with a wisdom not often found in these cases, they stood by until the girl herself saw that her marriage had been a mistake. When she and her child finally returned to her parents' home, the little girl was showing signs of disturbance. She was shy, withdrawn; there were other indications of detachment from reality which troubled the grandparents enough so that they called for consultation and subsequent testimony.

Despite the subtlety of the child's symptoms, a perceptive judge became convinced that there was serious trouble ahead for the little girl unless her future were carefully planned to meet her emotional needs. He granted complete custody to the young mother with the provision that the child should live with her and the maternal grandparents, whose home was in an Eastern city, until the mother might remarry.

The young mother's guilt and confusion were intense, as might be expected under the circumstances. Her guilt and the child's anxiety needed to be resolved. The judge's decision made it possible for the mother's family to use several resources in order to forestall serious neurotic consequences for the child.

Because of the distance of the child's new home from New York, she was actually treated only for a short period. Then for two years more, at long but regular intervals, the child and the entire family were given guidance. The family made every effort to co-operate with the young mother in surrounding the little girl with the love and security she needed. Under these new circumstances the father's rights of visitation were no longer the disturbing element to the family they had been before, and it thus became possible for the child to accept him as he was. Let it be said in passing that the working through of this acceptance of an absent parent, or a parent whose relationship is not satisfactory to the child, is one of the stumbling blocks commonly met in these situations.

What gives this story significance for us here is that it dates back not one or five but fifteen years, and we know the end of the story. After a few years the young mother married again, and her second marriage has been stable and secure. The troubled little girl of fifteen years ago has grown up with a new father and a young brother and sister and is now approaching marriageable age herself. She is as steady and well adjusted as any girl of eighteen who has had a more favorable history, and she has an equally promising future.

And so we can answer the question posed by our chapter heading: No, children of divorce are not bound to fail as adults. They can have as good a future as any child. They can make happy marriages and bring up happy children.

We can also say that there is no one way to assure them of this wished-for outcome, but a number of ways. Whatever way you as a parent find open to you—whether the child is to live with you or to visit you, whether he is to remain at home or go away to school, whether you can keep his old associations or must move him to a new setting—you can make that a good way for your child.

You can do it if you are concerned with the child, not as a pawn in your struggle with your former marriage partner, nor as a target for your bitterness, resentment, or grief, but for the child's own happiness. You can do it if you support him with your understanding, your alertness to his emotional needs, and your patient effort to see behind his behavior to his inner feelings.

9

WHERE DIVORCE BEGINS: THE LEGACY OF UNHAPPINESS

In the preceding chapter we have followed some children of divorce forward to the brink of adulthood. We will find it fruitful also to trace divorce backward along its winding roots into the past.

It is a truism that neurotic individuals seek neurotic mates, make neurotic marriages, and beget neurotic children. We have been told this so often that parents are occasionally trapped into repeating the precept fatalistically and accepting defeat in advance. "So I'm a neurotic, and my parents were neurotics, and my children will be neurotics, and that's that."

Not so. Many parents do not accept passively this unhappy fate for their children. Counselors who have listened to many troubled parents and have helped them come to grips with their problems are inclined to be a little more hopeful about averting the legacy of neuroticism.

Parents need not sit with folded hands. They have work to do. They can look behind the patterns of neuroticism and see *how* they are handed down.

There is in my files the story of one child whose experience presents so many of the facets of divorce, including its genesis in the childhood of her parents, that it perfectly suits our purpose.

Mary's story, as we shall see, comes to a dramatic climax: each of her parents has already had two divorces and three marriages. This is extreme.

But Mary's parents, Catherine and Peter, are not too unusual, apart from their excessive marrying and divorcing. Nor do they come of unusual families. Their parents were not divorced, but lived out their lives in apparent harmony and stability.

Where, then, is the neuroticism which was handed down from these parents to Catherine and Peter, and from them to their small daughter? And what are the mechanisms by which this legacy is bequeathed?

Mary and her parents and grandparents have much to tell us. We shall meet in Mary's story several familiar characters out of the dramatis personae of child psychology lectures: the dominating mother, the sibling rivals, the spoiled child, the indulgent father, the perfectionist parent. We shall try to see behind these labels the patterns which were laid down for Catherine and Peter by their parents, and which culminated at last in the violence by day and the terror by night of a six-year-old girl.

THE IDEAL FAMILY   When Mary was born she completed what was on all counts a perfect American family. Peter was a successful young lawyer with a secure future, Catherine a happy young wife. Jane, the first-born, was a sturdy two-year-old, and Mary was the second child rounding out the ideal picture.

With every comfortable infant chuckle the baby girl testified to the happiness of this family She was a beautiful child, as loved children are likely to be beautiful. She was healthy, happy, and good. Her young parents congratulated themselves on their success with their second child; they were no longer novices, no longer pacing the floor at night, calling up the pediatrician, going into a panic at each new unfolding of the baby's growth. Pink, round-cheeked little Mary slept like a kitten, ate on schedule, cooed and gurgled with inexhaustible gaiety when she was awake. Mary was the affirmation of her parents' love, the rosy embodiment of their dream of Family.

Today Mary is nearly six. She is pert and pretty as a Christmas angel, with great charm, a lively tongue, and the temper of a trapped wildcat. The charm she turns on and off as need be. The tongue she uses knowingly to lash or cajole, whichever method best serves her purpose. As for the temper, without warning the angel face becomes distorted, the pretty mouth pours forth a torrent of screaming filth, and the dainty hands and feet deliver kicks, scratches, and punches of incredible speed and variety.

Mary delights in telling gory stories, of witches who kill and bad men who torture little children, of dark evil caves, of tall mountains which dissolve and leave the climber floating in space forever and ever. Her fantasies, begun in playfulness, are so dramatic and convincing that they often end with Mary standing in the middle of the room, sucking her thumb, her blue eyes widened to circles of darkness, while her playmates around her sit frozen in fear.

Mary's nights are ordeals of terror from which she wakes screaming and fighting with whatever adult comes in answer to her cries. Mealtimes with Mary are rugged; she picks at her food, hoards it squirrel-wise in her cheeks, or flings it from her across the table, on the floor, at the wall.

The beguiling baby of a few years ago has become a seriously disturbed child. With all her generous gifts, Mary is a burden to her parents, a trial to her nurses and teachers, a menace to other children. She is, besides, and most important, a pitifully unhappy little girl, indeed, a very sick one.

"I HAVE THREE MOMMIES AND THREE DADDIES"   Mary herself tells us, unknowingly, how she came to this pass. She announces challengingly, "I have three mommies and three daddies."

This is the score. Catherine and Peter D. were divorced when Mary was three, and Catherine married again almost immediately afterward. After two years she divorced and married for the third time.

Mary now lives with her mother Catherine, her newest father John, her sister Jane, her young brother Jackie, by her mother's second marriage, and the baby Brucie, who is the child of Catherine's current union. Mary's father Peter, her second father Andrew, their new wives, who are her stepmothers, and their children who are half-brothers and half-sisters, are all lively, though not immediately present, members of Mary's family.

If this tangled family portrait is confusing to the reader, think how confusing it must be to Mary!

Even the young child fortunate enough to possess only one mother and one father has some difficulty accepting one or more brothers and sisters; we are familiar with the sharp problems of ordinary sibling rivalry. But Mary must struggle with too many of everything.

Again it is Mary herself who unconsciously tells us how important in her difficulties is this bewildering family constellation. She plays a game with her young stepbrother Jackie, a game which she invented on a long upsetting day when the nurse was out and their mother forgot her promise to be home early.

The game is in the form of a quiz. "What's your daddy's name? Your mommy's name?" she demands of Jackie, who is not yet three. "What's your big sister's name? Your little brother's name? What's his daddy's name? What's your daddy's wife's name?" And so on and on until Jackie is in a frantic state and Mary's eyes have an unhealthy glitter.

She delights in teasing Jackie, especially about the half-brothers and half-sisters, the less familiar progeny of the remarried fathers. There are half a dozen of these, and Mary knows them all. She insists on visiting them, and at home she chants their names in an unnatural high-pitched voice: "My cousins once removed, my cousins twice removed, my cousins three times removed . . ."

"Once removed" is a new language acquisition. Mary's use of it is inaccurate, but the phrase has a fascination for her because it so aptly reflects the successive "removals" of one after another of her families.

She sings it monotonously, and not for simple phonetic enjoyment. The overabundance of family in Mary's life not only sums up her emotional confusion. It is also a weapon to use against her mother. Instead of a bedtime story, Mary demands of Catherine almost nightly a recital of the family names and relationships. She listens in rapt concentration and then, to her mother's dismay, "No, I don't remember it yet—tell me again."

MARY'S PARENTS   What of Mary's parents, then? Are they heartless, inhuman, without feeling or understanding?

Not at all, although these six young people seem to be treating marriage like a game of musical chairs. That they marry again, and have children again, is evidence not of mere pleasure-seeking. As Catherine ingenuously would tell you, each new marriage is a fresh attempt, however mistaken, to find enduring happiness.

These young people refuse to let the failures of the past discourage them from seeking fulfillment of the human longing for home, family, and security in love. Each new marriage is undertaken in good faith. Each new child is an affirmation of the hope that this marriage at last is the good one, the one which will endure. To the observer it seems ludicrous that they cannot foresee how brief each experiment is doomed to be.

They continue to be friendly across the prickly emotional barriers of divorce and remarriage. They continue to take an affectionate interest in their own and each other's children by each marriage. They put aside resentments and recriminations. They make a brave attempt to be "civilized" in their old and new relationships, to be adult.

But the sad truth is that, while they can produce nice grown-up manners toward ex-wife and her new husband, and toward ex-husband and his new wife, they have been unable to show maturity in the one relationship which matters, the relationship of marriage.

Divorce does not just happen to people. Divorce is made, and it is a long time in the making. A divorce begins long before the marriage which it destroys. It begins in the childhood of one or both of the marriage partners, in the parents of these two, and if we could retrace the path far enough, probably in the parents of their parents.

The personal maladjustment which leads to the failure of a marriage is a legacy from generation to generation. Each marriage without love, each parent who cannot give love to a child, is preparing a new generation for marriage failure and for children of divorce.

To understand how this can be true, we must look more closely at the two young people who are responsible for Mary's unhappy state, her parents Catherine and Peter. What kind of woman was this Catherine, who could relinquish her life with Peter so soon after it was begun in such harmony, who gave up her marriage to Andrew within two years, and who is now trying again with John? What was lacking in Peter that he fled from a first marriage—a college indiscretion, it was called—even before he gave his faith to Catherine, and that he failed so signally with Catherine? For Mary's sake and for the ever-increasing number of Marys, we must try to discover where divorce begins.

PORTRAIT OF A "SPOILED CHILD"   Catherine was an only child, born of parents who married late in life. This in itself does not carry an implication of emotional deprivation. Older parents can give a child as good a quality of love as younger ones, and with thought they can supply to their only child the companionship which a child needs.

But Catherine's parents could not give her either love or companionship. Catherine's father waited until he had made a success in business before he undertook marriage, and he remained enslaved to the competitive drive, reaching always for a higher goal of material achievement. He was the kind of executive, familiar enough among self-made men, who could not delegate responsibility for the smallest detail of his firm's operation. Nor did he drop the heavy cloak of business in his home. He was a formidable person to his friends and associates, to his wife, and to his small daughter.

Despite his efforts at playfulness, Catherine stood in awe of her father. As she grew older she admired him, but at the same time she resented him for the unspoken standards which his example set for her and which she never could achieve. He cushioned her in luxury, acceded to her most trivial wish, but the one thing which he could not give her was the simple warmth of love.

Catherine's mother had waited long—until she was thirty-two—for her ambitious suitor to make her his bride. A beauty, she spent her twenties in perpetual expectancy, dabbling in the theater, taking courses in literature and music, in flower arrangements, continually burnishing her charm and her modest talents for that achievement which hovered forever in the future.

When at last she married and Catherine was born, achievement seemed finally within her grasp. In this at least she and her husband were temperamentally agreed: theirs must be the perfect home, herself the perfect wife, and Catherine the perfect child.

In Catherine's perfection they were doomed to disappointment. The little girl would not be molded into the ideal image. Catherine took refuge from her mother's code of perfection in a world of fantasy where she herself could make the rules. Cleverly, too, she learned to win her father to her side. Since his daughter was to him not a living, growing child but a symbol of his achievement and a diversion for his lighter moments, he found it easier to give her what she thought she wanted than to explore her deeper needs.

Thus Catherine became more and more tyrannical. Her mother, defeated, withdrew into the role of an ailing middle-aged woman, and died when Catherine was ten. During the years of her mother's semi-invalidism Catherine tried to compensate for the guilt which children take upon themselves for a parent's illness. She acquired hushed manners and a soft voice which, as it happened, contributed a good deal to her charm as a grown woman.

Meanwhile, left almost entirely to her own devices, Catherine reveled in elaborate games of make-believe, dressing up and playing parts into which she poured the feelings which found no normal outlet in her real world. In her parents and their friends she found unflagging admiration and applause for her performances. Indeed, apart from making childish demands for her father to satisfy, this exhibition of herself as a pretty showpiece became the largest part of Catherine's communication with the world in which she lived. No one, apparently, cared enough about Catherine herself to find out what she was really like, nor to win her into a more realistic relationship with life.

Here we see in full flower a demonstration of that gradual removal from reality which is often the fate of unloved children, which arrests their normal growth to emotional maturity, and which later leads to maladjustment, neurosis, and even more serious developments.

Catherine's childhood presents in capsule many of the elements which bring about a separation from reality, and in Catherine's case the process shows a hothouse growth to perfect bloom. Not every little girl who dresses up and play-acts, nor every little boy who dreams himself a hero in adventurous situations, is in difficulties. There is a large place for fantasy in the normal growth of children.

But if a child cannot share in the real life of the world through his parents, if he cannot identify with them in the day-to-day responsible life of the adult, then he has no pattern on which to achieve adulthood in his own right.

Without such an image of maturity the child cannot mature. Without the satisfactions of step-by-step achievement in terms of reality, the child cannot accept the frustrations of adult discipline and adult rules.

Catherine was a "spoiled child." We must explore the significance of this easy phrase.

ANYTHING SHE WANTS—NOTHING SHE NEEDS   Catherine rebelled against her mother—and with justification, since her mother's ideal of what a little girl should be was unrealistic, and had no relation whatever to Catherine as an individual, with her own personality and her own needs.

Catherine could take no share in her mother's responsibilities, since the home was an accomplished fact, sprung full-blown from her mother's dreams, and the small real acts of homemaking which a child can see and touch and share, the dusting and bedmaking and cooking, were all done by remote control, through servants.

Often a little child will express the normal longing to participate in adult activities by helping the maid with dustcloth and carpet sweeper, if the maid is friendly. But Catherine's mother could not countenance a dustcloth in her daughter's hand, and would not encourage a servant to be too friendly.

Thus the little child Catherine, finding no positive satisfactions in her mother to help her accept the discipline, early rebelled and turned to her father. But he was no help either. He was too rigid to bend to the level of a child's interests, to explore the mind and share the emotions of a child. His real love was his business and the power and prestige it brought him. He saw no need to share this major interest of his life with a child; if there were some aspect of it which a child could understand, he had neither the desire nor the imagination to present it to Catherine. His only means of communication with her was by the gifts he showered on her, the granting of her childish whims, and the pride he took in showing her off.

This is what we mean, then, by a spoiled child. A spoiled child is one who has been given what she wants, but not what she needs. She has had the world handed to her on a platter. She has been fed the illusion that she can have anything she wants, now and forever after, simply by demanding it.

She has never had to come to grips with reality; she has never been shown the positive side of maturity. She has never glimpsed the satisfaction of accomplishment, the joy of surmounting difficulties, the benefits of living by the rules, the happiness of recognizing and filling the needs of others, of loving and being loved.

She has been allowed, even encouraged, to live on in the self-centered chrysalis of the young child until, comes the day when she wants, for example, a home and children of her own, she crashes head-on into a wall of reality she never knew was there.

"YES, MOTHER" IN THREE VOICES   Peter, with whom Catherine was to suffer her first defeat in the real world, was growing up meanwhile in a different kind of deprivation. Peter's mother was a woman of enormous energy and competence whose own description of herself was: "Top man, always." As a child, later in school and college, still later in civic, political, literary, and social groups which she organized, she was a brilliant, forceful leader.

Her appearance was thoroughly feminine: modish hat, frilly blouse, softly tailored suit. But strip off the frills and you found the tough core of qualities usually associated with the male.

With a top man, frills or no, in the house, there is hardly room for a plain authentic man. But the question hardly arose. A woman like Peter's mother has a bloodhound's instinct for finding the meek, passive man. Let him cover himself with the toughest outer shell; no booming voice, no athletic physique, no masculine aggressiveness deceive the woman seeking the submissive victim for her own possessive, domineering drive.

The man she chose, and who was to be Peter's father, had already taken the line of least resistance in his relationships. He was a lawyer because his parents wanted him to be one. In the law he quickly removed himself from the human side of his profession into research. His encyclopedic brain was a byword in the vast legal organization of which he was a part; his colleagues turned to him for information, sure that he would save them a trip to the library.

Whatever urge Peter's father may have had to assert himself in his marriage was soon crushed. His tentative "Yes, dear, but——" presently became a chorus of "Yes, Mother" in three voices: Father, Peter, and Peter's younger brother.

The lines were laid down with a firm, if gloved, maternal hand for all three. But it was not so bad, really. If they could not have their own way, then neither were they obliged to take any responsibility for themselves. Everything was done for them, everything decided, everything made smooth and agreeable, provided they behaved themselves and did as Mother said.

For Peter it was harder than for his younger brother. The advent of a second child is rarely the occasion for rejoicing by the firstborn. Throughout the ages parents have dealt with sibling rivalry more or less adroitly as their own emotions would permit. The situation need not take on tragic proportions, and ordinarily does not, if the child has previously been secure in his parents' love. But with a busy "top man" mother and a meek, withdrawn father, Peter had small emotional resources for meeting the crisis.

As the elder and wiser, Peter was expected to "give in" to his brother. At the same time, since they were only three years apart, he was also expected to share with him uncomplainingly his friends, possessions, interests.

The patterns of submission were already set, and Peter submitted the more readily, since his mother's love (his father's love did not matter so much) seemed to hinge on his unconditional good behavior. The suppressed resentment with which he met his brother's arrival, and which grew with the injustices of their growing up together, seemed to wear off.

THE LATENT THREAT OF UNSPENT EMOTIONS   The design for human living would be much simpler if painful feelings could really wear off in time, leaving no imprint of destruction. But they do not. They become transferred, transformed. Buried, unspent, they turn up where least expected, as hardly recognizable yet powerful motivation in situations only remotely tied to the original.

You seem so fond of your brother. Yet deeply you resent him, you must surpass him—beat him, literally—in ways so compulsive and tyrannical that your whole life becomes distorted. Success must be yours, and such spectacular success that the effort toward it drains all your resources, leaving nothing for human relationships, for the wife and children whom you long to love and enjoy.

So it must have been in some fashion with Catherine's father, that man heavy with success and the need for success. So it was, too, with Peter, though in far softer terms, because Peter, mother-dominated, was a far softer character.

Peter did not work through and past that stage of childhood in which he must learn to share his mother's love with his brother. He continued to feel an overwhelming need for her love, which he had never had, and to depend on her. He did not work through his initial resentment of his brother and past it to the rewards of having a brother and companion. Thus resentment continued to seethe under outward submission, the submission demanded by his mother and demonstrated by his father.

His father also set a pattern of withdrawal and of high intellectual standards. He never cared to hear about the football team or the friendships, but only whether the boys had made a ninety average in their studies, nor, if they failed, did he stay to hear why, since he had neither interest nor patience for human weakness.

Thus Peter's birthdays eventually brought him to college age, but his emotional growth remained fixed in that period of crisis which had never been resolved. He had a drive to surpass his brother, also to win his father's and mother's approval. He became a first-rank student and in time a first-rank lawyer.

Away from home he found courage for a fierce but momentary mutiny: he married over his mother's objections. Still he was too dependent on his mother to persist and make a success of this marriage entirely on his own. His first divorce was a relief all around, and came to be regarded by Peter through his mother's eyes rather as an annulment of a hasty, unwise contract between two irresponsible adolescents. Fortunately there were no children.

Peter went on to serve his apprenticeship in his father's law firm, a personable and promising young man. His emotional scars did not show; from childhood he was adept at covering his inner feelings, even from himself. His surface warmth and charm were no deception. They were a genuine part of him. But they were simply not his whole self. In an emotional crisis his other self, the insecure, unsatisfied, dependent, and hostile child, could be counted on to burst through.

HOW THE CARDS WERE STACKED   Among the important clients of Peter's law firm was Catherine's father, and at one of the large impersonal parties in Catherine's father's home Peter and Catherine met.

Catherine by this time was in her sophomore year at college. Superficially she had weathered her mother's death well enough, although a cloud of questions hung over the event which seemed to have no answers. Had she been a good daughter? Had she eased her mother's burden? *Burden,* there was a troublesome word. What exactly had been her mother's burden?

Here again we find the same refrain of the child removed from reality. In a home like Catherine's, where there is no sharing either of responsibilities or of satisfactions, adulthood appears to the child solely in the light of a burden. The child herself, merely by existing, seems to add to the burden. How logical then that the child growing up should seek to avoid that unexplained but clearly unrewarding burden of adulthood!

Through her teens Catherine had grown into a lovely creature, with a skill at dramatizing her delicate looks. Her hushed voice, her pretty deference to her father's friends, her young fragility entranced Peter, perhaps because she was such a contrast to his forceful mother.

For her part, Catherine turned to Peter intuitively. He was an Older Man, yet boyish and young enough to belong to her own generation and talk her own language. He had been married and divorced, and thus he was also Experienced. He was so thoughtful of her, so sure of himself. He could visualize down to the last detail exactly the home they would have, safely within his income but delightful, just what she wanted. With Peter she felt safe, as safe as with her father.

What she could not see was that Peter had other resemblances to her father as well, traits which she had resented; for example, a certain rigidity and doggedness. And she could not detect the dependent child buried within Peter, with its power to negate all the apparent stability and maturity which she relied on in him. Nor could Peter suspect that this pliant, gentle-mannered girl who clung to him so flatteringly, feeding his hunger for manhood and independence, was underneath an iron-willed little tyrant who had never learned to give but only to take.

We see now that the cards were stacked against these two long before they met and loved and married. We see that with all their yearning toward permanence and security in love, with all their hope of making a good thing of their marriage, they had only the slimmest chance for success. They were concerned with the trappings of marriage but innocent of the realities of marriage. They carefully chose the outer furniture of their home, but they had no choice about the inner furniture they brought with them into the home.

THE MEANING OF INCOMPATIBILITY   Six years of marriage, two children were enough and more than enough to break through the surface harmony to the desperate conflicts beneath. Peter unknowingly sought in his marriage two opposites: independence, and also someone like his mother on whom he could depend. It is no use to speculate on whether Catherine could have given him the help he needed. It would be a task of some magnitude even for a mature and perceptive woman, and Catherine was neither. The spoiled darling of many adults had herself had very little chance to grow up.

Catherine meanwhile sought the sheltering protection of a strong male—her father—and at the same time rebelled against domination and demanded her own way. Since her own way, the only way she had ever known, was that of egocentric pleasure-seeking; since she had never experienced the gratifications of real-life experiences which demand effort and self-giving, she was almost immediately confronted with situations beyond her immature power.

While they were still two young lovers with no difficulties beyond the trivial ones of household management, Catherine and Peter coasted on the impetus of their strong attraction for each other. But they wanted children, the symbol of permanence and stability and also of maturity. Jane came before their first wedding anniversary, and Mary quickly followed. There is nothing like children to test a marriage, for the presence of children demands that there be adults to care for them. Under the pressure to be more mature than they were in fact, the real Catherine and Peter began to break through their unconsciously assumed façades.

Predictably, their conflict arose over the management of the children. Peter held out for strict discipline, the theme of his own childhood. Catherine, vacillating between the do's and don'ts of her mother and the anything-you-want of her father, was alternately indulgent and punitive.

Peter, trying to assert himself in the wished-for role of a strong male, would begin bravely by making a clear pronouncement. But Catherine's willful, spoiled-child stubbornness shook him, and he withdrew, each defeat adding to the growing rancor in his heart.

Arguments became sharper and crueler as each, out of insecurity and self-doubt, felt the need to best the other. Neither had the mature strength to be patient, reasonable; neither was capable of the considerable effort to keep the marriage going despite frustration, to resolve difference and strive toward understanding in order to preserve the relationship.

On the contrary, each was already seeking escape from a bond which seemed to promise only more hurt and more bitterness, which in fact demanded more than either had to give. Each was already considering, not how to make this marriage work, but how to make another try with a different partner free of the blemishes which to each now appeared so glaringly obvious in the other.

This is what is called, in another easy all-enveloping term, *incompatibility*.

10
A CHILD'S EYE VIEW OF
A FAILING MARRIAGE

How did these events in the adult world appear to Mary?

Mary is a child of superior gifts. She has greater than average intelligence and greater than average vitality, and she can tell us more about herself and other children than the average child is able to do.

Her tantrums—those tempestuous demonstrations which a psychologist blandly termed "motor expression of hostile feelings"—reveal an intensity of protest which many another child in a divorce situation would give vent to if he could.

Her dreams and fantasies, her outspoken play activities trace clearly the orbit around which a child's emotional disturbances revolve.

Let us not be misled by the extravagant form which marriage failure has taken in Mary's case, her "three daddies and three mommies." Multiple divorce is not average, but neither is it rare. This is an extreme case, but not an exceptional one; no new phases of human behavior are exhibited here, but rather the familiar ones raised to their *nth* power. Whether she had two daddies or four or six, this child would suffer the same hurt and use it as a whip against the world. Mary speaks for all children of unsuccessful marriage who have been left to find their own explanation of what is happening and to form their own defenses against it.

So plainly does she speak that we can watch the effects of her parents' discord on Mary step by step, almost day by day. We can trace the change in Mary from a rosy, happy baby to a bundle of fierce hostilities and desperate defenses at six.

On the surface it was a swift and sudden change. Mary was not quite three years old when her mother divorced and remarried within a few weeks. Those who knew Mary at that time witnessed a spectacular transformation in her personality, and did not hesitate to relate it to the breaking up of the home. But a perceptive observer of children would have picked up the danger signals which flickered on and off for many months before.

Mary began to stall a little over her food; she began to hang back from playmates she once ran eagerly to join. At the words, "time for bed," a keen watcher would have seen her pupils widen in fear; restless nights, bad dreams were beginning. The tempo of Mary's day, once so quick and joyous, was slowing. The gaily colored, steadily spinning top was losing its momentum, was wavering.

It was natural that these first signs of faltering should pass unnoticed by Mary's parents. So faint, so evanescent were they that Catherine and Peter would have had to be far more alert than they could possibly be now, enmeshed as they were in the tightening web of their own conflict.

Catherine wondered once or twice whether Mary was not going to begin biting her nails; little tense gestures, fingers to mouth, had come to her, as it were, out of the corner of her eye. But nail-biting was out of character with her bright happy Mary, and Catherine dismissed the thought.

Catherine and Peter were also lulled by that little knowledge which is sometimes dangerous. In discussing children from broken homes it is customary to date the maladjustment from the point of the break. Statistics painstakingly compiled, stamped, and passed through a tabulating machine are quoted with the weight of vast numbers to demonstrate that such children stand a good chance to go to rack and ruin—*after* their parents have dissolved the marriage contract and dispersed the home.

Tags and labels, classifications, inflexible demarcation lines are tools of some technical convenience, but they do not reveal the individual drama tucked away inside each pigeonhole. The drama begins long before a separation is even thought of. Divorce is not the beginning of the child's troubles. Divorce is the end result of a conflict which has already engulfed the whole family.

The child is warned of his parents' difficulties long before they broach the subject to him, if they do. He has his own means of detection, efficient though inarticulate. He knows that something is amiss and he feels threatened by some indefinite yet powerful source of danger.

He reveals this knowledge in unmistakable ways. To be sure, he does not come and say, "You know what? My parents are going to get a divorce!" But even from the outside some signs can be observed. He may become apprehensive, irritable, restless, aggressive, or, on the contrary quieter, less attentive, less interested in his usual activities. These changes, too small perhaps to be boldly revealing, yet say unequivocally, "Danger! Someone, do something!"

The real revelation, however, is not there. It makes itself legible and audible beyond doubt in another language, the language of the child's dreams and the child's play.

Here the child develops his new themes, expressive of what he fears may be going on between his parents. Here is enacted the drama of being abandoned, left to fight for himself in a friendless world. Here he sees his parents (or the king and queen or prince and princess of the story) going each his way, either childless or disputing over the child. Animals may be substituted for the human cast of characters, but the pattern and the message are the same. The child is attuned to the internal conflict of his parents, a conflict which they themselves may not yet have voiced or may have taken great pains to conceal.

WHAT THE CHILD SEES   So Catherine and Peter, anticipating no trouble from that quarter, saw no signs of trouble. They had no warning of the child's receptiveness to the emotional state of her parents. They felt secure that the secret of their conflict was well concealed.

After all, it should not be difficult to keep a secret from a three-year-old. Her parents may be suffering an upheaval, but the ordered routine of her life goes on as usual. And her understanding is surely very limited.

But let Mary tell it as she saw it—as countless children have experienced it and later revealed it in the course of treatment. Here we have the child's first inner reaction to something unusual:

Last night I woke up and I heard Daddy yelling and Mommy was crying. I never heard that before.

And again:

Today when Daddy came home he didn't pick me up, but he and Mommy started to whisper about something. They were too busy to play with me.

Catherine and Peter were trying their best to shield the children. They checked their quarrels in mid-torrent, to tiptoe down the hall and make sure the children were asleep. They smiled at each other and talked of everyday things in the children's presence. But a young child lives by feelings, not words, and is sensitive to the subtle expressions of feeling to which a grownup, dependent on words, has become dulled:

Mommy and Daddy are not the same as they used to be. When Mommy kisses me good night she's always in a hurry. When Daddy is telling me a story he stops in the middle and looks at me as if I wasn't there. Sometimes he squeezes me too hard when he says goodby. I get scared.

Mommy is always on the telephone. When I come in she starts to whisper.

Why doesn't Nanny like it here any more? Nanny was crying and she said she was going away.

I'm scared. Maybe I've been a bad girl.

These are some of the thoughts which assailed Mary's mind. She could not have said them in words; as "thoughts" they were barely formed. She gathered such bits and pieces of information over a period of months.

Through these months her security in her parents was being undermined. By the time Catherine brought herself to the point of telling her children the hard news, Mary was already shaken. Inwardly she quivered with fears; outwardly she had begun to bristle with childishly inadequate defenses against the situation which, without explanation and reassurance from her parents, could only be felt by the child as a threat of total destruction.

To Mary as to all young children, her parents were no ordinary human beings. They could do no wrong; they always knew the answers; they had the magic to dispel every fear, ward off every danger. They were all love, all help and protection; all power. They were God and more than God, because God is someone far away whom you never see, but parents are there and they are real to the touch, the sight, the hearing.

In so absolute an attitude there is no room for complexities and shadings, no ifs, buts, or maybes. At the same time, what Mary was witnessing during those months was in fact a situation gone out of control. Things were wrong for the first time in her short life, and apparently her parents could do nothing to set them right.

Worse than this, her parents themselves were *making* things wrong; they themselves were changing in inexplicable ways. But her mother and father could not be wrong. They were the very essence and substance of rightness, the final authority, the unshakable strength and support of her world. So it must be she herself who was wrong, who was bad. She was bad, and something terrible was going to happen to her. Inwardly the helpless protest had begun: *No, no, no, it must not happen to me!*

"DADDY CAN NOT GO!"   Like most adults, Mary's mother believed that a child so young cannot understand anyway, so why explain? When circumstances forced her to an explanation at last, she remembered reading in a magazine article that ideas can be communicated to children by way of fantasy. So one evening she began telling a bedtime story: A daddy bear went on a long journey and got lost, and another daddy bear came to look after the mother bear and the little baby bears——

She did not get far. Mary put both hands over her ears and demanded, "The other story, the one you always tell—YES, YOU KNOW!—about the little girl and the good fairy."

Catherine gave up the daddy-bear version, but the failure of this little excursion into modern psychology added to her feelings of inadequacy and tension—which, of course, were passed on to the children.

Her next attempt was the direct approach, one frequently used by parents in similar straits. To the beleaguered parents it appears, at least, to be direct, but so confused and inhibited are they by their conflicting emotions that even their most forthright effort comes out in the end as not direct enough.

A few days after the fairy-tale fiasco Catherine called the children from play into her room. She was going to tell them calmly and frankly that there was going to be a change in their lives. Their father must go to work in a faraway city and the family could not go with him.

The unhappy Peter had in fact decamped a week before. Powerless to cope with the crisis in his marriage, he had abruptly requested his transfer to the Chicago branch of his firm.

If this seems like an unfeeling way to deal a blow to children, we must consider that the action takes place in a setting of general confusion. The adult actors in the drama are deeply shaken, unclear about their own reactions, unable to face the stark realities of today and of the days which will follow.

It is an ancient protective device, as old as man, to run away as Peter did, and an equally time-honored method was Catherine's when she evaded the real issue. People have always tried to spare themselves and, they hoped, others by retreating from or denying a too painful contingency. More needs to be said, and will be elsewhere, about these protective devices, the function they serve and the scars they leave behind.

At this acute moment Catherine, besieged by conflicting impulses, seized upon Peter's removal to Chicago as the readiest explanation to give the children, one they would understand, one which would not hurt them too much. How frighteningly inadequate it must be, to the young who live not by intellect but by feeling and whose sharp perceptions have caught the deeper emotional undercurrents of the situation, she very quickly discovered.

As she heard herself say, "Daddy has gone away," these few words, openly spoken for the first time, threw her into a panic. Gone was her resolution to speak calmly and frankly. The rest of her message was delivered in a noticeably shaky voice as she became increasingly frightened at revealing her secret and aware at the same time that she was not telling the real truth of the situation. She watched the children's reaction with an apprehension which she was too deeply troubled to conceal.

Mary wriggled and fretted inarticulately; her mother's words carried little meaning to her, but her mother's mood was perfectly communicated. Jane, however, rebounded with the ingenuous enthusiasm of a child who for once has been able to beat a grownup to the draw: they would all go to Chicago! By car, by train, maybe they would even fly! She waited, breathless, certain that her wonderful solution would set them all packing trunks on the instant.

At this moment Mary, taking courage from her big sister, found her voice. "Daddy CAN NOT GO!" she screamed. Or if he went she was going with him, but he was not to go anyway, and that's all!

Catherine, trapped by the unforeseen inadequacy of her explanation, tried to improve on it. It was wartime; travel was difficult; they could not find a place to live in Chicago. Weaker and weaker, her excuses trailed lamely on. No one, certainly not the children and by now not even Catherine, had the faintest illusion that these diffuse apologies cleared the air or soothed the heart.

The issue fundamental to children, the question of whether their parents love and will take care of them, still remained unspoken and unresolved. A housing shortage in Chicago could scarcely explain the threatened end of the world.

THE UNSPOKEN QUESTIONS   Mary struggled to understand. No one had told her the truth about what was happening, so she sought the truth in her own terms.

Why has Mommy let Daddy go away? Maybe she sent him away. Can this be a punishment for being bad? Maybe Daddy was bad. But what could he have done?

Maybe—this was a terrible possibility—maybe Daddy went away because he didn't love Mary any more?

And if Daddy, why not Mommy too?

This was unbearable, unthinkable. Yet Daddy was gone; that, she knew, was really true.

The anguished questions buzzed in and out, giving her no peace, and meanwhile her outer world changed with dizzying swiftness. Daddy is gone. Mother leaves, but she is coming back (six weeks in Reno). Mary and Jane are left alone with a new nurse who doesn't believe in giving in to children's whims. Mother comes back and in a few days there is a new strange man in the house whom one is supposed to call "Daddy."

But he isn't my Daddy. My real Daddy's gone away. If I'm good maybe he'll come back and stay with us. Why can't I have two daddies? But will this new Daddy let him come back? Maybe he'll stop him!

Now the changes in Mary's behavior become dramatic and obvious. She is sullen and dreamy, absorbed in her own inner dialogue. She no longer asks questions. When her mother tries to draw her out, she is either unresponsive or actively belligerent. To every approach Mary's answer is, "Leave me alone!" or even, "Shut up!"

This "changed" mother can't help any more; why should Mary tell her anything? She has spoiled the chance of Daddy coming back by bringing this new daddy into the house. And many times it seems to Mary that her mother does not love her either.

Is Mary so very wrong about this? Catherine has just gone through the painful experience of divorce. All her efforts to protect the children from this upheaval, though often misdirected, have been nonetheless sincere, and have additionally taxed her already overtaxed emotions. Now she is trying to make a new start with Andrew.

Andrew is a kind, intelligent man. He is doing his best to pull things together for all of them.

And here is Mary, sulking, rejecting every advance. Mary is making things very difficult, and it is to be expected that Catherine is occasionally sharp and impatient with her. Catherine is groping for emotional stability; the failure of her first marriage hangs heavy over her and she is doubly tense in her effort to make a success of her second. Is it surprising that she sometimes resents this little girl who sharpens her own guilt feelings, and who by her troublesome behavior endangers the precious relationship with her new husband?

Mary and her mother clash like two pendulums swinging between the extremes of love and hate.

Mary both loves and hates her mother, but toward her mother's new husband Mary suffers no conflict of emotions. For her new daddy she has simple, unconfused hatred. Jane has been able to accept him to a degree, but not Mary. She sneers at his attempts to woo her, mocks his baby talk and corrects his language. His almost daily gifts she spurns or destroys. And when she sees her mother kissing him her sullen façade is torn by an explosion of the fears, the hatreds, the anguish pent within her. She screams, scratches, kicks; her child face is contorted and her child mouth spits filth and violence. She is an erupting volcano of boiling emotions.

During the first year of this second marriage Mary took no comfort; on the contrary, her agony and her protest sharpened. She dawdled endlessly at meals, cramming food into her mouth only to spew it at last over the table, the floor, the walls. Almost any small frustration could become the trigger for a temper tantrum; if she was unable to fasten the belt of her dress she became a raging demon of fury. She had sudden headaches, sudden spells of nausea.

In each of these episodes Mary was attempting to do the impossible: to reconcile her overwhelming feelings of love and hate. "Mommy, I have a headache." *Mommy will come and hold me, stroke my head, love me.* "Mommy, I have a headache." *Mommy wants to go out, and I am spoiling her fun and annoying her.*

At the end of the year Jackie was born, in Mary's eyes another rival. One way to compete with a baby is to become as helpless and babyish as he is. Mary, who had never sucked her thumb, now had it constantly in her mouth. She could not walk upstairs; she had to be carried.

She was deathly afraid of the dark, afraid to go to sleep and confront the terrors awaiting her in her nightmares. In the morning she was a tired, cranky little girl, fussing, crying, refusing to perform the smallest tasks.

MARY AT SCHOOL   At four and a half Mary was sent to nursery school. Catherine, still trying to do her best for her little girl, chose the school with care, and Mary's teacher was sensitive and soon became

aware of the depth of Mary's trouble. For the first month Mary
hung onto her skirt, and this warm and sympathetic woman encouraged the frightened child to stay close to her. For a time an
assistant teacher took over the rest of the group because of Mary's
incessant demand for her teacher's attention.

Every aspect of living had become an ordeal for Mary. For her
afternoon nap she had to be placed in a separate room so that the
other children might not be disturbed, and the teacher had to remain with her. There was an elaborate ritual: Mary would kiss the
teacher and demand to be kissed in return; then she would lie down
and sing a song to her doll; then she must have a song from the
teacher. A moment later she was up, kissing the teacher, beginning
the whole ritual over again.

The toilet was a problem: she would watch the other children, but
would not go to the toilet until they had left. Then she went in
alone, and remained so long she had to be coaxed to come out.

She took things surreptitiously, a toy from a child, a pencil or coin
from the teacher's desk.

In the course of the school year the affection and warmth of her
teachers began to bring results. Mary rested better and made less
of the toilet problem. She ceased to take things. She was able to
detach herself from her teacher for short periods. But usually she
fixed on one other child, a younger or smaller one whom she could
dominate or make the victim of her aggressive attacks, a substitute
for Jackie at home. She pulled this child from the others, disrupting
their play, and excited her chosen companion with wild fantasies.
Here is one from the teacher's record:

> Mary goes to the group which is building a city out of blocks.
> She gets hold of shy, timid Jimmy, her current bosom com-
> panion, and drags him to the bottom of the stairs leading to
> the roof.

MARY: You know what's up there?

JIMMY: What?

MARY: There's a big witch and it will kill you.

JIMMY: Yes, I can see her too.

MARY: See its black eyes. Now she's coming down. She shooted you and you're all dead.

JIMMY: She shooted you and you're all dead too.

MARY: No she didn't, but she bited me and she's going to bite you too. She's got big yellow teeth and she'll make you bleed.

JIMMY: Ooh! I'm all bleeding and you're bleeding too. She bited you on the leg.

MARY: Now he's sleeping and he won't hear us. Let's run away before he wakes up.

The children join hands and run off to hide under the teacher's desk, whispering excitedly.

This byplay was revealing in many ways, but for our purpose we need point out only one. It showed strikingly the fears that seethed inside Mary, and one of her methods of ridding herself of them—or at least diminishing their unbearable intensity—was by living them dramatically and sharing them with another child, scaring him too, and being at least temporarily the destructive witch.

THE THIRD DADDY   In the very last months of the school year, when Mary had actually become able to sleep several times during nap and had shown other promising signs, there was a second drastic change at home. Catherine's second marriage was even shorter-lived than her first. Again there was a divorce and again a quick remarriage, this time to John.

Catherine's handling this time was more adept, and Mary's reaction less violent, but the child slipped backward into her familiar tortured patterns. The patterns now followed old grooves. The fountainhead of Mary's anguished, protesting behavior was still and would always be that period of unexplained, uncomprehended conflict which came to its climax in the first divorce: the time when her "real daddy" went away, the time when her gods first failed her. That had been the first crack in Mary's world. From then on, she could only expect further crumbling.

Mary spent part of that summer with her father and his new family in Chicago, the rest with his parents—and still another new nurse—

at their summer home. When she came home her mother was pregnant again.

Back at school in the fall, a new teacher had to win Mary's confidence and soothe her fears, a task like the labors of Sisyphus; no sooner had the school pushed her part way up the hill toward recovery than events at home pulled her down again. Christmas brought presents to Mary from all her daddies and their wives, and from her own mother, among other gifts, came a new baby brother, Brucie.

Shortly after that New Year's, Catherine brought her troubled little girl for psychiatric help.

WHAT CAN BE DONE FOR THE MARYS?   At first, when her mother left the room, Mary would not sit down, nor would she take off her coat and hat. Under the jauntily tilted, bright beret her small drawn face was closed and suspicious. Yet almost her first words were revealing: "Mommy made me come here because I'm bad."

As she dared to show a little interest in the small dolls and doll furniture on the shelves, she allowed her coat to be removed. A bright new dime fell from her fist and she swooped to retrieve it.

"My daddy gave this to me," she said defensively, and snapped on a bright smile as she went on: "My daddy is the richest man in the world. He brings me a new present every day. I have a doll bigger than me. She weewees and she shuts her eyes. She's a good baby. Not like Jackie—Jackie's bad. Daddy gave her to me and he's got a thousand hundred zillion dimes. "

With this boastful description of her daddy, the kind of bravado many children display who are unsure of their parents' love, Mary picked up one of the dolls and seated it in a chair. The suggestion was made that the little girl—the doll—was in school.

Mary pushed another doll across the table.

"That's the mommy. She's coming to take her home. She's going to kiss her and kiss her and kiss her and then her nurse is going to read to her before she makes her take her rest."

She illustrated by banging the dolls together, a most violent version of kissing. A comment was made that these two, the mother and daughter dolls, were kissing pretty roughly, as if they really were not so loving to each other. A look of understanding and recognition was enough to establish that Mary caught a glimpse of her own feelings.

Then she began to build a scene at home, taking dolls from the shelf, and now naming each one literally: Mary and Mommy and Nurse, Sister Jane and Brother Jackie. But the fabulous daddy failed to appear.

Where was Daddy?

"Oh, Daddy's not home. He's too busy. He's at his factory. Daddy has the biggest factory in the world. It's a thousand million feet high and it's very far away in a big woods. It's full of giants and Daddy tells them all what to do."

"I wonder why this daddy has to be so strong and powerful."

Again Mary did not answer the comment directly. She tossed her head and added, too gaily, "I don't care whether Daddy comes home. It doesn't make any difference."

And now she stepped directly into the reality of her problems. She picked up the doll Jackie and began to spank and scold him.

Jackie, she explained, was bad. He jumped into her bed and woke her up at night. He was a scairdy cat. He had bad dreams "about witches with yellow teeth and big shiny knives. They're going to take him to their dark cave and cut him up into little pieces and eat him."

At first the bad dreams were all Jackie's. The repression of her own dreams she explained by saying, "I am not a good rememberer." But imperceptibly the defense went down and Mary slipped into the dreams: "Jackie dreamed about a beautiful fairy who took him to her house and then she changed into a big ugly witch. The house was all full of tigers and snakes and they started chasing me and I ran and I ran and I ran!"

Her face flushed, her eyes glittered with excitement, and the dreams poured out in a torrent. Mary had no time now for disguising their ownership: "One time I dreamed about a big witch that was going to eat me up and just before she was going to bite me she turned into Mommy. And it was Mommy and she was standing by my bed and I kicked her in the stomach and she squealed," Mary ended, triumphant. (Internally the wheels are spinning: *I love Mommy—I hate Mommy; I want Mommy to come and comfort me—I want Mommy to come so I can punish her.*)

When Mary went to the blackboard and took up a piece of chalk, she drew, again, her family. In its directness this was helpful; indeed, child psychiatrists know that a conflict does not often flow into an expression so free of symbolism.

Here was she, with Mommy. She went to the other end of the board, leaving a wide space between, and drew two more figures. "These are my daddies." She erased one, announcing that she had decided to have only one Daddy. But after a moment of painful hesitation she lifted her hand and scrawled the second male figure in again.

"Daddy went away because I'm a bad girl. Mommy made him go." (*This all happened because I'm bad. No, because Daddy's bad.*)

"He's my real daddy." (*I have a daddy who belongs to me—I must have one!*)

"He's not going to be away all the time." (*He will come back because he does love me—he must love me!*)

"Mommy told me." (*There! If Mommy says it, it must be so.*)

"What did Mommy tell you, Mary?"

"I don't remember." (*Did she tell me? And even if Mommy told me, is it true? Mommy has told me other things . . .*) "I don't remember," said Mary, closing the subject with finality.

But the subject would not remain closed. She had to talk about it, and with gentle encouragement she began again.

"My real Daddy is in Chicago. He has another wife. I love my Daddy."

"Who is the other daddy, there on the blackboard?"

To that, with the aggressiveness which covers defeat, she hurled her challenge:

"I have three daddies and three mommies!"

But three of each were too many; Mary wanted only one. She longed to go back to the time when she had only one daddy, a "real" daddy.

"I'm going to visit my real daddy after school stops. If I'm not a bad girl I can stay there all summer."

Thus Mary told her own confused, painful version of what had happened to her. If she could only be good enough, her real daddy would love her again and let her stay with him.

Meanwhile she loved her father and longed for him, boasted about his strength because she wished him to be strong and he had not been strong when she had needed his strength.

And she loved her mother and longed to have her, as she had had her briefly in babyhood, all to herself in a safe and comfortable world. She wanted her mother apart from all the new fathers and the baby brothers who were always coming between. But she did not want the mother who sent her father away and brought in these other fathers. She did not want the mother on whom she could not rely. She did not want the mother who, witchlike, threatened her with destruction for some "badness" which she did not understand.

THE ACCEPTANCE OF HARD REALITY   Can anything be done to help Mary?

Yes, a great deal.

Mary can be relieved of her anxieties, those inexplicable churning fears which make her nights and half her days a horror of dreadful fantasies. She can be helped to talk them out, to play them out, to see them in daylight and to get at what is behind them, and thus to free herself of the tug and pull of these anxieties.

Mary can be relieved of her guilt. She can come to accept it as a fact that her father does not think she is bad, that he did not leave because she was bad, that his leaving had nothing to do with her, that he was sorry to leave her and would like to have her with him.

She can come to understand that her father loves her and has always loved her, that he does not always expect her to be "good," that even when she is "bad," she is not so bad as she thinks, and he still loves her.

She can come to accept her father as he is, not a god, but a man, who can make mistakes and who is sorry if his mistakes hurt his little girl, who wants his little girl to be happy even though his search for his own happiness takes him far away from her.

Mary can come to accept and love her mother; though she can never again rely on her as all-knowing and all-powerful, she would in time be obliged to recognize her mother's human fallibility anyway.

Now, for her own sake, she must only recognize it sooner, and grow strong enough within herself to accept her mother's weakness.

All this is hard, and it takes time. Mary cannot undo in a day the elaborate defenses she has been months and years in building against her fate, and then in another day build a set of new, realistic, and healthy protections against hurt.

But it can be done. It has been done. Many children even more troubled than Mary have done it, when they have been helped through the tangle of their confusions and slowly led back toward reality, perhaps not an ideal reality but an acceptable one. Some children have made dramatic recoveries. Parents have even indulged in such words as "phenomenal." By such oversize descriptions they are in fact only giving the measure of their own relief.

These recoveries are not phenomenal. When parents can follow with warmth and sympathy the same path which the child is trying to follow, then these "phenomenal" recoveries become understandable.

At six Mary stands before us, emotionally maimed. She is ridden by fears and hatreds; her only defense is to attack. As we have come to know her, the chances for her future happiness look bleak indeed.

But they need not remain so. She longs to love and be loved. She can learn again that which, as a happy infant, she instinctively knew, but she will learn it on a more mature level. As with other children, the therapeutic process can in a sense help Mary develop a kind of maturity to deal with her parents' immaturity. She will have to accept realities which more fortunate children need not learn so painfully, nor so young. But she can learn to accept them.

Can we prevent what happened to Mary?

In one way we can prevent the damage which she has suffered.

We cannot undo the past. Catherine and Peter did not want or choose to fail at marriage; their failure was in the cards they were dealt at birth. They have married and divorced, not to harm their children, but because they could not help themselves. Parents like Catherine and Peter may, however, become troubled enough about themselves to seek the kind of help which could change their destiny. As part of Mary's treatment, both parents were brought in to participate, and they developed enough insight eventually to accept the suggestion of treatment for themselves.

BEFORE THE DAMAGE IS DONE   So far in this story we have been concerned with the aftermath of divorce, in a situation which required momentous changes.

But the Catherines and Peters can be helped to understand in advance what is happening to their children before the divorce stage is reached. Even what may appear small points in handling may have big consequences.

If Peter, for example, had perceived what his precipitate departure would do to his little girl, would he have gone in quite the same reckless way? If Catherine had known how her lame, shaking, inadequate explanations did not explain, but only reinforced the fears which had already begun to form in the child's mind, would she have plunged ahead into the morass of confusion?

And if either had realized, during the first crucial period of conflict between them, how badly their secret was actually being kept, would they not have stopped to take thought, to take counsel with each other, perhaps to seek advice?

Most parents would. Many parents have. When they have felt themselves inadequate, or when they have come to realize what the child has at stake, they have sought advice where they could find it.

Their very understanding of the child's need has guided them in better ways, often without outside advice. They have found ways to help their children even while they themselves have been caught in the débris of their shattered marriage.

III
THE COURTS AND THE AGENCIES

11
THE LAW'S DILEMMA

The parents, divorced or divorcing, who take unresolved problems concerning their children to court in search of a wise solution will rarely find it there.

You may ask your lawyer, "What can the law do for my children and me in this situation?" You are not likely to ask him, "What can the law do *to* my children and me?" If you did, he would probably be too discreet to attempt an exhaustive answer, and you are not likely to discover the answer until you are up to your neck in the legal quicksand, your emotional confusions far more tangled than before, your resentments sharpened, your grief and rage and frustration goading you to still more drastic forays in the courts.

What this does to the children—the whetting of bitter emotions between their parents, the pulling and hauling from one temporary solution to another, perhaps from one jurisdiction to another; the insecurity, often the direct appeal to the child to take sides and make choices which he is incapable of making—all this is too painfully obvious to need description.

In all the literature I have studied on the subject, the small amount which is written for the layman and a vast quantity for the legal profession, almost never have I seen this warning to parents. The path of wisdom does not lead through the courts, especially when your children's interests are at stake. Almost nowhere in the scholarly monographs have I found evidence that deeply troubled human beings have passed this way, seeking light on their perplexities.

I have seen scarcely a shadow of men and women who can suffer grief and anger, whose actions can be motivated by far more powerful forces than reason, and who have come here for understanding and guidance. A judgment, perhaps—this father is "irresponsible," this one an alcoholic, that mother is "unfit"—but except in certain special courts, no probing into the reasons why, no obligation on the part of the law to understand and to help.

Nor have I seen in the many learned pages more than a superficial estimate of the emotional needs of children whose future is being charted. A groping effort at insight sometimes, but of insight itself, none that I can discover.

Because of the damage parents may innocently inflict on their children and themselves, it seems necessary to include in this book a caution of the dangers they will meet when they take their children's interests to court.

This is not, I hasten to add, censure of the judges and the lawyers. For the most part they do their best within an antiquated structure not equipped to serve human beings in their deepest emotional struggles. They themselves are more acutely aware than anyone of the inadequacies of the law to solve the dilemmas put before them.

The movement to revise the divorce laws and the divorce courts is led not, as we might expect, by parents who have suffered there, but by judges and lawyers and law scholars. Parents could make a priceless contribution to future generations if they would enlist in this effort, which, after a most promising beginning, seems now to be stalled as we shall see in a later chapter.

Men and women must of course go to the law for their decree of divorce. But when settlements involving children are concerned, when custody and visitation, maintenance and the division of parental authority are to be decided, let them not bring these questions unresolved to court.

Nor should they be satisfied to settle them with the advice only of lawyers, as approximately nineteen out of twenty divorcing parents now do. Especially when resentments bristle and emotions are at the flood, should parents seek more than legal advice. Lawyers are not trained to deal with the emotions. They can barter rights and privileges and bargain with money, but they should not be asked to bargain with the welfare of children.

THE RELUCTANT PSYCHIATRIST   A few courts, known as Family Courts or Domestic Relations Courts, exist in the larger cities and serve for the most part families of low income. These courts have the services of psychiatric or social case workers and a few even have staff psychiatrists. But in most states divorce matters are handled in the regular courts devoted to civil suits of all kinds.

In these courts the dissolution of a marriage is granted because one party to a contract has proved that the other has breached the contract. Alimony, partition of common property, the custody and maintenance of children, and rights of visitation are argued in much the same way as disputes between business partners. From the records it is clear that they are customarily decided so as to punish the "guilty" party and reward the innocent, injured one.

This is the mechanism provided by the law. It is becoming increasingly clear that the court needs other professions besides the legal in weighing the social and emotional claims brought up in separation and divorce. Nowhere is this need more acutely felt than in cases involving children.

Psychiatrists are sometimes called in; their usefulness in situations which stem from personality and emotional conflicts is obvious. Yet many psychiatrists are reluctant to provide their services in court cases.

Parents may properly wonder why. Psychiatrists complain against the law's inadequacies in family problems, yet, given an opportunity to appear in court, they respond to the call with reluctance. A better acquaintance with the psychiatrist's experience in court would, however, discourage parents from bringing their family problems there.

To begin with, the psychiatrist in court is usually in an equivocal position. He is rarely called in by the judge as an aid in making a wise and impartial decision for the welfare of the children. More often one of the parents approaches the psychiatrist, and the parent, knowingly or not, is rarely looking for a solution purely in the children's interest. In most instances the parent wants the psychiatrist's support for his or her side of the case.

Occasionally the parent asks to bring a lawyer along to the consultation. This the psychiatrist resists, if only on the professional principle that a consultation with a physician is private. And the parent's request reveals the primary motive to be one of winning the case rather than discovering what is best for the child.

Even with a conscientious effort to be objective, a parent can scarcely help giving an unconsciously distorted version of the situation. Furthermore, the task of securing proper interviews with the second parent, when engaged by the first, often proves an insurmountable obstacle.

Add to this the multiform approaches of the law to divorce: no two states have identically the same laws applying to children of divorce, and different courts within the same state give different interpretations of the law. Add to this also the many cracks in the law which skillful lawyers know how to use, the distortions and misinterpretations to which scientific testimony is subjected by the opposing side—and it is obvious that psychiatrists have good reason to back away the moment the word *custody* is mentioned.

Custody is a legal word, presumably without emotional overtones. Yet at no stage in the emotion-filled course of divorce proceedings do emotions rise higher than when warring parents face each other over the custody of their children. At this crucial point in the battle no holds are barred, and the psychiatrist, because he is brought in by one or the other adversary, becomes another enemy objective in the theater of war.

What is needed, of course, is a psychiatric service attached not to either side but to the court itself, with the same impartial position as the court, with an unprejudiced opportunity to explore the situation with both parents, and with an obligation to provide the psychological basis for a decision in the interest solely of the child.

As we shall see, it is only in those few courts which are equipped with psychiatric and social services that the interests of the children are truly served. Not until all cases involving children are heard in courts equipped with these services will psychiatry be able to make its proper contribution to the protection of the child in court.

THE CHILD'S WELFARE AND THE JUDGE'S DISCRETION   Why, we are entitled to ask, is a psychiatrist necessary at all? Don't parents generally settle the custody of their children before they come into court?

Quite so. A committee of the American Bar Association reported in 1948 that eighty-five per cent of divorce cases are uncontested, and come into court with the parties already agreed on alimony, division of property, and the custody and maintenance of the children.

Lawyers take pride in being able to hammer out a settlement of these bristling differences in their offices. Judges are understandably relieved to find an agreement clipped to the plea for divorce. Such a paper, as the judge knows very well, represents many hours of wrangling and recrimination, of bargaining and compromise. He may or may not read it. Even if he reads it, his questions about it are likely to be routine: "Do you agree to this? Do you?" and at the assurance from both parties he accepts the accomplished fact and grants the decree with the agreement attached.

If a judge were to do otherwise than accept the agreement, it is not likely that he could improve matters markedly under the present state of the laws on divorce and custody and the poor faciilties of most courts for ascertaining the true "welfare of the child."

The law has lagged behind our changing social attitudes toward divorce. There is little in the statutes reflecting our growing understanding of what brings two people to the point of divorce. Legally, divorce remains a situation in which one party is guilty and the other wronged and innocent. Indeed in many states the guilt of one party must be proved in order for the decree to be granted. In New York, for example, an acknowledgment by one party that he has committed adultery is not enough. Evidence must be produced as in a criminal court (although, paradoxically, in a criminal case the wrongdoer's confession is enough).

If the court discovers, moreover, that the evidence has been manufactured with the consent of both parties, or that the plaintiff has known of and condoned the other's guilt, then the court is enjoined not to grant the decree. Collusion, connivance, condonation, recrimination are terms for these and similar "frauds" perpetrated on the court.

This concept of divorce as a proceeding in behalf of one party against another party guilty of breaking a contract has potency in the disposition of the children. While an assumption of guilt permeates the court's atmosphere, there is a tendency at least to grant custody of the children to the innocent spouse, and to deprive the guilty one either in punishment or because he is "unfit."

The common-law principle, which we inherited from the English system, grants to the father all rights over minor children, but this severe dictate is now generally set aside. The child under eighteen is a ward of the court, and the court is expected to award the custody in such a manner as will be best for him. This is the principle of the "welfare of the child," and in theory it governs all custody decisions.

But how is the court to determine what constitutes the welfare of the child? The answers to so complex a question, subject to the infinite shadings of each individual case and the fluidity of human living, could never be written into statute. In the end, and rather helplessly, the law leaves the matter to the judge's discretion.

THE JUDGE'S DILEMMA   Now the exercise of discretion cannot be considered simply a legal function. However learned in the law a judge may be, his discretion is far less a product of his learning than of his personality, his background, his interests—and, we must add, his prejudices, for every human being carries his unconscious burden of bias.

The more perceptive a judge, the more responsive to human needs and human weakness, the more troubling he will find his discretionary task. I remember a long-drawn-out custody case in which a high-minded judge eventually disqualified himself. He felt he was too sympathetic to the father, whose education and background were much like his own, and he quite properly decided that these factors, although they influenced his judgment, were not strictly relevant to the welfare of the children.

In another case the judge ordered the child placed in a neutral home, with a social worker to observe him over a period of two months. The same judge, studying the results of various psychological tests which had been made on the child, asked numerous questions as to their meaning. He was not content with a psychiatric report provided by one of the parents, because it was unilateral, nor was he satisfied with psychiatric testimony from both sides. Finally he called in a court psychiatrist for an independent opinion.

More than one conscientious judge has felt it necessary to go through this laborious investigation before deciding certain baffling cases. Yet, where the court facilities are not organized for the purpose, it is obviously impractical for the judge to do this for every child whose future is placed in his hands. Simply in order to get the work done, many courts find it necessary to cut through the complexities of custody cases with certain rules of thumb: Young children belong with their mother; beyond a certain age (seven, eight, nine) a boy needs his father; a parent whose way of life deviates from convention is not fit to rear a child (convention being of course defined by the custom of the community plus the moral code in which the judge himself was reared)—and so on.

Or a judge may doff the mantle of Solomon and ask the child to choose which parent he wants to live with.

On the surface this seems a kindly offer, and surely it is meant in kindness. But it is double-edged. It cuts to the heart of the child's most painful confusions. It confronts him with his already divided loyalty. It demands that he choose between two people who for him should never have been parted at all. Whichever he chooses, he is likely to be left with doubt, regret, and guilt toward the other.

Add one more factor to all these, the factor of accident. Lawyers know, and judges regret, that when the calendar is crowded, the last case of the day is more quickly disposed of than the first. Thus, with all the variables inherent in the situation, a child's future may in fact be determined by the time of day at which his case comes before the court!

This is no trivial threat to the child's interests. A distinguished Ohio judge, Carl A. Weinman, gives weight to this factor of accident. As the day wears on, the judge laboring through a heavy schedule reacts more and more, says Judge Weinman, "like a legal machine." Judges themselves realize how seriously this inevitable element of human fatigue can affect the destinies at their mercy, and many make a practice of withholding judgment until they are satisfied with their own decisions.

Judge Weinman also mentions the unwillingness of judges to leave the comparative safety of a legalistic approach and assume social responsibility. Social responsibility, he points out, is infrequently taught in our law schools, law books, or legal institutions. As a result of my own investigation I have ascertained that psychological and social sciences are not included in law school curricula.

Of course a decision can be appealed. But a higher court is reluctant to upset the decision of a judge who presumably has had a better opportunity to know the case. And an appeal costs money.

DECISION BY RULE OF THUMB   Let us examine the consequences of one of these discretionary rules of thumb, one which is, on the face of it, almost beyond question: A young child should remain with the mother. What if the mother remarries, and her new husband is unable to develop an affection for the child, may even actively reject the child?

Foolish woman, you will say, to marry a man who will not make a good father to her child. Certainly a woman who loves her child will be cautious in her choice of a second husband—*if she can*. This is a big *if*. The same unconscious forces which dictated her first marriage may dictate her second; people tend to repeat a pattern based on a conflict which has not been resolved. And the child of divorce may not be easy for the new husband to love. A troubled child can be troublesome.

I knew one such little girl, whose behavior was not much more difficult than that of many children whose parents are not divorced. Yet her stepfather could not accept her, and she was periodically banished to her grandmother's house, where her mother visited her once a week.

Another young child, a boy of four, was automatically given in exclusive custody to his mother by the court because of his tender age. The judge had no way to discover that the child also had a need of his father, and that the mother was not so much interested in the boy as in the additional support she could command from her husband for his maintenance. The records of the clinic to which this child was eventually brought show that he progressively lost interest in living; an unloved child does not want to live. Though he was a normal child to begin with, possessed of an intelligence well above normal, he was finally admitted to a school for mentally deficient children. A normally intelligent child may be so blocked by emotional conflicts as to appear moronlike.

Does the average judge know, or can he explain to hostile and wrangling parents, that while a two-year-old can be separated from his father with comparatively little harm, a child between three and five, whether boy or girl, has a more urgent emotional need of the father? A mishandling of that relationship may bring serious consequences.

The more conscientious the judge, the more likely he is to see that in cases involving the custody of children he stands on the edge of a field of knowledge in which he is not at home. He may be brilliantly equipped to deal with points of law, and may see through human behavior to the mixed and often conflicting motives underneath. He may know that he has only to lift a corner of the mask with which most adults face the world, to discover an unbelievable complexity underneath. His experience may have given him many clues to interpret what he observes—in adults.

But the child is not merely a smaller adult. Young children seldom use words to express directly what they mean. Older children more often conceal than reveal their deepest feelings. A child, wanting approval, tries to tell an adult what he feels the adult would like to hear.

If a child longs for his mother when he is with his father, and longs for his father when he is with his mother, how is he to tell the judge with which parent he will be happy? To him it seems he can be happy only with both of them together. And how is the judge to find the best division of the child's time between both parents unless he has the services of an investigator trained to observe and interpret the child's apparently conflicting needs?

The question of custody is not a question of law. It is a question of the child's integration in the family, whether the family is whole or is divided in two. The judge in the average court, handling a variety of cases, does not have the experience to deal with this special department in human error, the department of domestic discord. Much less is he equipped by experience to dispose of its innocent victims, the children, without the aid of trained workers.

Even the judge in a court devoted to domestic problems is wary of the problem of the children. Often he has considerable success in reconciling dissident marriage partners. Often he can bring a man and woman, who come for separation or divorce, to look down into the abyss at their feet. He can reveal to them the loneliness, the deprivation, the economic problems they will face. Often he can pierce their bitterness and hostility and show them the trivialities on which their marriage has been breaking. He can send them home more reflective and more determined to make a serious try at saving their marriage.

A judge experienced in domestic relations also comes to recognize an irreconcilable conflict between a man and woman, one which is based not on immature haste and impatience, but on deep personal maladjustment. When it comes to determining what is best for the children in such a case, however, the family-court judge is quick to turn to the psychiatrist or psychiatric social worker for the observations which only a trained student of child behavior can provide.

To say that the children of the poor get a better deal in the courts seems a frivolous gibe. But the truth is that family courts and children's courts, equipped with social or psychiatric services, are provided for the lower income population of large urban centers, and poor people bring their troubles to such courts more readily than rich people. Rich people go to their lawyers, and the lawyers usually, somehow, bring them to an "agreement."

Let us see how the children fare in the eighty-five per cent of cases in which their parents "agree."

WHEN PARENTS "AGREE"   We know that most of the men and women conferring with their lawyers about a divorce are, to say the least, confused. Feelings of defeat or outrage seethe in them. Fear, anger, bitterness, guilt at the failure of their marriage, hostility toward the other partner are barely concealed. Many feel wronged. Consciously or not, each is looking for opportunities to punish the other, to prove him wrong, make him suffer, make him pay, get the best of him. What better weapon to accomplish these ends than the children?

"Sure, we settle the children's custody before we go into court, just as we settle alimony and division of property. We settle everything, not in eight-five per cent, but in a hundred per cent of our cases. But sometimes the settlement—especially the deal the children get—is enough to turn even a lawyer's stomach."

The speaker is a successful lawyer in an American city of about 100,000 population. Listen to him further:

"Suppose we represent the wife, and another legal firm represents the husband. Naturally she demands custody. The way most women talk to their lawyers about custody, even a child could see that they are thinking not of the children but of the husband, how to punish him, or how to get the best deal out of him for themselves. If he won't pay enough alimony, she'll cut down on his visitation privileges. The father's wish to share in decisions affecting his children, his wish to see his children—these are her best bargaining points. I've seen women use their children to impoverish a man, or at least to strap him so that his new marriage has two strikes against it to start with.

"The men are no better. A man will chisel at his wife's alimony demands, and when he's gone as far as he can on that, he'll chisel at his children's maintenance. Naturally, if she has custody, he can get at her through maintenance too. He'll threaten to dispute her custody in court—if the children are older, he has a fighting chance of getting them, especially when she's the one who wants the divorce. He'll talk about bringing charges of immorality, incompetence as a mother, irreligiousness, any attack on her character which his lawyer can make something of. The pot calling the kettle black—she can do the same for him, and with as much justice. Who hasn't got a skeleton of some kind to hide? And he isn't thinking of the children, either. He's thinking how much he can keep of his bank account after the divorce.

"So there we sit, haggling. I represent the wife, or the husband. My colleague from another firm represents the husband, or the wife. Who represents the children?

"Not the parents, that's for sure."

And not the lawyers, we must concur. Struggle as they may—and as many of them do, even against their own clients—for what common sense and human feeling tell them is due to the children, still they are not engaged to look after the children's interests. They are engaged to get the client what the client wants in so far as they are able.

The lawyer we have quoted recalled several cases from which he had withdrawn in disgust over the rough handling of a child by parents in a battle of this kind. No doubt many other lawyers have done the same, or wanted to do so, in some of their cases.

Not all parents, nor even a majority of parents, make such ruthless display of their deeper motives. This lawyer and any lawyer could quote numerous instances of parents who seemed to be trying their best for the children. But inner forces of which they are not even aware still remain to confound them.

One wife sincerely believes that the less the children see of their father the better. How can she believe otherwise, when at this moment she sees the man who was her husband only as a heartless creature who has abandoned her for another woman?

One husband is convinced that his wife must be kept on a starvation allowance, and he fights over every dollar she demands for the children. How can he do otherwise when at this moment he remembers not one wise or tender thing she has ever done, but only her extravagance, her impulsiveness, and the fact that she never could learn to cook him a dinner which did not give him indigestion? (We can hardly expect him to know that his indigestion was a case of bad feeling rather than bad cooking.)

The lawyers for their part have no training to guide them in defining what is best for the children. A poll of leading law schools brought the information that no social or psychological sciences are offered to the students. With maturity and experience lawyers become astute in the judgment of human beings and their motives, but this kind of wisdom is not the same as insight into the hidden and

and often tortuous emotional needs of children. And even if a lawyer is exceptionally gifted with such understanding, his position in the service of one or the other parent handcuffs him in any effort he may make for the child's true welfare.

LEGAL ACROBATICS   The laws on divorce and custody provide innumerable cracks through which a skillful lawyer can draw an advantage for his client. There is no uniformity of law as between state and state, nor even uniformity of social attitudes which might influence the application of statutes or guide the judge in his discretionary role. Confusion is worse confounded by migratory divorce, to the extreme that a husband or wife may not even know he or she has been divorced, as in a Mexican decree.

A whole body of law exists, known as the Conflict of Laws, on which distinguished jurists have labored through the years, interpreting and reinterpreting, trying to bring order out of the chaos of differences between the states. The interests of the child can be seriously affected by these differences; his custody and maintenance may hang on one or another interpretation of, say, jurisdiction.

In one interpretation a state can exercise jurisdiction over a child's custody or maintenance only if the child's domicile is within the state. When parents live together, the child's domicile is easy enough to determine. But then his custody is not likely to be in question. It is precisely when parents separate, and when they are battling for the child, that his domicile becomes a controversial point.

And then, how is it to be determined? The law generally considers a married woman's domicile to be that of her husband, and a child's domicile that of his father. But according to the Supreme Court of the United States, a divorced woman's domicile is a place of her own choice, separate from that of her former husband.

Now suppose the mother has moved to another state and taken the child with her. Where is the child's domicile? Some authorities hold that the child still retains his father's domicile. Another view, considered more modern, suggests that the child takes his mother's domicile *if his father was to blame for the separation!* Here is a pretty problem for the lawyers to wrangle over, especially if the divorce was granted in a state where the "fault" of one party or the other is not necessarily established in the granting of the decree.

And suppose the decree has provided for joint custody? With the parents living in different states, where is the child's domicile? And in what state can one parent sue for relief from the other parent's refusal to hand over the child according to the terms of the decree?

A court in the father's state (or more probably in the state where the decree was granted) may issue an order to the court in the mother's state, requiring that the child be handed over. At this point the mother quietly departs with the child to a third state, where she is eventually discovered. Now the courts in this third state may respect the order of the first court, or they may find that the original order was handed down without jurisdiction, or that "changed circumstances" have affected the custody of the child.

And while the lawyers bring up argument after argument, quoting this and that authority or precedent; while the judge is forced to concern himself only with hair-splitting consideration of a point of law; while the pile of briefs and testimony and records mounts higher and higher—what is happening to the child?

We have read these stories of a child heartlessly dragged from place to place, snatched by one parent while the other's back is turned, going to and from school with hired bodyguards to protect him, not from evil strangers, but from one of his parents, or—and any newspaper reader will recognize this—held in a police station or jail for the parent who is en route with court order in hand.

For the hypothetical situations suggested by a study of the Conflict of Laws we are indebted to Professor Dale F. Stansbury of the University of Tennessee College of Law, writing on *Custody and Maintenance Law Across State Lines.* Ideally, as Professor Stansbury points out, the state where the child is eventually discovered will undertake to settle the heartless wrangle by investigating the fitness of both parents and deciding the child's custody in accordance only with the child's welfare.

Yet we may ask how many states, and how many courts, are equipped to arrive thus ideally at a decision for the child's best interest. And even when the child's custody is wisely decided, the loopholes in our laws offer ever more opportunities for an unreconciled parent to try and try again, provided only that he or she has the money and can find the lawyer to take the case.

Courts have been asked to award custody in a state where a child has never set foot. Courts have been confronted with a claim for custody of children who have been taken out of the country entirely. The California courts dealt with a famous case of this sort, in which the father, before the process server for his wife's divorce action had caught up with him, took the children out of the state and was living with them in Europe at the time of the hearing. Obviously the California courts had no way to enforce an award of custody to the children's mother.

With such loopholes for legal acrobatics, which parents are sometimes willing to exploit without regard to the child's welfare, it is comforting to realize at least that such cases are comparatively few, and too much concentration on them is in the nature of a distortion.

LAWYERS TO THE RESCUE   It is also comforting to discover that lawyers, quite on their own, sometimes take advantage of the confusion in jurisdiction for the sake of the child. Such a case is the refreshing one called fictitiously, "In Re Bologna et al." reported by William M. Wherry in the *Bar Bulletin* of the New York County Lawyer's Association of November, 1951.

The story of the two Bologna children is not unusual except in the concern of the lawyers for the children and the ingenuity exerted in their behalf. The children's mother had left home with "no concern," so the undisputed testimony went, for the care of the children in her absence. The father kept the children at home with a succession of hired housekeepers, then placed them for a period in a parochial boarding school. Both at home and away they were disturbed and unhappy. Eventually they were brought to Family Term of the Domestic Relations Court for a decision on their custody.

Custody cases in New York State are generally, indeed necessarily, heard in the State Supreme Court. In this court the case would have been fought out between two adversaries, the husband and wife. Since the wife had abandoned her children without evidence of any concern for their care, the husband would have had what is

considered a good case. As the innocent and injured party, he would
have enjoyed a better than even chance of being awarded the custody of the children.

But by bringing the children into the Domestic Relations Court
as "neglected children," these lawyers made sure that the interests
of the children would be given first importance, rather than the
claims and counterclaims of lawyers fighting for the rights of two
adults with no one to guard the rights of the children.

In the Domestic Relations Court the judge had the services of a
psychiatrist and a staff of social workers who studied the parents.
In the case of the father a diagnosis was formulated of "an inadequate personality, schizoid trends," and of the mother, "anxiety reaction." The mother's flight from her home was understood as a flight
from her husband's brutal behavior, which had brought her close
to "a breakdown." The judge's opinion, based on the psychiatrist's
findings, stated that her anxiety seemed less when she was no longer
exposed to the stresses of living with her husband, and that she
would improve further with therapy.

The court's Clinical Service brought additional evidence, of a
kind which would possibly not be acceptable in the standard procedure of the Supreme Court, and which would normally not be
available there. The children, without question, wished to live with
their mother. The latest of the housekeepers hired by the father, a
young widow who had lost her own two children in an automobile
accident, was found to be unstable and belligerently partisan to
the father. She could be expected to work hard at destroying the
children's relationship to their mother. These many careful and objective findings, plus the psychiatrist's opinion that the mother was
the more stable of the two parents, guided the court's decision.

The children were accordingly given over to the custody of their
mother in the fall of 1950. But this was not the end of the court's
interest in them. This court is equipped, as the Supreme Court is not,
to follow the effects of its decisions. In January, 1951, the court
handed down a supplementary opinion in the Bologna case: "Supervision of the children continues, with favorable reports as to their
welfare."

Thus through the exertions of lawyers who felt a strong social obligation, the welfare of these two children was effectively served. Interestingly enough, it was served through an artificial device: declaring them "neglected children." Nothing could be truer; they were emotionally neglected, though not neglected in the sense generally accepted by the courts.

The pity is that all children do not receive this attention. The children of parents in better circumstances are not likely to be adjudged neglected, and there exist few courts equipped with social services to deal with all family matters—divorce, separation, desertion, custody—regardless of the income of the parents.

In most courts today the judge has no such facilities to aid him in reaching a decision in the best interests of the children. In most courts the judge is virtually compelled to limit himself to deciding a point of law, or at best to do justice between two adult adversaries, without regard to what constitutes justice to their children.

12

CUSTODY IS NEVER SETTLED

In recognition either of the court's inability to solve the tangled human equation, or of the unpredictability of human beings, the custody granted by the court is almost never permanent. Except where final adoption proceedings have been taken, a custody case can be reopened. And in both court-decided cases and those agreed upon in the lawyers' offices, the issue of custody often is reopened.

Of the eighty-five per cent which are settled by agreement we have no way of knowing how many prove permanent. We only know that many of the settlements, which lawyers have labored to arrive at without a battle in court, come to such an eventuality after a few years anyway.

Ah, you say, then the welfare of the child does come to be considered after all, when the emotions of divorce are cooler and parents take second thought for the young in their keeping.

Unfortunately it does not seem to be so. Again we have no statistics, but the impression is inescapable that parents who reopen a custody agreement in court are generally fighting the same battle with each other all over again, with the helpless child as the pawn.

This is usually obvious in the cases which break into newspaper headlines, with their accusations of withholding of maintenance, furtive or forcible removal of a child from jurisdiction, and now and then a father or mother thrown into jail on a charge of child-stealing.

COURTS CAN BE CRUEL TO CHILDREN   A celebrated case comes to mind, the Jean Field case. The father had deserted his family when the boy was four years old and the girl an infant of three weeks. The mother later was awarded custody of the children with the divorce.

After ten years, in which the mother had cared for the children virtually unaided and the father had never used his visitation privileges to see them, the paternal grandparents asked that the children visit them in Oklahoma City for the summer, promising to return them in time for school in September. The mother complied, paying the children's plane fare herself. The paternal grandfather, by the way, was an assistant attorney general of Oklahoma.

Instead of returning the children at the end of the summer, the father kept them in Oklahoma City and instituted suit to have the custody withdrawn from the mother and awarded to him. The mother went to Oklahoma and took the children home with her to California before the custody hearing.

There followed a series of moves, by the father with the approval of the courts, which could not but have a disturbing effect upon the children. The Oklahoma court overturned the original award and gave the custody of the children to the father. The father arrived in Santa Monica with an Oklahoma deputy, first tried to pick up his son on the street outside his school, and then had the mother arrested for child-stealing.

When she was freed on bail, he had the children taken on a habaes corpus order and confined in the juvenile detention home. There they remained for more than six weeks until an award of temporary custody was granted to the father by a California court. Another California court later confirmed the Oklahoma award of permanent custody to the father.

The mother had cared for the children for ten years in an "exemplary" fashion—this was stated and not denied in court—despite financial difficulties. Except for the allotment during the father's war service, she had received a negligible portion of the $30 a month awarded her by the original decree. Reports from the children's schools and from the detention home described the children as healthy, well adjusted, well behaved, outstanding in their school work and in leadership in their school groups, and the boy, now fourteen, had won athletic honors. From this record it appears that the mother had done her job well. Nor was any suggestion brought into court against her character or morals.

On the other hand, the mother contended that her former husband had not only been financially irresponsible but also had a record of drunkenness and conviction for forgery. She described the home in which he and his second wife kept the children as "dirty" and stated that the children had no clean clothes to wear, although she had supplied them for the visit. In the ten years since he had left his wife and children—with a note in the typewriter and no money in the house—this father had not answered the children's letters nor come to see them. The mother had preserved the father's character with the children as best she could.

These facts, which have directly to do with the welfare of the children, were not heard in the Oklahoma court, but they were presented in both California hearings and were not disputed. The father's entire case was based on testimony that the mother had taught the children race equality and had expressed disapproval of the Korean war.

The judges did not explain their decisions with any reference to the welfare of the children. The Oklahoma court ruled that the custody should now be awarded to the father because the mother had taken the children out of the state and was therefore in contempt of court. The California judge, granting temporary custody to the father, ruled that he did so "in all the circumstances of the case." The second California judge simply upheld the Oklahoma decision.

One judge at least seems to have shown a callous disregard for the needs of children. He allowed the children to be detained in the juvenile detention home—to children the equivalent of being "in jail"—for the period from November 2 to December 14, when the case for temporary custody was completed. This was done on the father's plea that the mother might take the children out of the country if they were not held in detention.

During this time the children were at first not allowed to see their mother at all, and later only for one hour on Sundays and half an hour on Thanksgiving Day. When the decision was handed down that the children were to be delivered "forthwith" to the father, the mother's plea for a parting ten minutes with them was denied. Thus were children separated from their mother whom they loved and had lived happily with for ten years. It had been acknowledged in court that the children loved their mother and preferred to live with her.

At this writing the children remain with their father in Oklahoma. They apparently are not allowed to receive any communications from their mother. A Christmas letter in which she attempted to reassure them and express her love was returned by the father's lawyer to her lawyer with a rebuke.

Incidentally, Governor Warren of California, after a hearing in Sacramento at which both parents told their story, refused to extradite the mother to Oklahoma to be tried for child-stealing. Presumably, if she were now to go to Oklahoma merely to see her children, she could be arrested there and tried on this charge.

The legal confusions of this case appear to be infinite. The question has been raised whether the Oklahoma court had jurisdiction in the first place, when the children were legally in their mother's custody in California and held by their father after the promised end of the visit. If Oklahoma had no jurisdiction, not the mother but the father might be charged with child-stealing.

The Oklahoma court based its award of custody to the father on the mother's removal of the children from the state. A precedent has been pointed to in the Oklahoma Supreme Court which expressly declares that acts of contempt by parents in removing children from the state must *not* weigh with the court in determining custody: "the custody of the child ought not to be made the medium through which its parent is punished."

Whatever the legal considerations, it seems painfully clear that one consideration was given little or no weight in any aspect of the courts' handling of this case, either in Oklahoma or in California. This is the consideration of the children's welfare, the only consideration which should determine the decision of a custody case.

It is inconceivable that children who have lived well and happily with their mother for ten years should be separated from her for any but the most serious reason, such as inability to care for them further because of physical or mental illness. Any other basis for separation can have no relation to the welfare of the child.

THE TRUTH BEHIND THE TESTIMONY   Parents often seek the aid of a psychiatrist in reopening a custody case, but as we have pointed out, too often they are seeking better terms not so much for the children as for themselves. Too often, also, the law plays into the hands of parents whose emotions distort, for themselves no less than for the court, the question of the children's welfare. On the surface the child appears to be the focus of everyone's concern. We have only to scratch the surface and we find that the child is being tragically ignored.

Sometimes we have access to the truth behind the story that is told in court, as in the case of Evelyn.

Evelyn was six when her mother came to the court in the Midwestern city where they lived with the mother's parents. Three years earlier this young mother had left her husband, taking the child with her. In her youthful inexperience, she explained, she had agreed that her husband should have the child for Christmas and Easter and the long summer vacation. Now she asked the court for full custody of the child, with the father's visitation privileges either cut to a minimum or withdrawn altogether.

In brief this was her story: While in college and against her parents' wishes she had married a man in his late forties, a successful businessman in a small city adjacent to the college town. He had never been married before. He had taken his bride to the family mansion, where he lived with an aged housekeeper who had been there since his mother's day. After four years of what she described as virtual imprisonment in this grim and gloomy home isolated on a large estate, she had fled with her child to her own parents' home.

It was in this dark setting, with a morbid old man and an ancient crone to look after her, that Evelyn was forced to spend three or four months of the year. This was the picture Evelyn's mother drew, of a child crying for her mother, held against her will in a home which belonged in a Brontë novel, omitting only the mad relative caged in the attic. There was even a suggestion that the father was so excessively demonstrative in his affection as to be a potential danger to the child's sexual development; the idea of incest was implanted in the court's mind, though the word was not mentioned. The young mother impressed the court as genuinely despairing over the damage being caused to the child.

When the father came to the witness stand the contrast confirmed the mother's story. A man of dignified and distant manners, he was old enough to be his own child's grandfather. His face was dour and cold, and only monosyllables escaped his rigid lips. He seemed in the grip of violent emotion severely controlled, and it took not much imagination to suppose that the emotion was rage that his wife might succeed in freeing the child from his clammy grasp.

His own lawyer could draw nothing from him which would soften his wife's picture. To his wife's counsel he admitted, yes, the child did sometimes cry for her mother, and yes, he had once or twice taken the little girl into his own bed; alleviation of her fears was his justification. He sent the child little dresses; did she ever wear them? No, he could not say that he had ever seen her wear one of them. He sent the child toys; did she ever play with them? No, he had never actually seen her playing with one of those toys.

If the judge had any remaining doubts, he had only to glance from Evelyn's stony-visaged father to her mother, glowing with bright vitality, and to the kindly, gray-haired grandparents who sat close to their daughter as if to protect her. This pretty young mother would surely marry again and provide Evelyn with a suitable father. Meanwhile the grandparents could not be other than a bulwark of love and security.

So Evelyn was entrusted to her mother's care. Her father could see her occasionally, by appointment at her mother's home, a thousand miles or more from his own home and business; this concession, an impractical privilege at best, the judge made only because the man had no actual blot on his character which would abrogate even so slender a claim as was left him.

Evelyn's father went home a brokenhearted man, deprived of the one object of love and tenderness in his whole life. And Evelyn was parted from a father whom, despite the court evidence, she truly loved and needed.

We know this because some months before she took her case to court Evelyn's mother had consulted a psychiatrist in her city. He undertook the case with the understanding that his findings might or might not support her claim to full custody. He might come to the opinion that the child's emotional needs were better served by continuing the relationship with her father.

"Why, of course," Evelyn's mother blandly agreed, and added, unaware that she was revealing her motives, "If your opinion won't help me I won't use it in court, that's all."

The psychiatrist also interviewed Evelyn's father. He spent several sessions with Evelyn. He spent enough time with Evelyn's mother to observe, as the court could not, that she was determined to get the child completely away from her husband, that she had bided her time since the divorce until she could build a psychological case against him.

At the time of her divorce she could not have done this, having left him without any provocation which would make him the guilty party in court. He still loved her and would have contested the divorce. She had agreed to the liberal visitation privileges in return for an uncontested divorce. Now she felt strong enough to go back on the bargain.

The psychiatrist delved into the motives which prompted her marriage to this man, and he saw—as the court could never have seen—that she had married to escape a neurotic attachment to her father, that her choice of an older man was part of the same neurotic pattern, and her rejection of him after a few years of marriage was a further expression of it. He saw behind the kindly grandmother's façade a dominating woman who had thwarted her daughter's emotional development and was already at work on her granddaughter, putting confusion into the child's love for her father, breaking a natural and wholesome link in the child's emotional growth.

In the father the psychiatrist found a man who had lived an austere, high-principled life until his marriage to the beautiful young girl released all his capacity for tenderness. True, he was repressed and inhibited, and he had his sexual difficulties; but in his expression of love, first toward his wife and then toward his daughter, he had been able to give a great deal of himself. To this the little girl had responded, and the relationship was rewarding to both father and child.

During the marriage he had made a practice of shortening his business hours to spend more time with Evelyn. He had taken over many of the chores of baby care to spare his young wife, and because he loved the baby. Since the divorce he and his housekeeper had rearranged the house considerably to enlarge the child's play space and make her visits there happier. He described with strict factualness the rambling house, in which he had been born and lived all his life; he had prepared a sunny nursery for Evelyn, facing on the garden, with bright curtains and Mother Goose wallpaper.

Despite his rigidity, the father was responsive to suggestion. He had taken the little girl into his bed at night because she was afraid of the dark and he did not know how else to comfort her. When the psychiatrist pointed out that such physical nearness to her father might be disturbing to a little girl, he spontaneously admitted that he could learn new ways. He would, as the doctor suggested, leave her door open at night and a light in her room; he would sit by her bed and read or talk to her until she was ready for sleep. The psychiatrist was impressed with the man's dependability and, in contrast to the mother, with the genuineness of his concern for what was best for the child.

From the grandmother and the mother the psychiatrist elicited the information that it was not the little girl who rejected her father's presents. "Those dresses, such horrors!" the chic mother exclaimed, telling why she gave them away. And the toys the child brought home from her father's house or which he sent her were quickly replaced with "much nicer ones" by the grandmother.

Also, while it was true that Evelyn sometimes cried for her mother when she was with her father, when she was at home she begged to call up her father and ask him to visit them. This is a familiar response in children divided by two loyalties.

How different from the gloomy abode described in court does this father's house seem now, a warm and friendly home for a little girl, with a motherly old woman—the housekeeper—and a father who wanted only to be allowed to continue loving her. How different, too, is the young mother from the impression she made in court.

The psychiatrist not being amenable to the mother's purpose, his testimony was of course not called for in court. The father, an unworldly man, baffled by his wife's sophisticated lawyers, never realized that expert testimony was buried somewhere which might have been of help to him.

And the judge never knew that in handing down his decision he was abetting a double injustice, to the father and to the child. In this case, through the court's inability to get at the truth, the welfare of a child was plainly ill served by the destruction of a good and necessary relationship.

A HAPPIER ENDING   One more story remains to be told here of a child in court, one with a sinister beginning but a happy ending— happy, that is, if the child's welfare is our primary concern.

Jerry was four and a half when his parents were divorced, and his father, under strong guilt feelings because it was he who wanted the divorce, set Jerry and his mother up in handsome style in return for having the boy one week end a month.

Since then he had tried several times to reopen the custody case. When the court denied his plea, he attempted to persuade Jerry's mother by way of financial pressure. He refused to pay bills for the boy's wardrobe at an expensive shop. He stopped Jerry's attendance at a private after-school group. He refused to pay the fee of a tutor, demanding why a bright boy like his son needed remedial reading lessons. Finally he blew up over a series of bills from the neighbors for damage to their property, and at this point he sought a psychiatrist.

He was quite right to seek psychiatric help. From trouble in school Jerry at twelve had progressed to trouble in the community. He was the neighborhood bad boy, throwing sand in car radiators, deflating tires, riding his bicycle through shrubbery. One evening he made a systematic tour of the block, destroying porch lights. At home a passive, timid youngster, outside it he was the terror of the street.

Jerry's father candidly asked the psychiatrist's support in his effort to get the boy entirely away from his mother. She was making a sissy of him. An interior decorator, she was hauling the boy along on shopping expeditions, to help her choose draperies and wallpapers. She had no control over him; the boy was unmanageable when he came to visit his father. The list of complaints was endless.

Jerry's mother came willingly to the interview, eager to win the psychiatrist to her side. Jerry's father was to blame for the boy's behavior. He was bad only when he came home from one of "those week ends." She took him along in her business to keep him out of mischief, since the father was too stingy to pay for the after-school group and she could not afford to. The father was the indulgent one. Any rule she made, the father encouraged the boy to break. And the language he used! He could have learned it only from his father. The father's new wife was a silly woman, a bad influence on Jerry. She was trying to come between Jerry and herself—the mother could tell by the way the boy behaved toward her when he came home. Now she herself was ready to apply to the court to cut down those week ends. Perhaps to eliminate them altogether was better—what did the doctor think?

The case came to court. The psychiatrist, having given an opinion the father did not like, was not called by the father's lawyers. But the court subpoenaed both him and his records.

The judge, baffled by the convincing case which each of these parents made against the other, turned to the psychiatrist with unconcealed relief. After the inevitable badgering cross-examination to which an expert witness is subjected by the lawyers, the judge took over the witness. He asked many questions, some revealing frankly his lack of familiarity with the psychiatric approach, but all showing his eagerness to bring clarity out of an apparently hopeless tangle. He had studied the psychiatric notes and particularly the record of the sessions with Jerry himself. Jerry, needless to say, was a very disturbed boy.

For good measure a court psychiatrist was called in. When the decision was handed down, it followed the psychiatrist's recommendation substantiated by the court psychiatrist. Jerry's custody was not awarded to either parent.

This child, the decision said in effect, had been hurt by both his parents. Both were full of hostile feelings toward one another, and the child directly in the line of fire. The child was already a problem to himself and on the way to becoming a problem to society. Therefore, he was to be removed from both parents and sent to a boarding school where he would have psychiatric treatment. The court made both parents responsible for carrying out the order.

In Judge Weinman's previously mentioned discussion of the trial judge confronted with a custody case, the author deplored the reluctance of many judges to assume social responsibility. Jerry was fortunate in that his case came before a judge who perceived that he must do more than settle the amount of maintenance and the number of days of visitation; that the court, as society's representative, must in fact take responsibility for a child's future.

WHAT CAN PARENTS DO?   A parent who genuinely seeks relief for a child from an unwise custody agreement must truly despair before this array of confusion and inadequacy in our courts of law.

When both parents are sincerely agreed that the children's welfare is the paramount issue, they of course do not need to go to court to resolve their differences. They can find the best solution together, with the help of counseling agencies, clinics, or private consultation with a psychiatrist. Here they will learn not only what is best for the child but why it is best, and how to meet the new situations which may arise in the course of the child's development.

When the parents cannot together take the first step of seeking advice, it is still highly worth while for the parent who feels the need of help for the child to seek that help, though alone. Sometimes the counselor can bring the other parent into the effort, for the child's sake. If redress must be sought in the courts, a parent equipped with an objective knowledge of the child's needs is better able to protect the welfare of the child in court than one who is not so prepared.

Nor is it difficult for a father or mother, whose first concern is for the child, to find a lawyer who will strive in the same direction. As we saw in the Bologna case, there are lawyers who will exert every ingenuity to use the laws and the courts for the benefit of children.

Parents can help in this fight. In the next chapters we shall consider the courts and the mechanisms which now exist in some states for the protection of children of divorce, and how they function, as well as some of the agencies to which a parent can turn for emergency help.

13

THE DIVORCE COURT OF TODAY AND TOMORROW

There are courts existing today which take under their wing husbands and wives, parents and children who come to them with family problems. Variously called Family Courts or Domestic Relations Courts, and usually side by side with Children's or Juvenile Courts, they do not function on the Procrustes' Bed principle of fitting human behavior to an arbitrary legal pattern. They attempt instead to deal realistically with human behavior as it actually confronts them.

The aim of these courts is not to discover guilt and administer punishment, but to instruct people in how to manage their lives better. In effect there are no plaintiffs or defendants in these courts, only people in trouble. These courts point the way toward a better divorce court of tomorrow and one which parents could do much to bring into existence.

A COURT WITH CURTAINS ON THE WINDOWS   Anna Moskowitz Kross, a dynamic judge in New York City, sits in a shabby building on the lower East Side, in a courtroom like no other. She wears no black robe of authority, nor is her power symbolized by a guard of uniformed police. She has no dais and lofty desk to set her above the people whom she judges, but sits at a table across from them.

There are curtains on the reception-room windows of the Home Term Court. On their way into the courtroom the clients pass through a model apartment, with a nursery where they leave their young children in the care of volunteer play supervisors, and a kitchen where food for the children is prepared.

This, by another paradox of antiquated legal structure, is a criminal court. Technically, it deals with the same minor offenses as other magistrates' courts, such as assault, breaches of the peace, disorderly conduct. The cases on its calendar, however, are only those in which the disputants are members of the same family: husbands complaining against wives or wives against husbands, parents in difficulties with children above the age of sixteen (children under that age are dealt with in other courts).

Unlike most courts, criminal or otherwise, the primary aim of the Home Term Court seems to be not to take court action, but to prevent it. The probation officers go to work on a case before, instead of after, the case comes to trial, and their goal is to solve the human problems in the case so that it need not come to trial at all.

A trial in this court is in fact an inquiry into the causes of the trouble and how they may best be dealt with, by a judge thoroughly briefed in the circumstances and personalities of the family.

The wholesome effect of this approach is felt not only by the people who bring their conflicts to this court, but by the lawyers as well. As one lawyer put it, "As soon as we come into this court-room, we're human."

The lawyer who said this was sitting with the opposing counsel and Judge Kross at her table, and all three were agreed that the belligerent husband and wife represented by the lawyers were both in need of psychiatric treatment. This middle-aged couple, separated but still abusive, are quarreling over money. The judge reminds them that their children's welfare is at stake. "This is not a question of stock going up or down," she tells them. "It is a question of two human beings in the most formative periods of their lives . . . At any time the door of this court will be open to you," she adds as she sends them away for a "cooling off" period of a month.

In another room a young wife accuses her husband of beating her and going with other women; there are two young children. However long it takes, the probation officer listens, questions, listens again. Behind the bitter conflict warmer emotions gleam, though dimly. These two young people do not really want to break apart; they draw back in dismay from the vision of a shattered home which the court officer draws for them. But they cannot, unaided, find the way to live together in harmony. The officer mentions a church welfare agency for family troubles. The wife eagerly assents; she will go there and get her husband to go too. They leave the court side by side.

This may appear an overoptimistic picture, but surely to halt and pause will help them take second thought. With the enforcing authority of the court behind them, such efforts to turn people in the direction of their own and their children's greater happiness have a strong promise of success. So effective is the Home Term Court that its jurisdiction, at first limited to Manhattan, has been extended to include the five boroughs of New York City. It is hoped that eventually a similar court will be established in each borough.

THE "SPECIALIST JUDGE"   Not only the court's procedures but the personality of the judge distinguishes courts like these and makes them a promise of what can be done with the law as a therapeutic instead of a punitive power. By personality, by choice, and in time by experience, these judges are specialists in human problems. To them the paramount issue is not the point of law but the family as a unit, whose function it is to serve the welfare of its members.

Their concern is especially for the helpless members of the family, the children. They themselves are not trained in the psychological sciences, but they know how to use those who are trained in seeking a way out for the troubled people who come into their courts.

Some of these judges arrive at their interest in the family as a logical result of their professional concern with crime. Judge John Warren Hill, presiding justice of New York City's Domestic Relations Court, sees the adult criminal as a "bitter juvenile delinquent grown up," and behind him a childhood in a home emotionally shattered by the conflict of his parents.

"The child in an emotionally broken home is like a soldier in a beleaguered fort whose officers are quarreling," he said in the course of an interview. "He has no morale, no security . . . Children learn to meet trials by observing how their parents meet them. A girl who sees her mother laugh off the father's peccadillo in a kindly way will remember this lesson for her own marriage."

Judge John A. Sbarbaro of Chicago's Juvenile Court follows the same line from the juvenile delinquent back to the necessity for preserving the family. "The term 'juvenile delinquent' is inaccurate," he writes in *Marriage Is On Trial*. . . . "It might be better expressed, 'parental delinquent.'"

Judges of this caliber bring light also into courts in which the procedure is traditional, and give to the archaic label of "trial judge" a more human and realistic breadth. Judge L. N. Turrentine of California, writing under the title *The Trial Judge Decrees Maintenance*, shows how a trial judge can deal with human problems when, as he mildly describes it, "bitterness enters into the relationship between parents."

John and Mary Armstrong, he tells us, had been married twenty years and had seven children. They had weathered hard times together, but 1941 brought them sudden prosperity when they moved to California and the father and the two oldest boys went to work in a defense plant. Then the two boys entered the armed forces, and the father's salary of $47 a week was all the Armstrongs had for themselves and the five remaining children. John turned over to Mary each week all except $5.00 for the savings account, $1.00 for carfare, and fifteen cents a day "to spend in such riotous living as he saw fit." Mary put up his lunch and did the family buying, the cooking, cleaning, and laundry. So far, so good.

But Mary, a steady wife for twenty years, became unsettled. She sought the company of servicemen. Twice John forgave her. The third time he caught her, he filed suit for divorce and stopped giving her his earnings except an allowance of $10 a week to care for the children. Mary haled her husband into court to show cause why he should not give her $35 a week plus attorney's fees and costs.

THE TRIAL JUDGE MAKES A BUDGET   In court John showed, item by item, that he needed $29.25 a week to maintain himself. Mary itemized her needs and the children's: $38. Together these budgets came to $68.25. But John earned only $47.

So the judge made a budget for John. He would have to do his own washing ($2.00 a week for laundry disallowed), wear his old clothes ($2.00 a week for clothing disallowed), give up cigarettes and recreation ($3.00), let his old debts continue to irk him ($3.00), and put no money aside for possible illness ($2.00). He would thus live on $24.25. There remained for Mary and the children $22.75, and on that she would have to manage. This was the court's order for the five months which, because of a heavy calendar, must elapse before the trial.

Twelve weeks passed, and then John and Mary came together to see the judge. Neither of them, nor the children, could get along separately; they wanted to keep their home together. Would the judge work out a reconciliation?

John's main grievance was the servicemen. Mary answered, "Well, Judge, I will try to quit doing that, but it's going to be hard." Mary's grievance concerned the money. She wanted all John's earnings, except his carfare and his fifteen cents a day for recreation. If he still made the weekly savings deposit of $5.00 she wanted him to show her the passbook so that she could check up on him. At this John balked; "he'd be damned if he'd be henpecked."

Again the judge came up with a solution. Mary would promise never again to ask, but John would leave the passbook in the cupboard where Mary could look at it while John was away at work. Both thought this was fair. Mary's need for the reassurance of money in the bank was satisfied, and John would not be "henpecked." They kissed and left together.

At the end of two years they were still together and still, apparently, happy. This whole case seems to revolve around pennies, but many a marriage has come to this impasse over little more than pennies. Mary, confronted with the realistic problems following separation from her husband, was compelled to seek a reorientation in her family living. A patient and understanding judge gave her this opportunity.

He also provided these two people with a realistic demonstration of the inevitable hardship which all members of a family must suffer when two households instead of one must be maintained on the same family income. This is one of the factual problems of divorce which many couples who rush into divorce do not anticipate, and in the dismay which follows, the wife often accuses the husband of stinginess while the husband sees his wife as grasping. Post-divorce quarrels over money settlements are both an expression and an aggravation of the bitterness the partners feel toward each other, but they also grow out of realistic money stringency.

John and Mary Armstrong might have found their way back to each other alone. More likely, uprooted as they were from their original home, surrounded by the confusions and temptations of a war-plant town, Mary might have become increasingly irresponsible, and John might have been forced to find transient solace for his loneliness after twenty years of family life. And the juvenile courts might have had to deal with the consequences to the five children living at home.

Instead, having found a judge in whom they could place their confidence, they came to him for a solution. Naïvely simple as was his device, it served both Mary's need for security and John's right to the dignity of a responsible provider.

It happens, however, that the court may do its utmost and yet be inadequate to resolve the problems of a marriage and protect the rights of the children. Judge Turrentine tells of Peter and Clara Small, who also had been married about twenty years. When they filed suit for divorce, one daughter was in high school and the other about to enter college. Peter earned $10,000 a year as an engineer, and during their marriage the Smalls had acquired considerable property which was kept in bearer securities.

Clara asked for $350 a month for herself and the children, and also that her husband be enjoined from disposing of the securities. Peter agreed to everything. But two days before the trial, when the court order would become final, Peter vanished, taking the securities with him.

He was found in another state where failure to comply with the California court order and to support his children were not crimes nor offenses for which he could be extradited. Suit was brought in that state, and again he decamped. This time he was not found. Clara Small now works for a living. More significantly, so also does the older daughter, who has lost a college education.

For the Smalls, as for the Armstrongs, the trial judge did his best. But we see again as we saw in the case of the Bologna children how the children of the poor, whatever their other disadvantages, somehow derive greater protection from the law.

John and Mary Armstrong, with only $47 a week to divide, could not afford to have expensive lawyers come between them. They could go together to a humane and understanding judge and ask for help. Perhaps the rift between Clara and Peter Small was too wide to bridge. Yet if the trial judge had had the services of trained observers and investigators, and if the Smalls had had the benefit of consultation with psychiatrically trained officers of the court, Peter might not have been able to conceal so well from the court— and perhaps also from himself—his impulse to escape from the situation into which divorce was about to plunge him.

Thus, ironically, the Armstrong children, who had so little material wealth, regained their father, their economic security, and the most precious wealth of all, a united family. And the Small children, with $10,000 a year and considerable family property, lost father, material wealth, and emotional security all at once, plus the education which, with the standard of living set for them by their parents, they might reasonably have expected.

IN MICHIGAN, THE FRIEND OF THE COURT   Since 1918 the Circuit Court of Wayne County, Michigan, which includes the city of Detroit, has had a "Friend of the Court."

The Wayne County Circuit Court has jurisdiction over divorce. The population it serves numbers approximately two million, and about four thousand divorce applications are handled in a year. Many of these involve maintenance and custody decrees. About twenty per cent of maintenance cases and about fourteen per cent of custody cases are later reopened by petitions claiming "changed circumstances." It is one of the tasks of the Friend of the Court to investigate these changed circumstances.

According to the orthodox procedure, in Wayne County before 1918 and in courts throughout the country to this day, a parent desiring a change in a child's custody would file a petition, or in some cases he might cite the other parent for contempt. Lawyers would then find witnesses, prepare affidavits, and assemble their wordy ammunition for a trial.

At the trial witnesses would testify, and counsel would examine and cross-examine, make objections, and take exceptions. The judge would listen and perhaps ask questions of his own. He would also be obliged to rule out certain evidence, not because it was irrelevant to the human side of the case, but because it was irrelevant according to the rules of evidence.

Incidentally, this battle, from the parent's first consultation with a lawyer to the eventual decision, might take months, perhaps a year, during which his parents' antagonisms and the uncertainty about his own future could not but seep through to the child.

With the entrance of the Friend of the Court lawyers may still prepare their cases for the opposing parents, but there is at last someone—this neutral officer—to prepare the case for the child.

When the judge is faced with a custody decision and is unwilling to choose between two parents in the heat of battle, he can award custody to the Friend of the Court. Thus he gains time for emotions to cool and parents to take second thought, and the child meanwhile has a neutral guardian.

In one such case, reported by Edward Pokorny, who has been a Friend of the Court since 1918, the father asked this officer's permission to have the child for a summer vacation. At the end of the period he refused to return the child to the mother. Ordinarily this could be the beginning of one of those chases from jurisdiction to jurisdiction, with charges of contempt and accusations of child-stealing.

The Friend of the Court in the district of the father's residence persuaded the father to talk by long-distance telephone with the child's guardian. This officer impressed the man with the seriousness of defying a court order, and the father relinquished the child. The child was placed "in a very fine boarding school."

Says Mr. Pokorny, with a sympathy which this father might not find awaiting him in a court where he would be cited for contempt: "It was obvious that the father's reluctance to surrender the custody was based on his attachment and affection. It was a real sacrifice for him to part with his child."

What the writer does not say is that it might also have been a sacrifice for the child to be taken from a father who loved him, and be sent to a boarding school however fine. One may hope that the Friend of the Court later found a way to reunite this child with his father.

As a fact finder and neutral observer, an aide who can step outside the rarefied atmosphere of the law and confront a situation in real life, this officer's services are potentially valuable. We cannot expect the fundamental issues of a human situation to be resolved by this system. Only a follow-up study could give us a measure of the Friend of the Court's success in this respect.

In 1918 Mr. Pokorny's staff consisted of himself and one stenographer. Today he has 108 assistants and they can barely keep abreast of the population's need for their services. Since the establishment of his office, out of 160,000 applications for divorce, 56,000 never came to trial; thus thirty-five per cent of marriages were apparently salvaged. This record was maintained even through 1946, the peak year for divorces.

Again, without further study, we cannot assume that all these marriages were re-established on a sounder basis. And we cannot know how many children have been successfully guarded against the hazards of divorce's aftermath.

Mr. Pokorny points out that the Friend of the Court is available to poor as well as rich. We would reverse the phrase. What distinguishes the Michigan system from the family courts is that all applicants in divorce matters, whatever their income, and all children, rich or poor, have the services of this special officer who, alone in court, represents the family as a whole.

BLUEPRINT FOR THE FUTURE   We have seen in a previous chapter how the law's confusions and contradictions, the conflicts of jurisdiction across state lines and a host of other legal snarls, make it almost hopeless for the court to achieve and enforce a decree which is in the best interest of the child, *unless both parents understand and co-operate.*

In the effort to salvage a family on the way to divorce, the very way the law approaches the problem often offers the most serious obstacles to success. To begin with, the unrealistic grounds for divorce acceptable in most states can only aggravate the emotional distortion which already exists between two people in a divorce situation. A man who has had to go through a sham adultery with a hired corespondent is bound to feel outraged, his decent impulses thwarted.

This atmosphere of sordid farce with which the divorce proceedings begin cannot but pervade the future attitudes of husband and wife, through the divorce and after it. An enforced journey to another state where divorce is easier sets up almost as much resentment, and enfolds the divorce experience with the same unreality and disorientation.

Whether or not the marriage might have been saved, no one will ever know once the parties have been obliged to go through the battle of accusation and counteraccusation, the proof of innocence and guilt—or the at least equally destructive devices of falsehood and perjury—which the law's absurdities encourage.

In the face of such outrage to their best impulses and most decent feelings, even stable and mature men and women cannot maintain their balance except by shutting eyes and ears and getting through the ugliness of divorce as swiftly as possible so as to get back to the reality of living and looking after their children. When we have, as we are bound to have, more unstable than stable individuals in the divorce situation, and more immature than mature ones, the law itself becomes a hazard to these divorced pairs and their children.

To overcome the contradictions of divorce law between state and state, the Women's National Bar Association has for some time been actively advocating a uniform divorce law. A broader attack on the problem, and an effort to envision in detail the divorce court of tomorrow, is embodied in the Smith Report of the American Bar Association.

This came about as follows: In 1944 the National Conference on Family Life was born out of the concern generally felt for the survival of the American family today. In May, 1947, the conference conducted a noteworthy meeting at the White House in which 135 organizations participated, representing a membership of 40,000,000 in every relevant field: social work, education, religion, medicine and psychiatry, child care, labor organizations, law and legal aid. The American Bar Association accepted responsibility for the legal section of this meeting, and the Smith Report, prepared by the Bar Association's committee headed by Reginald H. Smith of Boston, is the significant result.

The Smith Report minced no words in characterizing the present state of the divorce laws:

"(1) That our present divorce laws are producing widespread evils and (2) that our laws in the field of domestic relations, instead of constituting a bulwark, are themselves a continuing threat to the stability of marriage in contemporary America."

The primary change recommended by the Smith Report is in the approach to divorce: The premise should be not punishment but prevention.

To this end the report takes a leaf from the juvenile courts, which first recognized that with child offenders against the law punishment presents more problems than it solves. The juvenile courts function on the principles of prevention and therapy, and use the resources of the social and psychiatric sciences to deal with the conditions which contribute to delinquent behavior. Says the committee:

"We suggest handling our unhappy and delinquent spouses much as we handle our delinquent children. Often their behavior is not unlike that of a delinquent child, and for much the same reasons. We would take them out of the quasi-criminal divorce court and deal with them and their problems in a socialized court . . . Instead of determining whether a spouse has misbehaved and then 'punishing' him by rewarding the aggrieved spouse with a divorce decree we would follow the general pattern of the juvenile court and endeavor to diagnose and treat, to discover the fundamental cause, then bring to bear all available resources to remove or rectify it."

The divorce court of the future which this report visualizes would have at its beck the services of case workers and psychiatrists, probation officers and investigators.

The judge of such a court would himself be a specialist in human relations and family problems. His point of view would be not to split legal hairs with opposing counsel, but to analyze and clarify the human conflicts which have resulted in the case before him. Such judges exist today, as we have observed, men whose own leanings have guided them into family rather than corporation or other branches of the law. These judges are among the most eloquent in protesting against the laws and procedures which handicap them in the effort to prevent unnecessary divorce and to rescue parents and children from the consequences of unwise divorce settlements.

Such a "specialist judge," as the report terms them, is Judge Paul W. Alexander whose model Family Court in Toledo, Ohio, has been widely written about. Judge Alexander was vice-chairman of the Smith Committee and later became chairman of the American Bar Association's Committee on Divorce Law. He is now chairman of the Interprofessional Commission on Marriage and Divorce Laws, of which more in a moment.

Such judges today are further hampered by the fact that in the law schools, in which both they and the lawyers arguing before them received their training, no enlightenment in the psychological and social sciences is provided. Without preparation in the use of social and psychiatric services they must learn by experience what these services can do in a court of law. The Smith Committee pointed out that "there are areas of life which the law can learn better to control by enlisting the resources and techniques of other social sciences."

The future divorce court, as the report points out with an eye to the practical, would have not only adequate staffs ("In fact, the salaries must be enough to attract and keep the best type of personnel") but adequate quarters as well. The privacy of a closed room may make all the difference in an interview with a husband or wife or child.

Naturally such a court would be more expensive than what the president of Detroit's Common Council aptly called "shotgun justice" in the ordinary divorce court. Says the Smith Committee:

"What must be made plain to the American people is that the total cost of the administration of justice is no more than a drop in the bucket of national or state expenses, and further that the cost of our present divorce system *in terms of human tragedy* has become too high to be tolerated any longer."

ENOUGH PSYCHIATRISTS?   A question which the Smith report did not ask, but which has been asked in other quarters, is: Where will all the psychiatrists for these ideal divorce courts come from?

There are at present between 6000 and 6500 qualified psychiatrists practicing in the United States, as estimated by the National Association for Mental Health. With the requirement of full medical training in advance of specialized psychiatric training, the time and expense of providing enough psychiatrists to serve as officers of the courts would seem to be a serious obstacle.

The greater number of psychiatrists practicing today are concentrated in a few large cities; their services are available to only a small proportion of the population. Efforts are being made by educational and professional agencies toward a redistribution of psychiatric services in terms of population quotas, by means of grants for traveling clinics in areas formerly deprived.

Even the present supply of qualified psychiatrists, however, would go far toward filling the needs of family courts if such courts were to be established on a nation-wide scale today. If more psychiatrists could be used before the cases came to court, fewer might be needed in the later attempts to repair the damages of divorce and its aftermath.

The moment when married pairs first file suit for divorce is not the beginning of their failure in marriage, as we have taken pains throughout these pages to establish. But in a majority of cases it is the *first overt recognition* of failure, and thus it is the significant moment at which all the efforts of society to save the marriage—or to guide its members into a wise divorce if divorce is necessary— may be most effectively exerted.

NEW DIVORCE LAW IN THE MAKING   In the Smith Report the American Bar Association spoke out for the first time as a body on the problem of divorce in our courts. Its recommendations were both sound enough and conservative enough to win public support. A vast mass of publicity in the press of the nation greeted the report—all of it favorable, according to Chairman Smith.

The committee's recommendation was followed, the President was asked to appoint a commission—and there the entire creative effort came to rest for nearly two years. When President Truman declined to appoint a commission, the American Bar Association Special Committee, with the co-operation of a group of national welfare organizations, organized the Interprofessional Commission on Marriage and Divorce Laws of which Judge Alexander is chairman. Funds were contributed by the American Bar Association and from foundations, and the commission was launched with a forum during the annual meeting of the Bar Association in New York City in September, 1951.

Since then the funds for the work of the commission have been exhausted, and again the momentum of this effort has somewhat slowed. However, as Judge Alexander writes me:

"The research upon which it is expected to base a model act is going forward under the guidance of Dr. John S. Bradway, of the Law Faculty of Duke University, which has been made research headquarters for the entire project . . . The various phases of the research have been or are being farmed out to law schools throughout the country."

Thus the legal profession persists in its program of reform, hampered by lack of funds, hampered by lack of support especially from those who might be expected to come forward most eagerly, the parents who have suffered and seen their children suffer in the courts.

Meanwhile, except for the family courts which serve a limited urban group, and except for attempts at improvement, like the

Michigan system, the divorce mills continue to grind out their frequently dubious and sometimes tragedy-laden decrees.

Parents who are concerned for the welfare of their children cannot yet look to the courts for help. They must still do the job themselves with what help they can command outside the courts, as we shall see in the following chapter.

14
LIFELINES FOR PARENTS

You can find helping hands outside the courts, and sometimes the help you need may be no farther away than your church or your children's school.

There are, of course, social agencies which offer guidance and sometimes material assistance to parents and children in trouble, but geographically they are most unevenly distributed. Some national agencies such as the Red Cross and the Travelers Aid have branches proliferating into all parts of the country, but these are intended primarily for emergencies and special situations and are not organized to carry out long-term guidance and supervision, although for the families of men in the armed services the Red Cross maintains social case workers in some cities.

The Family Service Association of America publishes a directory of its affiliated agencies, and a glance at its pages reveals that the large cities have a concentration of agencies to match their concentration of population. If you live in a large city, you have very nearly your choice of child guidance, legal aid, and possibly psychiatric consultation and access to clinical treatment if it is needed, although the facilities are still far from adequate. The large cities also have the majority of psychiatrists to whom you can go for private consultation, and who will advise what further steps need to be taken.

To a family struggling against emotional odds in a far corner of the state, however, or in a state where the population is thin, the existence of an agency or a private psychiatrist in a distant city is small comfort.

A letter to the health or welfare department of your state may bring you information about a counseling agency in your vicinity. The central offices of national organizations may also lead you to the kind of help you need. For example:

The Family Service Association of America, 192 Lexington Avenue, New York 16, New York (for family agencies).

The Child Welfare League, Inc., 24 West 40th Street, New York 18, New York (for child guidance agencies).

The National Association for Mental Health, Inc., 1790 Broadway, New York 19, New York (for psychiatric clinics or qualified psychiatrists).

THE MARRIAGE COUNSELOR   The profession of marriage counseling is a comparatively new one, and you may not be aware that it can be useful to you. If you think of marriage counseling as advice to young people about to marry or newly married, you are quite right. Or you may think of it as primarily for people aware of sexual maladjustments, and again you are right. Marriage counseling began in response to a growing need felt by married couples to space the arrival of children according to the family's economic resources. From there it broadened to include guidance to married couples who were having sexual difficulties.

From this base the marriage counselor has become a recourse for people having difficulties of other kinds in marriage. It would be the marriage counselor to whom you might go, when you are troubled about your marriage and wondering how to save it. And, if the marriage cannot be saved, he can guide you in the direction of a wise divorce. If he cannot himself give you advice on the management of the children during and after divorce, he can help you to clarify your own emotional confusions, and he can lead you to a source of specific counsel about the children.

Marriage counseling as a separate profession among the social services is new, but the practice is not new. Physicians, ministers, social workers and others have offered either scientific knowledge or the wisdom of experience or both to married pairs since long before such a term as marriage counseling was coined.

Today marriage consultation centers have grown up in the large cities, sometimes as independent social agencies, but also in connection with a medical or psychiatric institution, in a community center, or as an activity of a church.

An inquiry to the American Association of Marriage Counselors, Inc., 270 Park Avenue, New York, New York, will bring you information on any counseling service available where you live.

HELP FROM THE CHURCH   We began this chapter by saying that the help you need may be no farther away than your own church. Probably since the beginning of community living, human beings have turned to their men of religion when they were in trouble. Today you may find that your minister has prepared himself to help you with the tools of modern psychology. If you are a reasonably active member of the congregation and he has had an opportunity to know you, you may find that the perceptive modern minister knows you are in trouble before you tell him about it.

Ministers of religion and psychological scientists are attempting to open avenues of communication with each other. The first issue of a newsletter published by the American Psychiatric Association, *Psychiatry-At-Work*, reports on a panel of ministers and psychiatrists meeting to discuss the ways in which the special knowledge of each could be helpful in the other's work. The three predominant Western religions were represented. This novel approach was initiated at the Fourth International Congress on Mental Health in Mexico City in 1951.

A Pastoral Psychology Book Club was recently launched, also a journal called *Pastoral Psychology*. The trend has become so marked that Harry A. Overstreet, author of *The Mature Mind*, referred to it in a recent article, calling it, "this two-way movement." Individual ministers of all denominations have shown eagerness to use the new psychological knowledge in helping their parishioners. They seek new light on all aspects of human behavior. Marriage and marriage failure are of particular concern to them.

The subject of divorce might not at first glance seem an appropriate one to bring to a minister of the church. The prejudices of an earlier day would appear to make the very word unacceptable in his hearing.

But to the modern minister, dedicated to the welfare of his parishioners in the modern world, a marriage failure and the problems which follow in its wake are very much his business. He will help to save a marriage if the marriage can be saved. But if it cannot, or if it has already been dissolved, his concern is for the future of the children and their parents.

The minister of an Eastern community of about 12,000 comes to mind, one who must be representative of many. His church, like many churches and synagogues today, is not merely a house of worship but a center of social and educational activity for parishioners of all ages, from day-nursery groups for the toddlers to forums and study groups for their parents.

Thus he comes to know his flock from other vantage points besides that of the pulpit, and he has prepared himself to be more than a religious leader in its narrow sense. In his view, to live according to the ethics of religion requires a deeper emotional integration, and he spares no effort to bring the growing scientific knowledge of human behavior to the service of his people.

He has schooled himself for this role with intensive studies. He can, and often does, prod a young mother who is holding too close a rein on her son into giving the child more opportunity to become self-reliant; he signals to parents that they are out of touch with their adolescent daughter.

One cannot help being impressed with the dedication of this man to the happiness of his spiritual charges. Ministers with this approach, and with an individual gift for understanding and guidance, are in a unique position to help couples toward saving their marriages before they reach the divorce court, and to help mothers and fathers repair the ravages of marriage failure to themselves and their children.

If there is such a minister in your community, you may find the help you need in his parish house.

SCHOOL TO THE RESCUE   What is true in large measure of the church today is true also of the schools. The new knowledge of human behavior which the psychological sciences are bringing to light is adding breadth to the school's approach to the child.

Increasingly it is a child's teacher who first calls a parent's attention to the possibility that the child is in emotional difficulties. Observing a child's learning and his social behavior in school, a teacher may ask, "Is there any trouble at home?"

Sometimes parents are impelled by this question to take the first step toward investigating a hitherto buried or only dimly recognized disharmony in their relationship with each other. Taking the child for psychiatric consultation—and often this is first suggested, occasionally insisted on, by the school—may open the door on a parent's emotional discord. This may be the beginning of a search for insight and a better way of managing one's marriage and family.

Sometimes the school's query leads to the discovery of cracks in a marriage already headed for divorce. Or—and this is more frequent still—the school makes the first inquiry into the difficulties of a child suffering from the upheaval of a divorce, difficulties which a parent was too involved with his or her own problems to see. A parent can make advance use of a child's school to manage a divorce with the least damage to the child. Too often parents wait for the school to make the first move.

A teacher who is informed in advance of what a child will be going through is obviously in a better position to be sympathetic. A teacher forewarned will be more likely to meet a child's troublesome behavior or inattentiveness to studies with patience and an effort to help rather than punish. A teacher, a principal, a psychologist attached to the school staff, or some other qualified school adviser can also counsel a parent on changes which may be necessary, such as a move to another neighborhood or another city and hence a new school.

In making use of social agencies and consultation centers, of the minister and the teacher, the parent who makes the first move is likely to derive the most benefit. It is not enough that helping hands are available. You must reach out to grasp them. You must take a first step toward them, if for nothing more than to investigate the value of their help in your individual situation.

Unquestionably it is an effort for most people in the throes of a marriage failure to take their problems to a stranger. The need to talk about your troubles may seem to be more comfortably satisfied by pouring them out to a relative or friend. But the relative or friend, however sympathetic a listener, is not likely to be as well equipped to give guidance, nor to see the problems with that objectivity which is so difficult to achieve and yet so valuable.

For your own sake as well as the child's—and for the long-reaching benefits which a wisely handled divorce will bring to everyone concerned—the effort to find competent outside help is well worth making.

HELP FOR THE CHILD AWAY AT SCHOOL   In an earlier chapter we discussed the boarding school as a possible refuge for the child whose parents are going through a divorce. We emphasized then the need of making the situation clear to the child. It is important, we pointed out, for the child to feel that he is being sent away not so his parents can be rid of him, but so that he can be comfortable and cared for while his parents are working out their own difficulties, and until one or the other can again make a happy home for him.

Some boarding schools do more. There is a trend today among some directors of boarding schools to provide the essential elements of a normal home situation at school. Thus we have dormitories supervised not by a housemother alone or a male faculty member alone, but by a married couple, a substitute father *and* mother. We have children housed in small cottages instead of large dormitories. We find a headmaster and his wife combining efforts to provide a version of family relationships for the children. Where the school is small and the directors gifted with a warm understanding for children, this can be very successful.

The James School (the name of course is fictitious) is an example. Mr. James and his wife, with two children of their own, regard their school as an expanded home for the children who come to them. They accept not children with deep emotional disturbances, but children who may be upset by a specific situation. A considerable proportion of their children come from homes broken in one way or another. The director and his wife—and even, as will be seen, the members of the household staff—find opportunities to help the children toward understanding and acceptance of the difficulties of their parents.

We quoted earlier a luncheon conversation among a group of these children. Two of the children carried the discussion farther on another occasion. Whitey, as the reader will recall, had blurted that he was glad his father had committed suicide, because otherwise there might have been a divorce, "and that is worse than dying." When he repeated this assertion, his friend Pete took vigorous exception.

"No, it isn't!" Pete almost shouted. "Look at our mother and father. Before Mother got her divorce they were always fighting or just about going to fight, and it was horrible. John and me were scared all the time and sometimes I felt like dying. Now we're not scared any more. Mother and Father are good friends again. They're happy now that they're not married and we all get along together fine!"

Pete, who is nine, did not arrive at this healthy acceptance of his parents' divorce unaided. He and his seven-year-old brother John had suffered all the pangs of the tense home situation. In fact they had been brought to the school because, bright and capable children though they were, their schoolwork had deteriorated at an alarming rate and both had reached the point where they had practically stopped learning altogether. The parents discussed their family situation with the headmaster, and on their alternate weekly visits to the boys they continued to have separate conferences with him about their own problems and those of the children.

The boys showed almost at once that to be out of the home was a relief. The permissive atmosphere of the school, the avoidance of competitive pressure, which is part of the school's policy, and especially the warmth of the school staff had a beneficial effect on them from the start.

In addition they were encouraged to air their anxieties in informal talks with the headmaster and his wife. The boys learned about other divorces which had worked out well for parents and children. They came to realize that they were not unique, that others had gone through similar experiences, that divorce was not necessarily a catastrophe. They came to understand that a divorce might even be a good thing, the end of a bad time and possibly the beginning of a better one. Their school learning improved and they began to look like happy youngsters.

After the divorce the parents came together to see their sons, and the reunion was happy. The result of the school's good work is evident in Pete's positive, assured answer to his schoolmate, with which we began this story.

SALLY CONFIDES IN THE COOK   Sally, at the same schol, is ten. Helping the cook with the dishes, Sally began a conversation about a married woman with children who had a "boy friend" other than her husband. She wanted to know what Cook thought about it. Cook asked Sally what she herself thought about it. Sally came out with the comment that the husband-father also had a girl friend and that the quartet seemed to get along well together.

Underneath, however, the child seemed troubled, and the perceptive cook reported the conversation to the headmaster. He reported it in turn to Sally's parents. The parents then revealed a complex home situation, roughly on the model which Sally had drawn, and acknowledged that Sally and her young brother were in the school in order to keep them out of involvement in the parents' emotional tangle. They were upset to learn that Sally was, despite their efforts, aware and troubled. Both parents were undergoing psychoanalysis and struggling to find their way through their difficulties, but they had not been able to discuss any of this with their children.

The parents asked the headmaster and his wife to help acquaint the children with the facts; their analysts approved the decision that the children should be told. On their next visit, the parents took the children for a drive, told them the situation in simple terms, and brought them back plainly relieved. For the first time, when the parents left, Sally did not cry and Tom did not throw his customary tantrum. Being taken into the family problem relieved them of some of their feeling of rejection and helped them to accept the stay at school.

But they were both, of course, still anxious, still puzzled. It fell to the headmaster and his wife, in their casual daily contacts with the children, to continue the task of reassuring them and restoring their confidence in their parents' love. Thus, instead of suffering months of uncertainty and mounting tension, these children were given an opportunity to use the waiting time for storing up emotional resources which would help them face with strength whatever change might be in store for them.

HARRY AND HIS PARENTS   Harry came to the school because he had serious trouble in his former school, a battle with his teacher which resulted in his suspension. This was the stated reason. In separate talks the parents expressed their anxieties and feelings of guilt toward the boy for what might be failures in his early upbringing. The mother thought she saw in Harry some of his father's less fortunate traits. The father, voicing worry about his own strict discipline, implied criticism of his wife's softness toward the boy.

Conversations with the parents about Harry continued through the year, revealing more and more facets of the parents' tensions with each other. Gradually the tensions diminished. While this family may not have been headed for actual divorce, there were present the elements of an emotional divorce. It was to these unexpressed tensions that Harry had responded, as his parents came to see, and his consequent anxieties had expressed themselves in his behavior at his former school.

Father and mother, talking separately and then together with the headmaster, drew closer in their mutual effort to understand what was troubling their son. In time Harry was brought into the discussions, with increasingly good results. All three became better able to understand and accept each other, weaknesses and strengths alike. There can be little doubt that this family emerged from

Harry's first year away at school with a stronger unity and a sounder foundation for their future life.

Separation of the child from the tension in a troubled home can be a relief to child and parents, but separation is not enough. The separation in itself may cause the child additional pain unless he is helped to understand that it is not a rejection, and unless verbal explanation is confirmed by continued evidence of his parents' love for him in visits, in letters, in expressions of warmth and affection which are steadily comforting and without anxious outpouring.

So much, if it can be achieved, is already a good deal. But more can be done, as we have seen, at the right kind of school and with the right approach by parents and school together. In these stories of three children (plus younger brothers) at one such school, we have observed how children can be gradually brought to an acceptance of, in one case, actual divorce, in the second an impending divorce, and in the third a rift in the marriage which was capable of healing.

This is the difference between simply waiting out a storm—"We'll get Johnny straightened out after this mess is over"—and using the waiting time for positive purposes. A child cannot simply wait, holding his distress in abeyance (can an adult?), and the parent who puts off attending to the child's needs during a stormy period will find a much harder job to do later. Emotional wounds will have deepened, behavior problems sharpened, and the child's defenses will have been building walls which will be all the harder to break through.

When a child is obliged to face painful realities, he needs help, and it is never too soon to begin to help him with whatever resources can be found. Whether he is at home or away from home, the child's need for help begins when the trouble begins. Parents who look to the child as soon as they are aware of trouble in themselves will be rewarded by seeing the child grow in strength to deal with trouble.

IV
THOUGHTS ON THE FAMILY

15
TOMORROW'S PARENTS

On every side today we are told that the family is in crisis. To warn, as do some alarmed observers, that the crisis is unprecedented, and that the family faces imminent dissolution, is to undervalue both the evidence of history and the vitality of the family as a human institution. Through the centuries of recorded time, as far back as Greek and Roman history, as recently as the French and the Russian revolutions, the family has quivered under similar blows, and has survived.

Even today while we anxiously watch the divorce rate climbing on the graphs like the fever chart of a very sick patient, we are yet aware that the majority of men and women in America still marry and remain married, and raise their children in love and harmony.

Yet it would be folly to ignore the many distress signals. Parents confront with increasing self-doubt the task of rearing children in a troubled world. Teachers complain of aggressive behavior, disrespect, disobedience, disregard for principle and property among the children under their guidance. Adolescents range the cities and the countryside in destructive gangs, or engage in waves of self-destructive "fun"; on one day the headlines describe their wild games of reckless driving, on the next their addiction to narcotics. Each new hospital for the mentally ill is overcrowded before the paint is dry on its walls. And the divorce rate continues to rise.

We must face these evidences of widespread individual maladjustment, of the waste of human potentialities and the cost in human happiness. If the psychological sciences have indeed made the progress in understanding which is claimed for them, we should be able to trace the illness to its source and to stem the epidemic of personal tragedy and family failure.

Our best hope lies with the children. Laws may make divorce more difficult—or, as many now advocate, they may make marrying more difficult—but, until we learn how to revitalize the family in its essential role of rearing children to healthy adulthood, we are not grappling with the crisis at its roots.

To strengthen the family we must strengthen its adult members, the parents. Today's children are tomorrow's parents; it is to them that we must look for the better health of tomorrow's families and their children in turn. We must attempt to discover and restore to childhood some essence which has escaped from our philosophy of child rearing, and which children need in preparing for their future role.

In our consideration of children of divorce we have tried in these pages to explore and understand the inner world of children, to see how their needs for healthy growth can be met in the specific situation of family breakdown. The stories of children of divorce have shown us what happens when the family fails to meet the child's emotional needs. They have shown us, too, how the damage of this failure can be repaired. What we have learned from children of divorce can guide us in our effort to help the children of today toward becoming the more confident, more loving, more successful parents of tomorrow.

HAPPY CHILDREN, UNHAPPY PARENTS   Children in America have been said by European observers to be the happiest in the world. Certainly they appear to be the most carefree.

The whole concept of discipline in the rearing of children has undergone radical changes. The youth of today escape the toil of farm chores and farm labor to which in an agricultural economy they were automatically initiated as soon as they were physically capable; little girls in America are not the nursemaids of the younger children as they are in many primitive societies; young boys are not apprenticed to a craft or trade as in medieval times. Children in America are not schooled to reverence for adults, implicit obedience to adults, and service of adults as they still are in the typical families of Europe and Asia. Nor are they taught obedience and service to the State.

Indeed in the United States the roles of parents and children seem to be exactly reversed; it is the parents who wait on the children. There is the widely told story of the old lady who was asked by her host at dinner whether she preferred the white meat of the chicken or the dark, and who replied that she did not know, since she had never tasted the white meat. When she was a child the parents got the white, and when she was a grownup the children got the white.

For years now the children have been getting the white meat. Parenthood has seemed to confer no privileges, only obligations and responsibilities. In their zeal to protect the carefree happiness of childhood, parents have seemed willing to make themselves the slaves of their children. The first revelations of psychological science appeared to support this trend. The danger, parents were told, was repression. The urgent call was to liberate children from the rigid discipline of the past and its inhibitions.

There is evidence today that the era of untrammeled freedom for children is ending. Doubts have crept in: Is so much freedom really good for children? If a carefree childhood were ideal, would so many children grow up into unhappy adults? Would half our hospital beds be occupied by the mentally ill? And the most obvious question of all is asked: If children were being properly prepared for adulthood, would we have so many divorces?

DIVORCE, THE SYMPTOM   Thus we are brought back once more, as in so many discussions of the family, to that apparently most serious threat to its stability, divorce. Yet divorce itself is not the illness, but only a symptom of the illness. A glance down the perspective of history reveals sharp peaks in the rate of divorce in times of disorder; wars, revolutions shake the family as they shake all the institutions of a society.

We see also a gradual rise in the divorce rate as a sign of some gradual social change. Such a rise has been evident for the past century in the United States and more recently in other Western countries. Among the many complex factors contributing to this rise is the centuries-long struggle toward individual freedom of which we are witnessing the climax in our time.

Underlying the tensions, confusions, and anxieties which now beset the family, one great change becomes manifest. We mentioned early in this volume the dwindling of the family from the once spreading kinship group to the small conjugal group. Where once parents and grandparents, aunts and uncles and great-aunts and great-uncles and cousins of varying degrees were all part of a close-knit family structure, today we have parents and children, a stripped and nearly isolated nucleus.

Where once children grew up under the eyes of adults of two and sometimes three generations, took their discipline and learning from all of these, and distributed their affections and hostilities among them, today they have, typically, a father and mother only, and not always both.

If a grandparent or two hover in the background, they tend to be shy of "interfering." The "good" mother-in-law is one who brings presents, remembers birthdays, baby-sits when called upon, and never makes bold to impose her fuller experience upon the young parents. Again the roles have been reversed, and it is the older generation which is expected to speak only when spoken to and keep out of the way. There is no premium on age and a minimum of veneration for experience.

There are apparent advantages to this system. The young parents have freedom to find their own way, to question the merely traditional, to distinguish between chronological age and the wisdom of maturity. They can make for themselves the discovery that wisdom is not acquired by the mere accretion of years.

Unfortunately these advantages are more ideal than real. Few young people today enter upon marriage equipped to make all their decisions alone, or with the patience to learn from their own experience.

There is also a price for this freedom from family domination. The young mother who once could turn to her own mother, or an aunt or older sister or cousin, for help, now must go it alone. Mother, aunts, sisters, cousins are likely to be far away. Instead of taking root like the acorn close to the parent tree, each married pair set forth to found their own family, and in an occupation-based economy like the American their new home may well be in a town or city far from the original home of either husband or wife. Ready or not, the young birds fly the nest at an earlier and earlier age. The family today is ever less able to pass on enlightenment from one generation to the next, and to shelter the young adult from the consequences of his ignorance.

For children growing up today the change is equally significant. Instead of many adults from whom to draw their support and in whom to invest their love, they now are likely to have only two—if indeed they are lucky enough to have both. In these two, this one mother and this one father, they must place all their faith, and from these two they must draw all their strength and the images of manhood and womanhood which will shape their future lives. A teacher, a minister, an adult friend may enter, to some extent, into the emotional constellation which orients their growth. But in the early childhood years the mother and father are the nearest and most potent adults; in their orbits the young child necessarily moves.

And not only are the older and the side branches of the family now generally lopped off from the nuclear family group. There are also likely to be fewer children in the family itself. Inevitably there must develop, within this family stripped to its fewest and most intimate relationships, a compensating intensity in those relationships. There must follow an emotional concentration of husband and wife upon each other, of parents upon children, and children upon parents. The resulting emotional charge may emerge as positive or negative, loving or rejecting—and under such pressures the negative may be looked for to outweigh the positive in many families.

It is within this fragile framework, the modern family with its narrowed and intensified channeling of the emotions, that we must consider the children of today who are to be the parents of tomorrow.

EMOTIONAL DIVORCE IS THE DESTROYER   Our concern for the children of divorce is thus revealed as only one corner of a far vaster subject. True, it is an especially turbulent corner, a wilder whirlpool within the churning stream of change. Yet we cannot assume that today's children of divorce will automatically be the participants in tomorrow's divorce suits. Children of divorce are only more conspicuous because in their case the family, the natural nursery in which maturity is developed, has openly broken down.

Children of divorce are far from being the only casualties of marriage failure. They are not even its most serious casualties. As we have seen in these pages, all divorce begins with emotional divorce. And not all emotional divorce, nor even a fraction of it, ends in the open and sometimes cleansing surgery of divorce by law.

Not legal divorce but emotional divorce is the destroyer of children. Countless more couples live out their lives and rear their children in the destructive climate of emotional divorce. Among the hundreds of unhappy children who come to the attention of a child psychiatrist, I have seen many whose parents had no thought of divorce. But I have never found one seriously disturbed child whose parents were happy, well integrated partners in a harmonious marriage.

Appearances are deceptive. A man and woman may appear well married. Often we see a marriage in which the neurotic needs of each partner fit so well with the others as to make a mosaic, seemingly flawless on the surface, of which the jagged edges wounding to children appear only under closer examination.

Precocious marriages, hasty marriages, marriages undertaken on the impulse of a physical attraction can result in this way. A young girl may marry the gay bachelor, the life of the party, only to find him on better acquaintance to be most morose and melancholy. A more mature girl would wait, allowing the wave of physical magnetism to subside; she would try to know her man better before she committed her entire future to the union. Often in early marriages, in immature marriages, neurotic leanings tend to become soldered into permanent patterns. With more maturity a healthier basis for marriage would be found.

Emotional divorce may be the result of deep personal maladjustment in one or the other partner, or in both. But two people may also drift into a situation of emotional divorce without a profound dislocation as its source.

The hazards in the path of successful marriage and family life today are many, and the preparation for meeting them is far from adequate. Each partner may suffer many bruises to the spirit in his striving to share the entirety of life with another human being. Rarely do two people begin a marriage with the maturity which assures them at once of wisdom and tolerance toward each other. Rarely is the initial image of the other partner realistic; courtship does not generally provide an atmosphere conducive to realism. A lack of success in the sexual relationship is not unusual at the outset of a marriage; if not wisely dealt with, a poor sexual beginning can generate its own dissatisfaction through every aspect of a marriage.

Husbands and wives who allow discontent to mount, resentment to accumulate, hostility to dominate in a relationship begun in warmth and hope, are courting emotional divorce. That such negative emotions may arise in so intense and demanding a partnership is not remarkable. A marriage, like the human beings who make it, can scarcely be without a flaw. The danger is not so much in the human imperfections of its partners as in their attitudes toward those imperfections. If they can continue to accept each other with warmth and understanding, then the marriage continues sound. But if rejection becomes the pattern, then we have a widening chasm separating parents from each other, and a consequent widening chasm parting parents from their children.

This is emotional divorce. This is the situation in which parents lose communication with each other and with their children. Many a child grows up in circumstances of physical comfort, wanting nothing that pertains to his material welfare, his schooling, his social and eventually his professional opportunities—and yet he may be deprived of the emotional support essential to his growth because of the disharmony between his parents.

Such a child, however pampered, is a neglected, an underprivileged child. Such a child is likely to be the neurotic parent of the next generation. Emotional divorce is the medium through which maladjustment and neuroticism are handed down from generation to generation.

THE SEARCH FOR A FORMULA   It may be a quip to call America the land of happy children and neurotic adults. Yet it is ironic that in a land where so much is done for children, so many children grow up to insecure and anxious adulthood.

We live in an era of conscientious parents, when mothers and fathers exert themselves with unprecedented zeal for their children's sake. They attend lectures and meetings to discuss their children. The newspapers and magazines are full of articles for their instruction, and books about children stream from the presses onto the bookshop counters.

More words on this subject are poured out perhaps than ever before in history—so many words, and yet so little communication! For the truth is that with all their efforts to learn how to bring up their children, parents seem to feel ever more helpless before the tasks of parenthood, ever more perplexed and anxious. They seek frantically for experts, create an expert out of almost anyone who offers an opinion, and the next day denounce the expert they themselves have created, to follow one of an opposite opinion who in turn seems to offer them the magic formula to resolve all their problems.

Meanwhile, in apparent contradiction of their interest in their children, we see parents delegating more and more of their parenthood, so that very little is left of a direct relationship between parent and child. We see parents relying more and more on nursery schools, schools, and camps to take over their children's rearing. They offer mechanical entertainment as a substitute for shared activities, sitting the children down before the radio or television set, or sending them off to the movies. They crowd their children's days with lessons in music, dancing, painting, tennis, riding, again introducing a variety of outsiders. They pile up superficial accomplishments. Parents may delude themselves that they are fitting their children to live a richer life, but in fact these techniques are merely substitutes for the more important learning which children can acquire in no other way except by shared experience with their parents.

If they can afford them, parents also shower their children with expensive gifts. Many a child with a playroom full of fabulous toys complains that he is "bored."

All of these things can be enriching to children's lives. None needs to be a substitute if living itself is shared, if parents and children participate together in experience both joyful and frustrating. Childhood is the time of learning gradually to live as an adult in the adult world. The child's way of learning is by identification with the adults who have the greatest significance for him, his parents. Not so much the words they say, but what they do and how they feel, the way they face their own lives as adults, are most meaningful to him. Out of these parent images he unconsciously creates his own attitudes, his acceptance or rejection of the responsibilities and privileges of adulthood.

Thus it is quickly apparent that to shelter a child from the expected defeats of living, to surround him with illusion and spare him all frustration, is to do him no service. He is born into the world small, helpless, surrounded by dangers which threaten his very survival. He needs physical protection, and he needs the protection of his family's love. But within this physical and emotional shelter he also needs to make a gradual acquaintance with reality.

With the support of his family's love he can come to accept the rough as well as the smoother facets of living. He can learn the joy of a difficult task accomplished or a difficult challenge met. He can learn to find satisfactions for his own needs while yet accommodating himself to the needs of others, as he must in a community of individuals. He can come to tolerate the weaknesses of others, to develop his own capabilities and accept his own limitations. He can take these steps toward maturity one by one, under the guidance of parents who love him and who accept their double role as his protectors and his guides.

STRENGTH TO COPE WITH A COMPLEX WORLD   There is a growing awareness today of the concept of maturity and its significance in our world; witness the vast amount of current discussion on the subject. Parents, groping toward a formula for bringing up their children to live successfully, realize increasingly that more is needed than shelter, more than protection. This world, they acknowledge, is more complex, more confusing, more swiftly changing than was the world of their parents. They would like to know how to give their children the strength to cope with it, a strength which perhaps they have found lacking in themselves.

In their striving to prepare their children for this world, they run the danger of relying too much on words and generalizations, too little on direct experience and direct feeling. They run the danger of being further separated from the child by a barrier of words, of intellectualization. Lectures, discussions, study have their place, but they cannot supplant the loving parent's knowledge of his and her own child. The generalizations in books and courses are not so eloquent a lesson in the growth of a child as the child himself.

Parents tend to barricade themselves with recipes and formulas against their own feelings of inadequacy. This is part of a general pattern of conforming, of imitating, of following the leader, into which men and women retreat in a vain effort to escape their insecurity. They clutch at total answers to questions of living which can never be answered totally, but only by small day-to-day decisions for each individual family. The talk is of individual freedom, but the pattern is a slavery to conformism. Falling into this pattern, the individual loses more and more of his individuality. Having no longer any standards of his own, any values of his own, any principles or purpose of his own, he becomes ever more insecure, ever more inadequate and helpless to choose his own path.

As a parent, he is especially vulnerable. The rules of child rearing change with each new "expert." Between one day and the next, parents are confronted with exactly opposite admonitions and instructions. If they are not to flounder forever in a sea of contradictions, they will have to turn back to their own judgment, their own experience, their own feeling for the child and knowledge of the child, and measure the advice and instruction pouring in upon them by these realistic tests. In a time of frantic conformism it takes considerable exertion to maintain one's individual judgment in any area.

In the field of parenthood the exercise of judgment demands also that the parent both love and know his child.

IS IT HARD TO LOVE YOUR CHILD?   Is it hard for parents to love their children?

This is not an idle question. The simple direct love of parent for child seems today a rare and difficult achievement. Each step of man's progress has its price, and in our era one price we have paid for material progress is a loss of direct experience.

The young mother today is robbed of much of the direct experience of motherhood. In the sterile atmosphere of the hospital where her baby is born, she has little chance to feel the warmth of the infant body against her own. At home she boils bottles and measures out formulas instead of nursing the baby at her breast. She opens little jars of prepared food instead of preparing his food with her own hands, and she would be shocked at the simple mother of a less germ-conscious world who gives the baby his first solid food from her own plate.

We do not argue against the hospital methods which save so many lives, nor the prepared baby foods which save so much labor. But at the same time we must measure the cost. The modern mother does not even know the sensuous pleasures of which she has been deprived, as she makes her way through the mechanized techniques of modern baby care—so many teaspoonfuls, so many minutes of cooking, and her eye forever on the clock instead of on the baby.

If the mother has lost the direct knowledge of her baby, how much more has the child lost, growing up in a mechanized world! Like the milk delivered at the kitchen door each morning, everything is brought to him sterilized, predigested. He lives in a physical setting so incomprehensible to the young child's mind that most of his learning about his environment must wait until he has reached the intellectual level to grasp it.

But there is a learning which has not changed, which the child can acquire, now as in times past, in only one place, the home, and from only one source, his family. The emotional verities have not altered. The young child learns to take satisfaction in work, in responsibility, learns to adjust himself to others, learns slowly to use his individual judgment, and he learns these things as he has always learned them, in the family. Mother and father, brother and sister are his teachers. The simple act of living together, in its whole and not merely its physical sense, is the young child's emotional school.

We have talked of the isolated family of today as though it were unique in history, but we have only to glance back a short distance into the past of this country to see that it has its precedent. The pioneer family which made its way into the wilderness was surely isolated from its kin, and it was also beset with dangers and well nigh overwhelmed with hardships. Yet that family has left a record of unequaled strength and sturdiness. Its emotional life, though rarely emerging to the surface level of words, ran in a deep undercurrent beneath the shared daily labors necessary to survival, carrying strength to all its members.

Shall we say, in defeat, that love can survive only under the challenge of hardship and danger? Shall we not rather observe that hardship in some degree is the lot of all human beings, that to live is to struggle, and that reality is for all of us a blend of defeats and successes, of pain and pleasure, of grief and joy, all to be shared with the support of love?

Parents who struggle to learn the long words of psychological science are missing the essence of their function. Not the words in lectures or in books, but the small daily experiences, happy and unhappy, lovingly shared with the child—these are the materials of a child's growth to emotional hardihood.

A CHANCE FOR TODAY'S CHILDREN   Today's generation of parents—and today's psychologists, psychiatrists, educators, ministers, doctors—are justified in their concern for the children who will be the parents of tomorrow. The legacy of ill-prepared, immature adulthood has swollen to menacing dimensions in our time. It is a considerable task to break the chain and give today's children a chance for the emotional maturity which will make them the happier parents of tomorrow. But the task is not a hopeless one.

Many illustrations have been recorded, a number of them in the pages of this book, of how something can be saved for the child's emotional wholeness even in the most destructive situations. Parents who have seen their marriage end in divorce often feel that they are dealing with shards and fragments; they despair of ever putting together an integrated emotional world for their children. But if the family is broken, there still remains the relationship of each parent to each child as individuals, and in this the child can still find the support which he needs to grow to emotional maturity.

Parents may be so disturbed that they are not able to help their children unaided. With and without divorce there are times when parents are too involved, too distressed. These are the times when they may well turn elsewhere for help. They need not feel that their failure has done their children irreparable harm; something can always be retrieved. It is the part of parents to recognize the time to seek help, and the kind of help to seek

If there is any doubt, it is better to look for help. The services of the psychiatric counselor should be more freely used. There are still many parents who feel that to take a child to a psychiatrist or social agency at once marks that child as "sick" or "disturbed," a "problem child." But there is also a growing recognition of the broader uses of the psychiatric services, and particularly in situations where the need is for clarification, not necessarily for treatment.

Thus a parent does not automatically take a child for treatment. In many cases he does not take the child at all. He takes the *situation* to a counselor trained to know about children and children's needs. It is up to the counselor to decide whether it is necessary to see the child.

It is well for the adviser to see the child, and most advisers prefer to do so. A parent is rarely in a position to tell what is troubling a child. A parent in a state of personal distress is especially at a disadvantage in the effort to give an objective account of the child's situation. It is probable that he will unconsciously distort the fundamental issues.

The more we grasp the patterns of children's emotional growth, the more hope we can offer to parents, who themselves may be suffering from personal maladjustment, that their children's emotional health can be safeguarded. Many parents, aware of their own emotional difficulties and troubled lest these should harm their children, have found reassurance together with advice on how to guide their children's development toward a happier adulthood than their own. Even children whose only knowledge of marriage is of their parents' failure can be prepared for marriage with a prospect of success.

PREPARATION FOR LIFE   Under the stimulus of the soaring divorce rate the subject of preparing young people for marriage has become the focus of much recent attention. Courses in home management and child rearing appear in college catalogues. In some states sex education has been introduced into the schools over agitated opposition.

All this is good, but it is not enough. Preparation for marriage is only another aspect of preparation for mature living, and it begins not the day before the wedding, not in college or in high school, but in the cradle.

The practical aspects of home management—budgeting, nutrition, child care—can be taught to future mothers in school and college, but the deeper lesson of a mother's emotional attitudes toward her tasks is learned in childhood and in the home, from the living example of a mother who takes joy in her family and her responsibilities. The anatomy of sex and its techniques can be taught, but anatomy and techniques dwindle in importance in an area so inextricably interwoven with emotion.

It has been said over and over again that preparation for the sexual relationship in marriage can never be entirely delegated to the schools. The best education of children for sexual love in marriage derives from the healthy sexual relationship between their parents. It is in the climate of the parents' satisfaction with each other that children find their own growth toward happiness in sexual love. Here they learn at its source the joyful emotional approach to sex which makes the techniques of sexual satisfaction easy to achieve after marriage.

Preparation for marriage is preparation for life. It is the slow growth of emotional maturity through childhood and adolescence for which the family is designed. The sheltering, guiding, and liberating love of emotionally mature parents is the child's best insurance that he will develop his own maturity for marriage and child rearing, for his work, his leisure, and all the many aspects of living.

The subject of love in the family in our time goes far beyond the scope of a book designed, as this one is, for parents whose marriage is foundering or has foundered, and who seek guidance in safeguarding their children from the damage of divorce. It is a subject which must wait to be explored in greater breadth and depth in a volume of its own. In this chapter I have attempted only to sketch its outlines, and to suggest to parents who have suffered a wounding defeat that their children and their children's children need not carry the scars.

With our present knowledge of children and our growing insight into what makes for solidly based happiness in childhood, we have the tools for helping the children of today become the emotionally mature parents of tomorrow. Admittedly the task is vast, and the efforts of society are often diffuse and lagging. Yet the individual parent can take heart. It is not beyond the powers and the present resources of fathers and mothers to build in their children the foundation for future happiness in marriage and parenthood.

16
LOVE IS ENOUGH

I want to tell a love story. It is not such a love story as the reader may be accustomed to reading in the pages of a shiny-paper magazine. But it is a story of love, this story of the Lewises.

To sophisticated parents struggling with the fragments of a broken family life, this story may at a glance seem farfetched, perhaps even an unkind taunt.

It is not meant to be so. In the story of Benjie Lewis I ask the reader to see with me not the superficial differences from his own life—the rural setting, the large family, the closeness of children and parents even when the children are grown and established in their own homes. I ask the reader to see through these obvious differences to the essential likeness between his own life situation and that of the Lewis family: the struggle for security, the coping with hardship, the need for purposefulness, the daily demand for making choices large and small. Beyond these I ask him to see the essential motherliness and fatherliness for which all parents strive.

It is a story from which I hope the reader will draw this comfort, that even in a world in which material progress outraces the human spirit and leaves it panting far behind, it is possible for each of us in our homes to nurture the warmth and closeness of human beings to one another, husbands and wives, parents and children, a warmth which is needful to all of us and on which we thrive. It is possible for us to nurture this essential humanity toward each other in any era, in any setting, so long as we recognize our need for it—and its priceless rewards.

I tell the story of the Lewises in the hope of showing that central heating, though desirable, cannot take the place of human warmth; that bought entertainment, though enjoyable, is no substitute for human companionship; that sterile cleanliness is efficient for shutting out germs, but need not also shut out love. Let us, like the Lewises, dare to make our own choice of what we can and what we cannot use of a dazzling modern technology of living.

THE MOTHER I first met Mrs. Lewis on a sleety December afternoon which was turning bitter. I was driving back to New York from a professional meeting in Boston, and I had promised to stop in this Massachusetts village on my way, to see to a friend's property for which my friend had recently engaged a new caretaker. The meeting had run overtime, the weather made driving slow, and I was hours off schedule. I was cold, tired, annoyed with myself for making the promise, impatient to get the task done and be on my way.

The new caretaker's name was Lewis. The postmaster had a friendly smile for the name, and I found the house as he had described it, a "mixed-up sort of house" up an icy hill from the village.

It was sprawling, shapeless, some of it brown brick, some red asbestos shingles, some bare two-by-fours and black tar paper. It was a house which could not have been much to begin with, and had grown mushroomlike through many years with whatever materials were at hand—an ugly house, an anomaly after the chaste New England cottages with dates on their lintels, houses which I had been passing all day. This was a house without a pedigree.

But the windows had crisp curtains in cheery colors, healthy potted plants were green on the sills, and smoke plumed beckoning from the chimney under the forbidding sky. The front door, with simply a flat rock for a doorstep, was obviously not much used, so I picked my way over the ridges of footsteps frozen in the mud to

the back. Chicken houses, a pigpen, a yard without litter lay neat
and tended in the grip of winter.

Mrs. Lewis came to the door, a big woman with a broad placid
face. She gave me no time to state my business. "Come in, come in,
you'll have a cup of hot coffee," she urged. Who I was and what I
wanted were secondary. The only possible first thing was to make a
human being warm and welcome, her manner said as she went at
once to the stove.

It was a large, handsome range, so new that it must only recently
have replaced on old-fashioned coal stove. She was pleased when I
commented on this efficient modern version of a kerosene cookstove.

"My children bought it for me," she said. "They shopped a long
time before they decided that this was the best."

Something good was simmering in a big pot, a soup or a stew. Its
aroma had comforted me the moment I stepped inside the door. She
lifted the lid and stirred, with the automatic efficiency of a woman
who has been stirring things in pots for many years. But there was
nothing automatic in the way she sniffed the steam from the pot,
tasted from the spoon, shook in a little seasoning, stirred and tasted
again, nodded, and replaced the lid. She was a woman who enjoyed
good food and enjoyed cooking it.

The coffee which she placed before me was good too, and she
came back to the table to resume the work which my coming had
interrupted. Afterward I saw that she was repairing tiny wooden
figures of people and animals for a Christmas crèche. With work-
roughened, sausage-thick fingers she fitted here a matchstick for a
leg, there a minute chip of wood for a cow's ear; she fastened one
with thread, another with glue, touched it with a bit of paint,
smoothed the paint with her finger, and set it aside to dry.

This was a crèche not just to look at, but to play with, too. If anything was broken, Mother could always repair it. The toys were
already very, very old.

Before she sat down now, she glanced around the room as though
looking for someone.

"Where are you, baby?" she called. Then she stooped before her
own chair. "Come out, Benjie, we have company," she coaxed.

From under the chair the face of a child of about two looked out at me, not frightened, but with the bright eyes of a small animal who sits at a safe distance, watching. He was too young to be her own child. A grandchild? She offered no explanation. Her attention was all for him.

I said, "That's a nice safe little house you have, isn't it, Benjie?" and bent to my coffee.

Mrs. Lewis held out her hand to him, and the child took it and crept out between the chair legs. When he stood before her she enfolded him with an indescribable gesture of reassurance, lifted him, and sat down with him in her lap to continue her work.

She was Maya, sitting there with the child in her lap. She talked like any rural woman, chatting to entertain me while I waited, telling me about the village, about her children and grandchildren, who all lived near by and whom she saw almost daily, telling me about the house and how it had grown as the family had grown. There was nothing out of the ordinary about her speech, or her clean worn house dress, or her plain, friendly, earth-brown face.

But she was Mother Earth, unthinkingly accommodating her big soft body to the child as he snuggled into warm comfort, enclosing him in safety with her big arms while still her thick fingers worked skillfully with the toys, and above the child's head she talked and nodded and laughed with me.

The marks of children growing and children grown were everywhere in that room, a room clean and wholesome and with the surface disorder of busy human life about it. Benjie's cart lay where he had left it, a homemade, hand-me-down toy which had been repaired and repainted many times like the toys of the crèche. An older child's mittens lay on the window sill. The sewing machine had some bright printed cotton tumbled on it, a child's dress in the making. In a corner stood a battered crib, where others before Benjie had napped, and a high chair bearing the honorable wounds of many small heels banged against its legs and many spoons pounded in rhythmic percussion on its tray.

Of all this, and the aromatic pot on the stove, the potatoes mounded by the sink to be peeled for dinner, the bowl of applesauce cooling, the loaf cake still in its pan with a corner taken off for Benjie, no doubt, to taste—of it all, the woman, sitting serene with the child cradled in her lap, was the center, the pervading spirit. A warmth as from an invisible sun glowed from her, and like sunlight it was life-giving.

"MAMMA WILL MAKE YOU COMFORTABLE" Mr. Lewis came in presently, a short wiry man a few years older than his wife, with grizzled hair and a grizzled mustache and ruddy color on his cheekbones. His eyes were small, bright, and merry.

"Well, sonny!" he said, patted the child's head, and kissed him audibly before he turned to me.

Mr. Lewis drove me in his truck to my friend's house and we finished our inspection tour quickly. Everything was in order. Mr. Lewis impressed me more every moment: practical, conscientious, a solid man, and honest. I could assure my friend that the place was in good hands.

In the nearly ten years since I first met him I have never had reason to change my opinion of Mr. Lewis. Despite a lifetime of the greatest possible economic insecurity, he is a man like a rock. Without special skill or talent beyond a native ingenuity with mechanical problems and a sound common sense, with a minimum of formal education and no superior intellectual attainments, he possesses as his only capital the clanking, patched, cut-down truck which is both his business vehicle and his family's transportation.

For forty years he has supported his family on the hand-to-mouth living of a general trucker and Jack-of-all-trades in a none too prosperous community. Yet he has no anxiety, no envy of another's lot, no frightened need to chisel, cut corners, take advantage of an absentee owner away in the city. He has known lean times, but the family has never been on relief. He has self-confidence and dignity, and the community respects him. He has no other talents, perhaps, except the most precious one, a talent for living. Today he is a capable, virile old man, joyfully and on occasion exuberantly full of life.

He drove me back to his house, where I had left my car, and I asked him where I could get a bite in the village before driving on to Worcester, some twenty miles farther, where I would spend the night.

He couldn't let me do that, he said. It was already dark; the roads were icy and getting worse, with sleet coating the windshield faster than it melted off.

Then I would stay in my friend's house, I decided. The oil burner was on, though turned low, and there was water.

"We'd find you frozen in the morning," he warned, chuckling. "Don't worry, Mamma will make you comfortable."

It had been his intention all along to put me up, and although nothing had been said, apparently it had been in his wife's mind as well. An extra place had already been laid on the big kitchen table. Mrs. Lewis showed me the bedroom which was being warmed for me with a portable oilstove. Benjie, though he had still not said a word to me, came with us to see the room, holding a fold of her tentlike skirt.

Three young women were in the kitchen, and each looked up pleasantly to greet me from some task which had to do with the preparation of dinner. They were three of the eight Lewis daughters: Loie, the youngest, was engaged but not yet married; Gladys, the next older, was living with her parents while her husband did his service in the Navy; and Helen, the eldest, worked in the near-by mill town. Helen had never married. Ed stopped in on his way home from work. He was one of three grown sons.

The Lewises had eleven children, and those who did not still live at home lived in the village or the near-by town. Ed was a garage mechanic, Harry a farmer; the youngest boy was away doing his Army service. The five other daughters were all married and mothers of one, two, or three children. Mrs. Lewis named all her grandchildren, twelve of them, and two more coming in the spring.

Benjie was still not accounted for. He was no longer silent, however. He ran about among the young women, calling them by name, chattering to them, and each one had time to speak to him, pick him up, and fondle him. Though each of them was handling pots and pans or carrying dishes and food to the table, and he was under foot, none scolded him, and none found him in the way.

He climbed into Ed's lap, was dandled there for a while, and clambered down again. He went to Mr. Lewis, whom he called "Papa." Finally he came to rest in Mrs. Lewis' lap. He called her

"Mamma," as did everyone there including Mr. Lewis. In effect, Benjie, making the rounds of the kitchen, had been attended to and cuddled by four mothers and two fathers in that room.

All the while dinner was being set on the table, and all through dinner the talk went around the room. Everyone had something to tell, or some comment to make on what someone else told.

Gladys mentioned a new book she had brought from the circulating library. Loie had read it, Helen planned to, and Ed thought it sounded like something his wife might like, though he himself didn't care for novels. Ed had time to make a few good-natured thrusts in what was apparently a running political argument he was having with his father, and then he departed for home and his own dinner. Our dinner was the stew I had already appreciated in the cooking, plain but delicious, and there was plenty of it. Everyone ate with relish, the old people, the red-cheeked robust girls, and Benjie most of all.

A FAMILY DEMOCRACY   After dinner Loie put on her coat and bundled Benjie into his jacket with the hood, and the two of them went out to feed the pigs, Loie with the big kettle of mash, Benjie proudly after her lugging his small pot of greens from the family's dinner vegetables. When they came back, Helen gaily picked Benjie up and carried him off to bed. Loie hung up her coat and took a dish towel. Gladys and Helen had already cleared the table and Gladys was washing the dishes.

Whenever I saw a group of Lewises together, I saw the same self-assigned division of labor in the home. No one was told what to do or asked to do anything, but each found a task which needed doing and proceeded to do it. Through the years I have been to more than one family party. I remember a Christmas, with a huge ham in the oven, golden-crusted oversize pies cooling on the table, and the crisp cold when someone opened the door to get something from the covered porch where the icebox stood, and the heaped baskets of potatoes, carrots, turnips, apples from the summer crop gave a feeling of abundance though by economic standards the Lewises are poor people.

Even then, with babies in arms and toddlers underfoot, there was no scolding, no jangling, never a temper. Everyone seemed to know what to do, the older grandchildren gravely helping the adults, half a dozen young women around the stove without confusion or traffic congestion, while Papa jovially called his sons and sons-in-law to share a pre-dinner nip with him, and Mamma, like the goddess Ceres, brooded lovingly and serenely over the steaming, aromatic kitchen. Benjie, momentarily weary of trotting, his eyes big in dreamy anticipation of good things to eat, lay at ease in the ample cradle of her lap.

In that large family, celebrations were always being planned, for everything was an occasion, engagements, marriages, baptisms, graduations, and if there was nothing else there was always a birthday. I was present at Loie's wedding the following June, and the supper afterward, with the endlessly long table set up in the Lewis back yard and all the Lewis daughters and daughters-in-law and a few granddaughters moving about in their bright dresses, some home-sewn, some bought by mail order, but all crisp and pretty, serving the guests. For the Lewises alone any party was the equivalent of a banquet, but when one of the Lewis girls was married the entire village came and a good many friends from the town.

A whole roast pig was the succulent centerpiece, one of the Lewis home-grown ones. Around it food was heaped high on the platters, plentiful and good, and all of it prepared by Mrs. Lewis and her girls.

HOW BENJIE CAME   Benjie's growth from babyhood could be measured by the tasks he found to do in the family. By the time he was four I found him cracking nuts with a big stone for Mamma's cookies. The next year or so he was chopping kindling with a hatchet for a family barbecue. In the fall a year later he went hunting with Ed and Harry, and a year after that, when he was past seven, he was allowed to handle a gun himself. He was patiently taught and he has never hurt himself.

On this first night, when Helen had carried him off to bed, I heard the story of how Benjie came to the Lewises. With all the children grown up and Loie a few months from marrying out of the house, they were lonely.

"Mamma isn't happy without a baby in her lap," Mr. Lewis said. They had heard about Benjie, an orphan in a near-by foster home. He was not thriving there. The Lewises had brought him home a few months before, and at the end of a year they would be able to adopt him legally.

"They didn't treat him right in that home," Mrs. Lewis said. "He didn't learn to say Ma-ma or Da-da first. All he knew to say when he came here was 'Oo debbil.' What kind of people could they be who would call a baby 'You devil!'"

Mr. and Mrs. Lewis were both past sixty and they had raised eleven children. But in this house, as a traveler like myself with no possible claim on them had just discovered, there was always room for one more.

"That trick he has, getting under the chair," Mrs. Lewis told her husband, "he did it again today. He's been doing that when anyone comes to the house except the family," she explained to me. "I don't know why he does it. None of our children ever had a trick like that." She was puzzled and just a little impatient.

Helen came back into the room after putting Benjie to bed. She was the eldest, the one daughter who had not married. The eldest in a large family is traditionally sacrificed. She must help as the new babies come along, and often she is needed at home until it is too late to make her own life, her own family. I looked at Helen curiously to discover, if I could, what her sacrifice for the family had cost her.

In her middle forties, Helen was a full-blown, womanly woman, with her mother's big frame; a handsome woman, with her father's high color and merry eyes, and a quick spirited manner. There was nothing deprived, nothing dried up or spinsterish about her. As she sat with us at the kitchen table, telling a funny story of something that had happened that day at the mill, gossiping with warm friendliness and not a trace of malice about the people with whom she worked and about the neighbors, it was clear that the words *sacrifice* and *resignation* could never be applied to her. She was full of life and the enjoyment of it, and if she had been prevented by circumstance from taking one path to happiness, the path of marriage and children, she had found another which suited her equally well.

As would happen in any village, gossip had been busy fabricating an explanation of Benjie's adoption. Fiction had it that the owner of the mill where she worked had become interested in her some years before, but he had an invalid wife and could not marry Helen. Their friendship, it was said, went on for years, until his wife died and then, tragically, the man too died soon after. And so Benjie was explained as Helen's child by this man.

Such gossip grows readily in a small and rather narrow community, an inept effort by the unimaginative to explain why two old people, who must have had their fill of child rearing, should do so surprising a thing as adopt a baby.

Supposing there were any substance to this fantasy, it would reflect still more credit on these parents' abundance of love. They are not sophisticated people. They are conventional; they accept without protest or discomfort the morality of the rather isolated rural community in which they live. In such a community an unmarried mother is a blot upon a family, and the conventional solution is for the girl to take her child and leave her parents' home and village forever, or else to abandon her child to strangers.

In such a situation people like the Lewises would still be obliged to bow to convention to the extent of keeping Helen's secret and protecting her child from the stigma of illegitimacy. But they would not turn their daughter out into an unfriendly world. And they would not, could not abandon her child. To continue to love their daughter, and to extend their love to her child, would be to them not condonation of sin but a natural and human expression of parental love.

THESE COMFORTS THEY HAVE   I slept that night in a warm bed, but when I awoke the room was icy. Beyond my door I could hear the family stirring, going about their normal lives without special fuss because there was a guest. They had not strained, the night before, because there was a stranger, someone from the city. They had absorbed me easily into their midst, and their talk could hardly have been more cheerful and uninhibited if I had not been there.

Through my door came also the tempting smells of coffee, fresh hot muffins, fresh pork frying. It was no hardship to dress quickly in the cold with such an invitation to breakfast.

Before we pity the Lewises for the luxuries they did not have, we should savor the real comforts they enjoyed. The wind howled outside, frostflowers bloomed on the panes, but in the kitchen it was warm and on the table there was hot, nourishing, tasty food. In the setting of deep emotional comfort which their unstintingly motherly mother created for them in this house, they could enjoy the simple physical pleasures.

They could not be sluggish, weary, or bored here. There was work to be done always, and always the reward of work. No one here could ever be alone or lonely. This awkward rambling house with the busy, loving parents was full of their past as children, full of the work and play of growing up, the happiness and the pain, all shared, all understood with the heart—and no other understanding is needed if this one can be depended upon.

Families like the Lewises are not unusual in American life, only inconspicuous because they never make trouble for the community and never call attention to themselves. I have known such families in New England and New York State and the South, in the Middle West and the Far West; in the country and in small towns and cities and, less frequently, in big cities. Families like these are the stability of the United States, the continuum on which the American way of life is solidly founded.

Surprisingly, the Lewises are not natives of their Massachusetts village. They began their family life in a city tenement.

"We're newcomers—we only came here forty-some years ago," Mr. Lewis likes to say. They moved here when there were two babies in the family, Helen and Ed, and the third was on the way. Mr. Lewis was born and brought up in a Boston slum and it was there he took his bride when he married her. He earned his living driving a truck.

"I couldn't see my kids growing up like gutter rats," he said, explaining the heroic decision to move to the country.

And it was heroic. The house into which they moved—this family with two babies and the mother three months pregnant—was a tar-paper summer shack, without heat, without insulation, which they could rent for $20 a month. That winter the wind tore through the flimsy paper walls, and the parents prowled the house through half a winter night, patching, stuffing the holes with rags. They melted the ice in the water bucket on the stove each morning.

Yet the Lewises survived, and more, they prospered. Year by year the wire-muscled, vigorous man exerted his skill and ingenuity to make the house more livable, building as birds build their nests, bit by bit with whatever scraps were to be had. Year by year the mother, however burdened with her growing family, radiated the warmth of love which made the house a refuge no matter how cold the wind or unwelcoming the world.

ENVIRONMENT CREATED FROM WITHIN   Mrs. Lewis—Mamma—must have had wonderful parents, an ideal childhood, a perfect start in life, one would think. The truth is quite otherwise. Everything was against her from birth.

She had no parents whom she had ever known, no family that belonged to her. She was an orphan, first in an institution and then, quite early, in a foster home. The one piece of good fortune to fall to her thin lot was in her foster parents, a kindly man and a big hearty woman, with children of their own—and this, we must believe, was enough to shape her character for future happiness though she was deprived of everything else.

She was a strong girl and hired out early to earn her own way in various farm families. A young man from the city, tough and smart in the ways of survival which poor city children learn, came to hunt with friends in the neighborhood where she worked. He responded to her soft, generous warmth, married her, and took her back to a city tenement.

Possibly some feeling for a better way of living and bringing up a family than he had known had begun to unfold in him since his visit to the country. Possibly he had yearned toward the direct knowledge of earth in his own childhood of hard city pavements.

Possibly the girl he had chosen, her loving embrace of life in any form like the embrace of Mother Earth herself, stirred in him a recognition of the setting in which she more properly belonged, as a painter sees in the model the mood of his whole composition and chooses the background accordingly, as a musician hears a theme in his inner ear and builds the movement of a symphony

around it, or as a writer discovers a character and creates a world
in which the character can live.

The young truck driver Lewis could not articulate any of this,
but he did not need to. He could act on it. There were practical reasons enough to support his decision. Children are healthier in the
country (or so most city folk believe although it is not statistically
true). Children have more freedom in the country (this is true).
Living space is less expensive in the country—certainly true—and
one can eke out an uncertain cash income by growing food. They
didn't have to be rich, once they could be sure they would have
shelter and enough to eat. So he argued.

But the compelling argument was not rational in the materialist
sense. It was intuitive, creative: "I couldn't see my kids growing up
like gutter rats." He wanted for his children not the shabby make-
shifts of growing up in an artificial urban world. He wanted for
them the direct experience of reality, the simple reality of the
sources of man's living, which a child can grasp and which builds
in childhood a foundation of reality and security.

Then, we might be saying, families should all move out to the
country, and all country families must produce happier or at least
more secure and better-integrated children.

And, we might be saying, from the example of the Lewis children, what we need is large families again.

Certainly there are good arguments both for bringing up children
in the country and for raising them in large families. But neither
the country nor the multiplicity of brothers and sisters is a guarantee
of anything.

I think of the Simpsons—which was not their name—a native farm
family who lived across the road from a country place where I
visited often. The father had died of pneumonia, the result of sleeping off one of his drinking sprees by the roadside on a cold night,
and left his widow with six half-grown children.

The eldest was an exceptionally bright boy, and the mother sacrificed herself and the other five children to send this one to college.
He never got to college; he got to jail first. When last heard of, he
had spent a total of fifteen years of his life in prison. All the others
were in more or less serious trouble at one time or another. When

the mother finally sold her farm, there was little enough money above the mortgage, and one of her sons managed to get even this little away from her for his own use.

Large families? I think of the Gordons, which is not their name either, who had sixteen children. Every social worker knows families like the Gordons. Every social worker has tripped over the stack of bottles, not milk bottles, which litters the entrance to their flat. Every social worker has struggled with the insoluble problem of men and women who breed children as pigs breed little pigs, but do not care enough even to suckle them as a sow suckles her young in the sty.

We tend to talk of the country, of large families, of this or that environmental factor as though it were external and objective. But environment is subjective too. Whole and happy men and women have come out of dreadful environments, and we know—how well we know it—that children who have everything, that is, everything material, everything external, everything that money can buy, are often the most deeply and tragically deprived.

THE FLOWERING OF A FAMILY As do all of us, whether we know it or not, the Lewises created their environment from within. The tar-paper shack was home from the first, and the physical comforts which came later were only the outward expression of the emotional well-being into which each of their babies was born.

The very way in which they acquired their physical comforts confirms their independence of external props to happiness. Their grip on reality never wavered. From the first they dealt with it; however harsh, it was only the outer reality which was harsh, and its harshness was a challenge. They moved into inadequate shelter because that was what they could afford. They improved their shelter as they could afford to do it.

They did not choose to build their physical comfort on a gathering of possessions on credit. They did no buying on the installment plan; to them it meant mortgaging their future for present pleasure. They saw too many neighbors acquiring a shiny electric refrigerator or radio—or later a television set—at so many pennies a week forever, or until the truck came and carried it away. To them credit meant debt, and debt was a threat to their peace of mind. They preferred to wait until later for what they considered luxuries, and to invest the work of their hands and their little cash in the essentials of shelter and food.

One may disagree with them. One may call them naïve and old-fashioned. But it was their choice, just as rural living was their choice in preference to the comparative convenience of city living.

They insulated the shack before another winter, and in time gave it a shell of brick. They added rooms for the increasing family. They brought water into the kitchen, later put in a bathroom along with electricity. They bought a cow, pigs, and chickens, vegetable seeds and seedlings and young fruit trees. In time they bought the acre on which stood their ungainly but happy home.

At each stage they made their choice of what was to them the next necessity. Others make other choices. Other families budget their installment buying so that they can have comforts and labor-saving appliances while the children are small. If they plan purposefully, and the debt does not become burdensome and a strain on family living, then their way is the right way for them.

From the first the Lewises had a telephone. With young children they wanted the comfort of a doctor within quick reach. Besides they were friendly and gregarious; they liked people. Church suppers, clambakes, grange picnics, the volunteer fire department fair—they always managed money for those, enough for the whole family to go.

Every event within the family was a celebration to which neighbors were invited. There was always money for parties, enough money, however little, because it could be made to go so far with willing hands. The Lewises always brought their share of cakes to the cake sales, and salads to the suppers.

The telephone did in fact become more of a social convenience than a medical necessity; the doctor was rarely needed. The Lewis health record is the local doctor's proudest boast. Except for a few serious illnesses, and only one requiring surgery—a sudden appendicitis—the Lewises were almost never sick. More revealing still, they almost never had accidents; we know the meaning of accident proneness as a sign of emotional disturbance. The Lewises had, from parents to the youngest child, an uninhibited will to live and to enjoy life. They were not in rebellion against life nor against themselves.

LEARNING THE PHYSICAL SKILLS   Teaching children to be careful is no problem if there is no anxiety. Anxious warnings and prohibitions— "Look out! Be careful! Don't climb there—you'll fall! Don't touch that—you'll hurt yourself!"—have never taught children very well. The Lewis children learned to handle tools and guns with skill because those skills were a real and necessary part of their lives. They learned to climb the roof without falling, because they climbed not for reckless adventure or to draw their parents' anxious attention or to rebel against parental prohibition, but to help their father fix the roof, which was leaking.

I saw Benjie helping his father fix a rain gutter at three, carrying a piece of galvanized tin as big as himself. Before he was six he was chopping kindling with a hatchet, and an observer who restrained anxious comment long enough to watch him do it could see that he was in less danger of hurting himself than a grown man who had no practical acquaintance with hatchets. As naturally as animals learn to survive in their environment the Lewis children learned to meet the physical demands of their rugged life.

LEARNING ABOUT SEX   Knowledge of sex, so often a source of anxiety to children—and to parents who are ill at ease in conveying this knowledge—came naturally to the Lewis children. They enjoyed the advantage, common to country children, of observing as a matter of course the procreation of farm animals. They watched chickens hatch and calves being born. Benjie at four was not surprised when a calf was born. Of course, he said, he had seen the cow and the horse together all the time in the field, and they had made the calf. He was misinformed about the species, but not in the least confused about the sexes.

City children do not have these daily lessons offered to them, but, alone, these lessons in nature would not suffice either. More significant than the things they could learn out of doors was the fullness of the love between their parents. They would not know the whole meaning of their parents' sexual relationship, but they would feel intuitively that all was right between father and mother. Children everywhere are capable of such insights.

The warmth, the understanding, the satisfaction in each other, the respect for each other's well-being which radiate from a good union—these were constantly demonstrated by the elder Lewises. They maintained the sunny climate of the children's sex learning as of every other aspect of their learning. Even without the example of field and farmyard, the love of their parents for each other is enough to give children the emotional setting in which sex learning has its wholesome beginnings.

LEARNING DISCIPLINE   Not that their life was one unbroken idyl. The children bickered as children must. Papa grumbled when he came home hungry and dinner was not ready. Papa also administered discipline.

But when a quarrel was over it was over. When a child was spanked the incident was finished. There was no coldness of parents held over; there were no "bad" and "good" children. A child might do something troublesome to parents, something unfair to brother or sister. He would be corrected in whatever way was feasible at the moment. But his wrongdoing did not make him a "bad" child.

Discipline to these parents was what discipline should be, a way of teaching children how to live within a community of human beings, beginning with the family. When children grow up so close to the realities of living, discipline does not need to be explained to them in words. The demands of reality are the first discipline they learn, and it is the healthy basis of all discipline.

One day Benjie made a mistake. Playing, he moved the stepping stones which Mr. Lewis had laid to the kitchen door. Mr. Lewis stepped over the puddles which Benjie had created, and called the child to account. He was angry and his voice was loud as he explained in very few words that he had laid the path for a purpose, that these stones were not toys.

Benjie listened seriously but without fright. He understood his father's anger and the reason for it. But he also had the assurance from past experience that nothing terrible would happen to him because of his mistake. The sky would not fall on him. The stones would be relaid, he would not move them again, and life would go on serenely as before.

Such parents need no books and lectures to tell them how to "handle" their children. They do not handle their children at all, in the self-conscious, intellectualized meaning of the phrase. They do what is necessary to teach their children the things the young human creature must learn in order to live in the world. Their child rearing is informed by reality, within the warm protecting love which the young creature needs. They fulfill the primary function of the family, not thinking or talking or reading about it, but doing it.

The children did not need to be assigned to chores. The chores were there to be done, as each child could see, and each child undertook what he was able to do as his natural contribution to the whole family. They did not need to be competitive; there was enough for each to do to the best of his ability, and their parents' love was not contingent on behavior, performance, skill, or anything else whatever. It was distributed with the equality of rain. A child only had to exist, and he was bathed in love.

BENJIE UNDER THE CHAIR   On that very first visit I was lucky enough to see, in Benjie's "trick" of hiding under his mother's chair, a situation of interest to a psychiatrist. None of Mrs. Lewis' children had ever done a thing like that, and she was disconcerted by it. As I was leaving in the morning, when she looked for him to say good-by, he was under her chair again, concealed beneath her voluminous skirt.

"Benjie, come out of there! Don't be so silly!" she exclaimed.

By now I knew, of course, what was bothering Benjie. In the foster home from which he had come, he must often have been looked over for possible adoption. Now, when he was where he wanted to be, loved and cared for in a family where he was made to feel he belonged, he was apprehensive only about one thing: Any stranger might be a threat to his new-found security. Any visitor might be coming to take him away. So he hid—under Mrs. Lewis' chair, under her skirt, as close as he could get to the source and pillar of his security and at the same time out of sight. He curled up there in a fetal attitude, safe as in the womb.

I said, "It feels good under there, doesn't it, Benjie? No one can take you out of there, can they?" And I walked to the door, showing no further interest in him.

He came out by himself in a moment, and shook hands with me, holding to Mrs. Lewis' skirt. When I saw the Lewises again at Easter time, Mrs. Lewis told me I had "cured" Benjie of his trick. He had never again gone under the chair when strangers came.

Perhaps I had cured him. I had stated the meaning of his symbolic behavior, brought it out into the open. But he was ready to give up the trick before very long anyway, or he could not have given it up then.

His real security had already begun to dissipate this surviving fantasy from the past. He was surrounded by love and reassurance and no longer had to retreat into fantasy. Mrs. Lewis might never understand what Benjie's trick meant to him, but she had no need to. The love she gave him was the right medicine, and he would have been cured without a word from a visiting city psychiatrist. The cure would only have taken a little longer.

No expert can tell a mother how to be motherly. Troubled mothers ask psychiatrists what to do, what to say, even what words to use. The significance is not, however, in *what* they do or say, but *how*, and for that there is no recipe. The *how* can come only from within. No one can be told how to communicate the warmth of love to a child.

UNLIMITED LOVE PLUS LIMITING REALITY   When life is realistically lived, love need have no limits. You cannot spoil children with love. Reality provides the discipline for their behavior and the boundaries to their desires. When they have love, they do not need what they cannot have. When they have love, they will learn to make the most of what they do have.

If a recipe could be given to parents, it would be this simple one: Give your children unlimited love, and share with them your experience of limiting reality. The recipe is not, of course, as simple as it sounds. No one can tell you how to experience reality in the first place; that is your own affair. And on your experience, your acceptance of reality—of your own limitation and capabilities as well as the outer limitations of your life—depends the quality of what you share with your children.

Your values are your own. Your standards are the ones they will accept or rebel against. Whether they accept them or rebel against them makes actually little difference; in either case your example, good or bad, realistic or unrealistic, will dominate their future lives.

The Lewises did not trouble about putting their realistic philosophy into words for their children. They did better; they lived it. They lived their pleasure in life and their acceptance of its challenges.

Each person's reality is his own; there are almost as many realities as there are individuals and individual combinations of circumstance. The assembly-line worker who must turn so many bolts in so many hours for forty hours a week, always the same bolt, may find his reality a grinding monotony. Or he may find in the companionship of his fellow workers, in factory welfare and trade union activities, in his home and garden and growing family, a richness which more than compensates for the limiting work of his hands. He turns a bolt for forty hours a week, but it is up to him to decide what he will do with the rest of his waking hours. And that decision determines his acceptance of his personal reality.

The bank clerk's reality is the necessity of accepting his boss, whatever kind of boss he may be, and of accepting the frustrations of white-collar work, the limitations on his personal ambitions while daily he deals with the bank's wealthy clients and handles the cryptic symbols of their wealth. When we read of a cashier who has embezzled for years or absconded in a sudden reckless bid for freedom, we are reading of a man who was not able to accept his individual reality.

The civilian who becomes a GI faces drastically changed life conditions. This new reality is temporary—since he will presumably return to civilian life—but in its alternation of deadly monotony and sudden danger its revolutionary contrast to his normal experience may be shattering to all previous patterns. The sergeant, the lieutenant, the division commander all have taken over the man's responsibility for himself in a chain of command which leads right up to the President of the United States. A mere private can grouse and grumble, and he can also feel well taken care of with so many fathers. Some welcome this relief from personal responsibility, some rebel against it, some are permanently shaken by its anonymity which obliterates the individual's freedoms and potentially the individual's life itself.

For the Lewises reality was harsh and bleak, a reality such as most Americans have not been obliged to face since pioneer days. Their hardships were principally physical, their problems largely a matter of how to make fifty cents stretch to two dollars.

Yet each small decision was part of the whole policy of their lives. Each choice was weighed in the balance against a single purpose, the good of the family. About this purpose they suffered no doubts and no uncertainties. The good of the family was everyone's good.

Their unshakable faith in their purpose gave them signposts at every turn and crossroads on their difficult way. And, as with the traveler who knows he will reach a safe haven if he only keeps on, the hardships of the way seemed never so hard because they knew where they were bound and were certain they would get there.

NO SUBSTITUTES FOR LOVE   We have talked in an earlier chapter of the giving of lavish gifts; often these are a substitute for love. The Lewises always were giving each other presents. Christmas and birthdays, graduations, engagements, weddings, baptisms, all were occasions for gifts as well as parties.

Except for the house presents which the children gave Mamma later on, these many gifts which were exchanged year in year out were of the simplest kind. There was very little outlay of money, but an enormous expenditure of loving thought.

The girls learned early to sew and knit because these skills were necessary to keep the family in clothes. But they learned to make things with skill and taste, too, because the learning had purpose to them, and it was seasoned with love and the joy of accomplishment. When one wants to learn a skill, one works with the tools and materials, not against them.

They had watched their mother buy a better doll undressed than she could afford to buy with clothes, and then sew a complete wardrobe for the doll out of scraps and bits of material which she had saved from their own clothes. A little girl who has watched her mother sew lovingly for her doll does not need to be urged to sew.

The presents they made for each other were created out of knowledge of each other's needs and wishes. The presents they bought for each other were tirelessly shopped for, though in the ten-cent store; each choice was measured against the person for whom it was intended—"She could use a new one"—"She would like the blue"—"The one with the bigger handle would fit his hand better." Not much money, but unstinted time and thought and care went into the smallest gift.

Gifts should be an expression of love, not a substitute for love. And no one who received these gifts could doubt that they were an expression of love.

I happened to be there one Christmas Day. Benjie came running to me and lifted up his foot: "Look, my Christmas socks!" They were inexpensive little cotton socks, which he had probably needed anyway. But they were special, bright for Christmas, with many colors. Benjie preened himself in them as though he had received a gift of inestimable value. And of course he had. He had received a gift of love.

LIVING THE AMERICAN DREAM REALISTICALLY   The realism of the Lewises extended into every aspect of their lives, including their aspirations for their children. None of the children, for instance, went to college. None aspired to go.

Is this a negation of the American dream that every boy can be President of the United States—or of United States Steel? It is so only if we mistake the symbol for the reality. Every boy and every girl can make a good life in this country within the bounds of his or her own reality.

Why should every boy want to be President? Why should every boy want to be rich? Incalculable harm is done to children by setting up standards for them which are unrealizable because of cir-

cumstance or ability, and the realization of which would not actually
be for the child's best interest or greatest happiness.

If one of the Lewis children had displayed a special talent or the
drive to push on to higher education, he or she would have found a
way to go in that direction. These boys and girls learned early that
you work for what you want. But to push one child at the expense
of the rest, for prestige, for the satisfaction of parents' ambition, for
any unrealistic reason, was impossible with the Lewises. There could
be no tortured sacrifice of a whole family so that one might have
more or reach higher than was possible for all.

We have seen such sacrifices. Psychoanalysts hear the stories of
them. Sometimes it is hard to decide who suffers more, the one who
makes the sacrifice or the one who receives its benefits. And the
mental hospitals are overcrowded with people who live in a dream
world.

The Lewises do not live in a dream world, whether of the
American or any other variety. They live in the real world of an
American rural community, and their children, to them, were always real personalities growing up to live in the same real world.
As their parents accepted their limitations, so did the children. What
would a college education do for one of them? They did not need
to be rich, or famous. They needed only to earn a decent living, to
be decent members of the community, to meet trouble sensibly when
it came and to enjoy happiness to the fullest.

They are, without exception, solid citizens. They read and discuss the affairs of the day and vote for what they believe in. They
are strong and competent individuals, looking after themselves and
making their steady responsible contribution to the life of their community and the nation. The Lewis women are real women who accept and enjoy their womanly role.

They are not deceived by spurious values. Just as they rode in
the cut-down truck as children, with no envy of the neighbor's sedan,
so now the girls buy their spring coats and Easter bonnets from the
mail-order catalogue. They are well dressed girls. They choose
bright colors for their clothes, but not flashy; they do not need to attract attention by noisy colors, but they please their own happy tem-
peraments by wearing cheery ones.

The same high spirits shine in the house. The furniture the girls picked for Mamma's parlor is cheerful in color, as well as solidly made and comfortable. There are plants in the windows all winter, and flowers around the house in summer. And the house is always full of people, talking, laughing, enjoying themselves. Not only the Lewis children, the in-laws and grandchildren, but the neighbors too like to drop in.

Out of such a cheerful home, with such a background of joy in work and joy in human companionship, the Lewis boys and girls found it no hardship to go out to work every day in all weather, sometimes walking up the hill to the house because the steep road was too icy for the community-pool car. All of them began to work as a matter of course as soon as they finished high school.

The work they did, in the stores of the village, in the mills of the near-by town, might seem dull to an outsider. To perform a monotonous repetitive task eight hours a day, five days a week is not troubling to people who live fully and positively the rest of their waking hours. Even the work is rewarding. It pays them their necessary livelihood, and to sweeten the uncreative task they have the companionship of the people working beside them, the shared experience of other human beings.

The girls had their problems. There was not much choice of prospective husbands in the community. By other girls' standards they did not have many of the lures that would win a husband. A Lewis girl would be scouring the pots or feeding the pigs before she dashed into her room to dress for a date. She would have to pick her way down the muddy path and get into the cut-down truck to ride to a party. Her dress would be homemade, her coat and hat and shoes ordered by mail from the catalogue.

But the Lewis girls always looked nice in their clothes, with a boutonniere of artificial flowers on the coat and a veil on the hat for special occasions. Their high color, their high spirits, their healthy capacity for enjoying themselves must have been enough of a lure for a good man. Whatever the reason, all but Helen found themselves responsible husbands, and Helen found happiness without one. A farmer, a farm manager, a trucker are among the Lewis sons-in-law; the others have various jobs in the town.

Mamma is getting heavy now and does not move around as briskly as she used to. But the house is still always welcoming. There is still always something good cooking on the stove, and the high chair is still the most conspicuous piece of furniture in the kitchen, ready for the youngest of the thirty-odd Lewis grandchildren.

The rooms may often have a look of disorder, with children and grandchildren popping in and out and strewing their things about, but Mamma never had any compulsion toward surface neatness, nor any time to fuss over it, and the place is always cleanly.

Outside, the garden is well kept, the chicken house and the pig house trim and tended as always. The brown brick and the red asbestos shingle and the other ill-assorted surfaces of the house have weathered together, and though it fits no known style of architecture, the house spells cheerful comfort, with the curl of smoke forever feathering out of the chimney.

Benjie is ten, a sturdy friendly boy who is at home in his family and out. He gets along well at school. He will learn a trade like Ed, or follow Harry into farming, and like them he will be competent at whatever he does and content with the fullness of his life. Benjie in his hand-me-down clothes, riding beside his foster father in the ancient truck, has little of material value. But he has love, and love is enough.

THE BEDROCK OF A NATION   In a day of virulent attack on the American family, the American home, the American mother, families like the Lewises are the optimistic note. The fly-by-nights, the birds of passage, are our constant anxious concern, their flaring successes fill the newspapers and their failures crowd the clinics and the mental hospitals.

Families like the Lewises may not contribute to the headlines, but neither do they add to the American neurosis. They are the stable core of the country, the bedrock of the nation. They live purposefully, and their purpose is to cultivate the human values which alone provide lasting satisfaction. Their wealth is the wealth of love and companionship, of joy in living, and in the work and play which are the solid sustenance of living.

Neither their homes nor their minds are closed to progress, but they are immune to fad. They judge the new and take from it what serves their purpose. Their life does not depend on the products of the machine age for its enrichment nor on a display of possessions for its dignity. They are conservative in the true sense of conserving the values by which they live, and they have earned their conservatism.

The Lewises moved to the country because this was, for them, the environment which best served their purpose, but this does not mean that we must all move to the country. They had many children, but the answer is not in large families. As Helen Lewis shows us, one need not even have a family of one's own at all to live successfully. The Lewis children did not aspire beyond high school, nor train for the professions, because it would not have served their purpose to do so.

They are not an argument for curbing aspiration, but they are a plea that aspiration should have its roots in reality. Each of us has his own reality, and each of us begins his education in living by learning early what his reality is. Without this first lesson, the greatest wealth and the finest education cannot bring that inner comfort and security, that ability to live to one's fullest capacity, which we call happiness.

A man may learn to acquire millions or to split the atom, but he cannot learn to be happy and he cannot bequeath the capacity for happiness to his children unless he has and shares with them the experience and the acceptance of reality.

John P. Marquand, in *B. F.'s Daughter*, writes of Polly Fulton whose father, an industrial genius, rose from a small-town hardware business to fabulous wealth, who bought English country houses and French chateaux and brought them in crates to add to his home near New York. Polly, full of the capacity to love, yet spends her life groping for a happiness which forever eludes her.

"There was once a brief time," Mr. Marquand tells us, "when Polly Fulton had been very happy." That was when she was ten, and went with her mother to the little town of Willett, New Hampshire, from which her father and mother had originally come. Her

Aunt Martha wore an apron, but she was not a maid, and they did their own cooking and washed their own dishes.

"Those two weeks at Willett of bringing kindling from the woodshed, of making her own cot bed, of sweeping out the kitchen and drying the dishes, formed the only occasion in her childhood when she was useful to other people, or even an essential part of anything. It was surprising that her parents, though they had been brought up in just this way, could have completely overlooked that aspect of a child's development."

For parents who live in cities, parents whose work, interests, and standard of living are far from the simple realities on which man's life is based, it is harder to give their children the direct experience which is necessary to their learning. But it is dangerous for them to overlook it as Polly Fulton's parents, loving and otherwise thoughtful for her happiness overlooked it. This is the potential tragedy of children in a modern industrial civilization. Emotionally they may live forever on the top floor of a skyscraper and never know the solidity of earth under their feet.

Families like the Lewises teach us what children really need. The attractive and comfortable home, the beautiful wardrobe, the toys, the parties, the expensive school and the learning of accomplishments are nice, but they are not essential, and the individual television set—the substitution of mechanical entertainment for individual creative effort—can be actually harmful.

Beyond nourishing food and shelter from the elements, children need little that is material. But their needs of the spirit, though simple, are absolute. If these are not met, nothing else can serve in their place. If they are met, nothing else matters.